PASSTRAK

SERIES 6

INVESTMENT
COMPANY/VARIABLE
CONTRACTS LIMITED
REPRESENTATIVE

QUESTIONS & ANSWERS

18TH EDITION

Dearborn
Financial Institute, Inc.®

MW00718583

At press time, this 18th edition of PASSTRAK® Series 6 contains the most complete and accurate information currently available for the NASD Series 6 license examination. Owing to the nature of securities license examinations, however, information may have been added recently to the actual test that does not appear in this edition.

This publication is designed to provide accurate and authoritative information in regard to the subject matter covered. It is sold with the understanding that the publisher is not engaged in rendering legal, accounting or other professional service. If legal advice or other expert assistance is required, the services of a competent professional person should be sought.

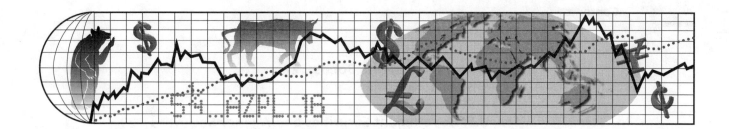

Contents

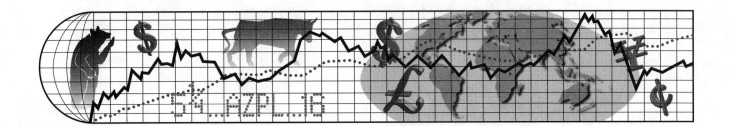

Acknowledgments

Hundreds of Dearborn students, instructors and customers contributed to this 18th edition of *PASSTRAK*® *Series 6 License Exam Manual* and *Questions & Answers*. Special thanks go to Barry Dempsey, Stuart Egrin, Gib Larson, Lynn Nessa and Marc Katz for their participation in creating this new edition. I'd also like to extend my particular gratitude to production editors Nicky Bell, Brian Fauth, Rebecca Milos, Rebecca Hicks and Nancy Whiteley, whose talent, patience and persistence made this book.

Wm. Linton Farrelly, Editor

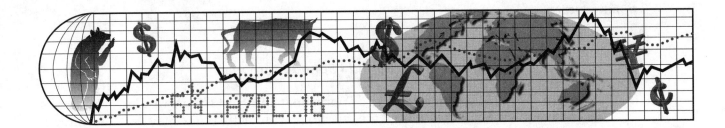

Introduction to PASSTRAK® Series 6

Welcome to PASSTRAK®. Because you probably have a lot of questions about the course and the exam, we have tried to anticipate some of them and provide you with answers to help you prepare.

The PASSTRAK® Series 6 Course

PASSTRAK® Series 6 is divided into two volumes: a textbook and an exam book. The textbook, titled *License Exam Manual*, consists of four lessons, each devoted to a particular area of investment company/variable contract products trading and regulation that you will need to know in order to pass the Investment Company/Variable Contract Products (IC/VC) Limited Representative Qualification Exam (the Series 6). Each lesson is divided into study sections devoted to more specific areas with which you need to become familiar.

The exam book, titled *Questions & Answers*, contains review and lesson exams that test the topics covered in the *License Exam Manual*; it concludes with three comprehensive final exams composed of questions similar to those you will see on the Series 6 exam.

What Topics Are Covered in the Course?

The Series 6 exam and PASSTRAK® Series 6 address the following topics:

Lesson 1 Securities and Markets, Investment Risks and Policies

Lesson 2 Investment Companies, Taxation and Customer Accounts

Lesson 3 Variable Contracts and Retirement Plans

Lesson 4 Securities Industry Regulation

How Much Time Should I Spend Studying?

You should plan to spend approximately 30 to 40 hours reading the material and working through the questions. Your actual time may vary depending on your study habits and professional background.

Spread your study time over two to three weeks before the date on which you are scheduled to take the Series 6 exam. Select a time and place for studying that will allow you to concentrate. There is a lot of information to learn, so be sure to give yourself enough time to understand the material.

What Is the Best Way to Approach the Review and Lesson Exams?

Take each review and lesson exam after you have read the corresponding section or lesson in the *License Exam Manual*. Read each question carefully and write down your answer. Then check your answers against the key and read the accompanying rationale. Take each test entirely, rather than reading each question and skipping directly to the rationale; this will increase your comprehension and retention of the information in the book.

Do I Need to Take the Final Exams?

Yes. The final exams test the same knowledge you will need in order to answer the questions on the Series 6 exam. By completing these exams and checking your answers against the rationale, you should be able to pinpoint any areas with which you are still having difficulty. Pay particular attention to the rationale for questions you missed. If needed, review the section(s) of the *Licence Exam Manual* covering those topics. At the end of each rationale, you will find a page reference that directs you to the page in the *License Exam Manual* where the information is covered.

The Series 6 Exam

Why Do I Need to Pass the Series 6 Exam?

Your employer is a member of the National Association of Securities Dealers (NASD) or another self-regulatory organization that requires its members and employees of its members to pass a qualification exam in order to become registered. To be registered as a representative qualified to sell investment company and variable contract products, you must pass the Series 6 exam.

Are There Any Prerequisites I Must Meet Before Taking the Exam?

There are no prerequisite exams you must pass before taking the Series 6.

What Is the Series 6 Exam Like?

The Series 6 is a 2-hour-and-15-minute, 100-question exam administered by the NASD. It is offered as a computer-based test at various testing sites around the country. A pencil-and-paper exam is available to those candidates who apply to and obtain permission from the NASD to take a written exam.

What Topics Will I See Covered on the Exam?

The questions you will see on the Series 6 exam do not appear in any particular order. The computer is programmed to select a new, random set of questions for each test taker, selecting questions according to the preset topic weighting of the exam. Each Series 6 candidate will see the same number of questions on each topic, but a different mix of questions.

The Series 6 exam is divided into four broad topic areas:

Securities and Markets, Investment Risks and Policies	23%
Investment Companies, Taxation and Customer Accounts	36%
Variable Contracts and Retirement Plans	16%
Securities Industry Regulations	25%

What Score Must I Achieve in Order to Pass?

You must score at least 70 percent on the Series 6 exam in order to pass and become eligible for NASD registration as an IC/VC representative.

Additional Trial Questions

During your exam, you will see up to ten extra trial questions. These are potential exam-bank questions that the NASD is testing by having examinees answer them during the course of an exam. These questions are not included in your final score, and you will be given extra time in which to answer them.

What Is PROCTOR®?

The Series 6 exam, like many professional licensing examinations, is administered on the PROCTOR® computerized testing system. PROCTOR® is a nationwide, interactive computer system designed for the administration and delivery of qualifications examinations. Included with your PROCTOR® enrollment, you will receive a brochure describing how the exam is formatted and how to use the computer terminal to answer the questions.

When you have completed the exam, the PROCTOR® System promptly scores your answers and within minutes displays your grade for the exam on the terminal screen.

How Do I Enroll for the Exam?

To obtain an admission ticket to the Series 6 exam, your firm must file the proper application form with the NASD, along with the appropriate processing fees. The NASD will then send you a directory of Certification Testing Centers and a PROCTOR® enrollment valid for a stated number of days. To take the exam during this period, you should make an appointment with a Certification Testing Center as far in advance as possible of the date on which you would like to take the test.

What Should I Take to the Exam?

Take one form of personal identification with your signature and photograph as issued by a government agency. You are not allowed to take reference materials or anything else into the testing area. Calculators are available upon request; you will not be allowed to use your own calculator.

Scratch paper and pencils will be provided by the testing center, although you will not be permitted to take them with you when you leave.

How Well Can I Expect to Do on the Exam?

If you study and complete all of the sections of the course, and consistently score at least 80 percent on the review and final exams, you will be well prepared to pass the exam.

Examination Results and Reports

At the end of the exam, your score will be displayed on your computer screen, indicating whether you passed. The next business day after your exam, your results will be mailed to your firm and to the self-regulatory organization and state securities commission specified on your application.

Successful Test Taking

Passing the Series 6 exam depends not only on how well you learn the subject matter but also on how well you take tests. You can develop your test-taking skills, and thus improve your score, by learning a few simple test-taking techniques:

- Read the full question.
- Avoid jumping to conclusions—watch for hedge clauses.
- Interpret the unfamiliar question.
- Look for key words and phrases.
- Identify the intent of the question.
- Recognize synonymous terms.
- Memorize key points.
- Eliminate/short-list Roman numeral choices.

- Use a calculator.
- Beware of changing answers.
- Pace yourself.

Each of these pointers is explained below, including examples that show how to use them to improve your performance on the exam.

Read the Full Question

You cannot expect to answer a question correctly if you do not know what it is asking. If you see a question that seems familiar and easy, you might anticipate the answer, mark it and move on before you finish reading it. This is a serious mistake and can result in errors. Be sure to read the full question before answering it—the questions are often written to trap people who assume too much. Here is an example of a question in which an assumption could produce a wrong answer.

> What is the term for an investment company whose shares are traded on an exchange and that invests more than 80 percent of its assets in many companies within a single industry?
>
> A. Closed-end
> B. Open-end
> C. Diversified
> D. Nondiversified

The answer is C—the question describes an investment company that meets the 75-5-10 test for diversification. This is an easy question to answer only for someone who has read the full question, because the point is made in the second half. If you read the question too quickly, you might get to the words "traded on an exchange" and assume that you are being asked whether an exchange-traded investment company is an open-end or a closed-end company.

Avoid Jumping to Conclusions—Watch for Hedge Clauses

The questions on the Series 6 are often embellished with deceptive distractors as choices. To avoid being taken in by seemingly obvious answers, make it a practice to read each question *and each answer* twice before selecting your choice. Doing so will provide you with a much better chance of doing well on the test.

Watch out for hedge clauses embedded in the question. Examples of hedge clauses include the terms *if, not, all, none* and *except*. In the case of *if* statements, the question can be answered correctly only by taking into account the qualifier. If you ignore the qualifier, you will not answer correctly.

Qualifiers are sometimes combined in a question. Some that you will frequently see together are *all* with *except* and *none* with *except*. In general, when a question starts with *all* or *none* and ends with *except,* you are looking for an answer that is opposite to what the question appears to be asking. For example:

> All of the following are characteristics of Treasury bills EXCEPT that they
>
> I. mature in more than one year
> II. are sold at a discount
> III. pay interest semiannually
> IV. are very safe investments
>
> A. I and II
> B. I and III
> C. II and III
> D. II and IV

If you neglect to read the *except,* you will look for the choices that are characteristics of T bills. In fact, the question asks which choices are *not* characteristics of T bills (that is, the exceptions). T bills mature in one year or less and do not pay periodic interest; therefore, choices I and III are incorrect and the answer is B.

Interpret the Unfamiliar Question

Do not be surprised if some questions on the test seem unfamiliar at first. If you have studied your material, you will have the information to answer all the questions correctly. The challenge may be a matter of understanding *what* the question is asking.

Very often, questions present information indirectly. You may have to interpret the meaning of certain elements before you can answer the question. The following two examples concerning bond yields and prices highlight this point.

> What is the effect of a decline in purchasing power on the current yields of outstanding bonds?
>
> A. The yields decrease.
> B. The yields increase.
> C. The yields stay the same.
> D. This cannot be determined with the information given.

This question is asking you to apply your knowledge of economics, investment recommendations and the relationship between bond prices and yields. Consumer purchasing power declines during periods of inflation. Inflation causes interest rates to rise, and this in turn causes prices of outstanding bonds to decrease. You will learn that when a bond declines in price or sells at a discount, the current yield increases (answer B).

This same content could have been tested in a different way, as illustrated by the next example.

> What is the effect of tight money on bond prices?
>
> A. Bond prices decrease.
> B. Bond prices increase.
> C. Bond prices stay the same.
> D. This cannot be determined with the information given.

When you study the sections on economics, you will see that tight money is closely related to high interest rates. When money is scarce (tight), interest rates rise. When interest rates rise, prices of outstanding bonds decrease (answer A).

At first glance, the two questions appear very different, but in fact they test the same relationship—the relationship between a bond's price and its yield. Be aware that the exam will approach a concept from different angles.

Look for Key Words and Phrases

Look for words that are tip-offs to the situation presented. For example, if you see the word "prospectus" in the question stem, you know the question is about a new issue.

Sometimes a question will even supply you with the answer if you can recognize the key words it contains. The following is an example of how a key word can help you answer correctly.

> Whose Social Security number must appear on an account under the Uniform Gifts to Minors Act?
>
> A. Minor
> B. Donor
> C. Legal guardian
> D. Parent

Looking at the answers, answer A is a likely candidate. You will learn that under UGMA, the minor is the owner of the securities. As the owner, the minor's Social Security number must be listed on the account. Few questions provide clues as blatant as this one, but many do offer key words that can guide you to selecting the correct answer if you pay attention.

Be sure to read all instructional phrases carefully, as illustrated in the next example.

Rank the following persons in descending order of their claims against a corporation's assets when the corporation is forced into liquidation.

I. General creditors
II. Preferred stockholders
III. Bondholders
IV. Common stockholders

A. I, II, III, IV
B. I, III, II, IV
C. III, I, II, IV
D. III, II, IV, I

The most important aspect of this question is identifying the key word—*descending*. A descending order ranks a list from highest to lowest—in this question, the highest claim on assets to the lowest claim on assets. (The answer is C: bondholders, general creditors, preferred stockholders, common stockholders.) The question could have asked for the *ascending* order—lowest to highest. Or it could have asked you to rank the choices from junior claim to senior claim or vice versa. Take time to identify the key words to answer this type of question correctly.

Identify the Intent of the Question

Many questions on the Series 6 exam supply so much information that you lose track of what is being asked. This is often the case in story problems. Learn to separate the "story" from the question. For example:

You have decided to buy 100 shares of ArGood Mutual Fund, which prices its shares at 5:00 p.m. every business day. You turn in your order at 3:00 p.m. when the shares are priced at $10 NAV, $10.86 POP. The sales load is 7.9 percent. What will your 100 shares cost?

A. $1,000
B. $1,079
C. $1,086
D. 100 times the offering price that will be calculated at 5:00 p.m.

A clue to the answer is presented in the first sentence—the fund price at 5:00 p.m. Orders for mutual funds are executed based on the next price calculated (forward pricing); therefore, the answer to this question is D. You do not need to calculate anything.

Take the time to identify what the question is asking. Of course, your ability to do so assumes you have studied sufficiently. There is no magic method for answering questions if you don't know the material.

Recognize Synonymous Terms

The securities industry has a tendency to abbreviate terms and use acronyms. Several terms may be used interchangeably throughout the test, and you should be able to recognize them. Examples include:

- NAV = net asset value = bid price
- POP = public offering price = ask price
- periodic payment plan = contractual plan
- buy = long = own
- sell = short = owe
- registered representative (RR) = account executive (AE)
- tax-sheltered annuity (TSA) = tax-deferred annuity (TDA)
- Uniform Gifts to Minors Act (UGMA) = Uniform Transfers to Minors Act (UTMA)
- VLI = variable life insurance

Memorize Key Points

Reasoning and logic will help you answer many questions, but you will have to memorize a good deal of information. In particular, you should try to memorize these key points: sales charges for investment companies; sales charge refunds for contractual plan withdrawals; the difference between refunds from spread load plans and those from front-end load plans; and the difference between sales literature and advertising.

Eliminate/Short-List Roman Numeral Choices

Roman numeral (or *multiple-multiple)* questions are common on the Series 6 exam; they require you to distinguish between several likely answers. When you are confronted with Roman numeral choices, try to eliminate one or two of them. Doing so helps to narrow your choices. For example, if you can eliminate choice II in a Roman numeral question, and three of the four answers contain choice II, you have successfully narrowed down your options to the correct answer by the process of elimination. For example:

> An owner of <u>common stock</u> has which of the following rights?
>
> I. Right to determine when dividends will be issued
> II. Right to vote at stockholders' meetings or by proxy
> III. Right to determine the amount of any dividends issued
> IV. Right to buy redeemed shares before they are offered to the public
>
> A. I, III and IV
> B. II
> C. II, III and IV
> D. II and IV

The answer to this question is B. Stockholders have the right to vote on certain corporate matters and the right to dividends if and when declared.

Stockholders do not vote on when a dividend is to be paid, nor on the amount of dividend to be paid. Knowing this, you can eliminate answers A and C. You are now left with only two answers from which to choose.

Use a Calculator

For the most part, the Series 6 exam will not require the use of a calculator. Most of the questions are written so that any math required is simple. However, if you have become accustomed to using a calculator for math, you will be provided with one by the testing center staff.

Beware of Changing Answers

If you are unsure of an answer, your first hunch is the one most likely to be correct. Do not change answers on the exam without good reason. In general, change an answer only if you:

- discover that you did not read the question correctly
- find new or additional helpful information in another question

Pace Yourself

Some people will finish the exam early; some will use the entire time allowed; and some do not have time to finish all the questions. Watch the time carefully (your time remaining will be displayed on your PROCTOR® screen) and pace yourself through the exam.

Do not waste time by dwelling on a question if you simply do not know the answer. Make the best guess you can, mark the question for "Record for Review," and return to the question if time allows. Make sure that you have time to read all the questions so that you can record the answers you do know.

To give yourself an indication of how much time you need to answer a 100-question exam, time yourself on the final exams provided in the *Questions & Answers* book. Your ability to take an exam within an allotted time will improve with practice.

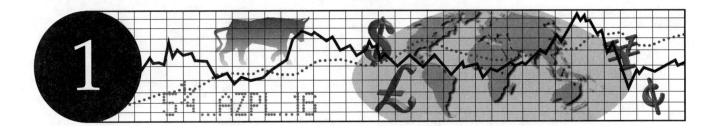

Common Stock

1. Five directors will be elected at the annual meeting of Consolidated Codfish. Under the cumulative voting system, an investor with 100 shares of COD would have

    A. 100 votes that she could cast for each of five directors
    B. 100 total votes that she could cast in any way she chooses among five directors
    C. 500 votes that she could cast for each of five directors
    D. 500 total votes that she could cast in any way she chooses among five directors

2. Which of the following statements describe treasury stock?

    I. It has voting rights and is entitled to a dividend when declared.
    II. It has no voting rights and no dividend entitlement.
    III. It has been issued and repurchased by the company.
    IV. It is authorized but unissued stock.

    A. I and III
    B. I and IV
    C. II and III
    D. II and IV

3. Stockholders' preemptive rights include the right to

    A. serve as an officer on the board of directors
    B. maintain proportionate ownership interest in the corporation
    C. purchase treasury stock
    D. pay a subscription price on stock

4. Common stockholders' rights include a

    I. residual claim to assets at dissolution
    II. vote for the amount of stock dividend to be paid
    III. vote in matters of recapitalization
    IV. claim against dividends in default

    A. I
    B. I and III
    C. II and III
    D. III and IV

5. The holders of which of the following securities are considered owners of the corporation?

    I. Mortgage bonds
   II. Convertible debentures
  III. Preferred stock
  IV. Common stock

  A. I, II and III only
  B. III and IV only
  C. IV only
  D. I, II, III and IV

Answers & Rationale

1. **D.** With cumulative voting rights, this investor may cast 500 votes for the five directors in any way she chooses. (Page 6)

2. **C.** Treasury stock is stock a corporation has issued and subsequently repurchased from the public in the secondary market. It does not carry the rights of other common shares, including voting rights and the right to receive dividends. (Page 4)

3. **B.** A *preemptive right* is a stockholder's right to purchase enough of any newly issued stock to maintain his proportionate ownership in the corporation. (Page 6)

4. **B.** As a corporation's owners, common stockholders have the lowest claim against a company's assets at dissolution or bankruptcy. Holders of common stock are entitled to vote on matters that affect their proportionate ownership. Recapitalization—the alteration of a corporation's capital structure—is an example of a situation that requires a vote of the stockholders. (Page 5)

5. **B.** Common and preferred stock are equity securities. Bondholders are creditors of the corporation. (Page 2)

2

Preferred Stock

1. Which of the following are considered to have equity positions in a corporation?

   I. Common stockholders
   II. Preferred stockholders
   III. Convertible bondholders
   IV. Mortgage bondholders

   A. I and II only
   B. I and III only
   C. II and III only
   D. I, II, III and IV

2. In a portfolio containing common stock, preferred stock, convertible preferred stock and guaranteed stock, changes in interest rates would be MOST likely to affect the market price of the

   A. common
   B. preferred
   C. convertible preferred
   D. guaranteed

3. Which of the following statements is true of a company offering cumulative nonpartici-pating voting preferred stock?

   A. It pays the preferred dividend before paying the coupons due on its outstand-ing bonds.
   B. It pays past and current preferred divi-dends before paying dividends on common.
   C. It pays the current dividends on the pre-ferred, but not the past dividends on the preferred, before paying a dividend on the common.
   D. It forces conversion of the preferred that is trading at a discount to par, thereby eliminating the necessity of paying past-due dividends.

Answers & Rationale

1. **A.** Owners have equity positions. Common and preferred stockholders are owners. (Page 8)

2. **B.** Preferred stock most closely resembles bonds and would be most affected by a change in interest rates. (Page 8)

3. **B.** The company must pay current and unpaid past dividends on cumulative preferred stock before common stockholders can receive a dividend. (Page 9)

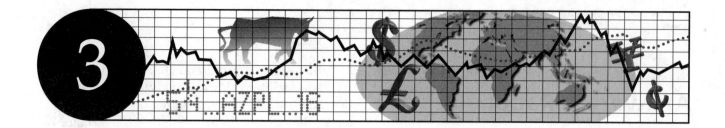

American Depositary Receipts

1. ADRs facilitate which of the following?

   I. Foreign trading of domestic securities
   II. Foreign trading of U.S. government securities
   III. Domestic trading of U.S. government securities
   IV. Domestic trading of foreign securities

   A. I and II
   B. III
   C. III and IV
   D. IV

2. Which of the following statements is(are) true concerning ADRs?

   I. They are issued by large commercial U.S. banks.
   II. They encourage foreign trading in U.S. markets.
   III. They facilitate U.S. trading in foreign securities.
   IV. They are registered on the books of the bank that issued the ADRs.

   A. I and III
   B. I, III and IV
   C. II
   D. II and IV

3. ADR owners have all of the following rights EXCEPT

   A. voting rights
   B. right to receive dividends
   C. preemptive rights
   D. right to receive the underlying foreign security

Answers & Rationale

1.   **D.**   ADRs (American depositary receipts) are tradeable securities issued by banks, with the receipts' value based on the underlying foreign securities the bank holds. In this way, Americans can trade foreign securities in the United States.
(Page 12)

2.   **B.**   Large commercial U.S. banks issue ADRs to facilitate U.S. trading in foreign securities. ADRs are registered on the books of the banks that issued them.   (Page 12)

3.   **C.**   If the foreign company issues additional securities, the ADR owner does not have the right to maintain proportionate ownership of the company.   (Page 12)

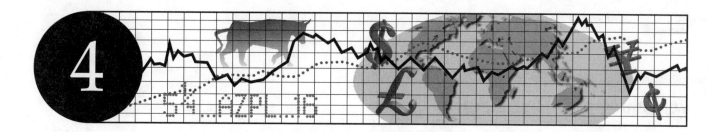

Tracking Equity Securities

1. ALFAtronics closed at 42⅝. The closing price per share was

    A. $4.26
    B. $42.63
    C. $426.25
    D. $4,262.50

2. Anchor closed at 30 and pays a dividend of 1.60. Thus, the current yield would be

    A. 3.1 percent
    B. 4.8 percent
    C. 5.3 percent
    D. 18.6 percent

3. Acme Sweatsocks's volume was reported as 178; the number of shares traded was

    A. 178
    B. 1,780
    C. 17,800
    D. 178,000

Answers & Rationale

1. **B.** 42⅝ = $42 + $⅝ or .625, which is rounded up to $.63, for $42.63 per share.   (Page 14)

2. **C.** 1.60 ÷ 30 = 5.33%.   (Page 14)

3. **C.** 178 × 100 = 17,800.   (Page 14)

Rights and Warrants

1. How would a corporation benefit by attaching warrants to a new issue of debt securities?

   A. Dilution of shareholders' equity
   B. Reduction of the debt securities' interest rate
   C. Reduction of the number of shares outstanding
   D. Increase in earnings per share

2. A corporate offering of 200,000 additional shares to existing stockholders is what type of offering?

   A. Tender
   B. Secondary
   C. Preemptive
   D. Rights

3. A new bond issue includes warrants to

   A. increase the spread to the underwriter
   B. compensate the underwriter for handling the issue
   C. increase the issue's price to the public
   D. increase the issue's attractiveness to the public

4. All of the following pay dividends EXCEPT

   A. common stock
   B. preferred stock
   C. convertible preferred stock
   D. warrants

Answers & Rationale

1.   **B.**   Usually, the warrant is issued as a sweetener to make the debt instrument more marketable. This enhancement allows the issuer to pay a slightly lower rate of interest. A warrant may be issued together with bonds or preferred stock, entitling the owner to purchase a given number of common stock shares at a specific price for a certain number of years.   (Page 17)

2.   **D.**   The question defines a rights offering.   (Page 16)

3.   **D.**   Warrants are used as a sweetener to increase a new issue's attractiveness to the public.   (Page 17)

4.   **D.**   Warrants do not pay dividends under any circumstances. The other instruments listed pay dividends when declared by the board of directors.   (Page 17)

6

Introduction to Options

1. An investor is in a position to acquire stock under which of the following circumstances?

    I. She buys a call.
   II. She buys a put.
  III. She sells a call.
  IV. She sells a put.

  A. I and III
  B. I and IV
  C. II and III
  D. II and IV

2. An investor is in a position to sell stock under which of the following circumstances?

    I. He buys a call.
   II. He buys a put.
  III. He sells a call.
  IV. He sells a put.

  A. I and III
  B. I and IV
  C. II and III
  D. II and IV

Answers & Rationale

1.   **B.**   The holder of a call has the right to buy stock at the strike price; the seller of a put is obligated to buy stock at the strike price if exercised.

(Page 18)

2.   **C.**   The holder of a put has the right to sell stock at the strike price; the seller of a call is obligated to sell stock at the strike price if exercised.

(Page 18)

Characteristics of Bonds

1. Your customer holds a 10M KLP 6s bond callable at 102 in 1995 and maturing in 2001. How much money will the customer receive in total at the debenture's maturity?

   A. $10,000
   B. $10,200
   C. $10,300
   D. $10,600

2. All of the following are true about bonds registered as to principal only EXCEPT that

   A. coupons are attached
   B. the registered owner may sell the bonds before maturity
   C. interest payments are sent directly to the owner twice a year
   D. such bonds can be purchased today in the secondary market

3. A corporation calls in its debt during a period of

   A. rising interest rates
   B. declining interest rates
   C. volatile interest rates
   D. stable interest rates

4. Max Leveridge purchases $50,000 worth of 10 percent corporate bonds at par. At the end of the day, the bonds close down ½ a point. Max has a loss of

   A. $25
   B. $250
   C. $2,500
   D. $5,000

5. Your customer has two $5,000 bonds. One has a coupon of 5.1 percent; the other has a coupon of 5.3 percent. What is the difference in annual interest payments between the bonds?

   A. $1
   B. $2
   C. $10
   D. $20

6. Which of the following is a characteristic of bearer bonds?

   A. They come in registered form.
   B. They have interest coupons attached to the bonds.
   C. They have interest coupons detached from the bonds.
   D. They pay interest quarterly.

7. Which of the following statements is true for an investor who purchased $50,000 face value of 5.10 bonds at par due in 2002 and held them to maturity?

    A. The investor received $50,000, the final two interest payments and 5.10 market gain at maturity.
    B. The investor received $50,000 less 5.10 market discount at maturity.
    C. The investor received $50,000 plus 5.10 at maturity.
    D. The investor received $50,000 and the final interest payment at maturity.

8. The difference between par and a lower market price on a bond is called the

    A. reallowance
    B. spread
    C. discount
    D. premium

9. Which of the following factors is LEAST important in rating a bond?

    A. Bond's coupon
    B. Amount and composition of existing debt
    C. Stability of the issuer's cash flows
    D. Asset protection

10. Texas Powerful Light Company issued mortgage senior lien bonds at 8⅞, price 96.353. Each $1,000 bond pays annual interest of

    A. $85.00
    B. $85.51
    C. $88.75
    D. $96.35

Answers & Rationale

1.   **C.**   The holder of a 10M bond will receive $10,000 in principal at maturity. Each bond pays 6 percent annual interest, or $60; thus, 10 bonds pay a total of $600 per year in two semiannual payments of $300. At maturity, the bondholder will receive the $10,000 face amount plus the final semiannual payment ($10,000 + $300 = $10,300).
(Page 20)

2.   **C.**   A bond registered as to principal only has a certificate registered in some person's name and has bearer coupons attached to the bond certificate. Only the person to whom the bond is registered may sell the securities. Interest is paid on the bond only if the interest coupons are sent to the bond's paying agent.   (Page 21)

3.   **B.**   A corporation generally calls in its debt when interest rates decline. It can then replace old, high interest rate debt with a new, lower interest rate issue.   (Page 25)

4.   **B.**   The customer holds 50 $1,000 bonds. If each bond decreases by ½ point, the loss is $5 per bond; multiplied by 50 bonds, this equals $250.
(Page 22)

5.   **C.**   To determine the dollar difference between the bonds, calculate the two interest payments and find the difference between them. (In this case, $5,000 × 5.1 percent = $255; $5,000 × 5.3 percent = $265; $265 – $255 = $10.)   (Page 22)

6.   **B.**   Bearer bonds, also called *unregistered bonds*, must have the interest coupons attached to the bonds.   (Page 20)

7.   **D.**   Because the investor purchased the 2002 bonds at par ($1,000 per bond) and redeemed them at par ($1,000 per bond), the investor received $50,000 plus the final six-month interest payment of $1,275 at maturity.   (Page 22)

8.   **C.**   The difference between a bond's par (or face) value and a market price lower than par is known as the bond's *discount from par*.   (Page 22)

9.   **A.**   The coupon rate that a bond pays is not a factor in rating the bond, although the rating that a bond could receive may significantly affect the interest rate the issuers must set.   (Page 23)

10.   **C.**   A coupon of 8⅞ represents an annual interest payment of 8⅞ percent of $1,000, or $88.75.   (Page 20)

Bond Yields

1. If interest rates are changing, which of the following terms would best describe the relationship between prices and yields for corporate bonds?

    A. Reverse
    B. Inverse
    C. Coterminous
    D. Coaxial

2. With fluctuating interest rates, the price of which of the following fluctuates most?

    A. Common stock
    B. Money-market instruments
    C. Short-term bonds
    D. Long-term bonds

3. How do you calculate the current yield on a bond?

    A. Yield to maturity ÷ Par value
    B. Yield to maturity ÷ Dollar market price
    C. Annual interest payment ÷ Par value
    D. Annual interest payment ÷ Dollar market price

4. The current yield on a bond priced at $950 with a coupon bearing interest at 6 percent equals

    A. the nominal yield
    B. yield to maturity
    C. 6 percent
    D. 6.3 percent

5. The current yield on a bond with a coupon rate of 7½ percent currently selling at 95 is approximately

    A. 7.0 percent
    B. 7.4 percent
    C. 7.9 percent
    D. 8.0 percent

6. A customer purchases a 5 percent corporate bond yielding 6 percent. A year before the bond matures, new corporate bonds are being issued at 4 percent and the customer sells the 5 percent bond. In this case, which of the following statements about the bond are true?

   I. The customer bought it at a discount.
  II. The customer bought it at a premium.
 III. The customer sold it at a premium.
 IV. The customer sold it at a discount.

A. I and III
B. I and IV
C. II and III
D. II and IV

7. A bond at par has a coupon rate

A. less than current yield
B. less than yield to maturity
C. equal to current yield
D. higher than current yield

8. Which of the following happens to outstanding fixed-income securities when interest rates drop?

A. Yields go up.
B. Coupon rates go up.
C. Prices go up.
D. Prices go down.

Answers & Rationale

1. **B.** As interest rates increase, the price of outstanding debt decreases and vice versa. Because the face and coupon on a debt instrument remain unchanged, the market value fluctuates to account for changes in yields. (Page 27)

2. **D.** Long-term debt prices fluctuate more than short-term debt prices as interest rates rise and fall. When an investor buys a note or a bond, he really buys the interest payments and the final principal payment. Money has a time value: the farther out in time money is to be received, the less it is worth today. (Page 27)

3. **D.** A bond's current yield equals the annual interest payment divided by the current market price. (Page 27)

4. **D.** The current yield is the coupon ($60) divided by the bond market price ($950) equals 6.3 percent. (Page 27)

5. **C.** Each $1,000 7½ percent bond pays $75 of interest annually. Current yield equals the annual interest divided by the bond market price, or $75 divided by $950, which equals 7.89 percent, or approximately 7.9 percent. (Page 27)

6. **A.** If a bond's current yield is higher than its coupon rate, the bond is selling at a discount from par. If interest rates of newly issued bonds are lower than a secondary market bond's rate, it is likely that the older bond could be sold at a premium. (Page 27)

7. **C.** When a bond is selling at par, its coupon rate, nominal rate and current yield are the same. (Page 27)

8. **C.** When interest rates drop, the coupons on new issue bonds decline in order to offer lower yields. The price of outstanding bonds rises to adjust to the lower yields on bonds of comparable quality. (Page 27)

Corporate Bonds

1. In case of bankruptcy, debentures rank on a par with

   A. first-mortgage bonds
   B. equipment trust certificates
   C. unsecured debts of private creditors
   D. collateral trust bonds

2. Which of the following statements are true regarding corporate zero-coupon bonds?

   I. Interest is paid semiannually.
   II. Interest is not paid until maturity.
   III. The discount must be prorated and is taxed annually.
   IV. The discount must be prorated annually, with taxation deferred to maturity.

   A. I and III
   B. I and IV
   C. II and III
   D. II and IV

3. In the liquidation of the assets of General Gizmonics, Inc., in what order would the following organizations and individuals receive payment?

   I. Internal Revenue Service
   II. Holders of subordinated debentures
   III. General creditors
   IV. Common stockholders

   A. I, II, III, IV
   B. I, III, II, IV
   C. III, I, II, IV
   D. IV, III, II, I

4. Which of the following is NOT true concerning convertible bonds?

   A. Coupon rates are usually higher than nonconvertible bond rates of the same issuer.
   B. Convertible bondholders are creditors of the corporation.
   C. Coupon rates are usually lower than nonconvertible bond rates of the same issuer.
   D. If the underlying common stock were to decline to the point where there is no advantage to convert the bonds into common stock, the bonds would sell at a price based on their inherent value as bonds, disregarding the convertible feature.

5. What is the conversion ratio of a convertible bond purchased at face value and convertible at $50?

    A. 2:1
    B. 3:1
    C. 20:1
    D. 30:1

6. Angus Bullwether purchases two newly issued $1,000 par, 5 percent convertible corporate bonds at par. The bonds are convertible into common stock at $50 per share. During the period in which the investor holds the bonds, the $50 common stock market price increases by 25 percent. The parity price of the bond, after the increase in the common stock price, is

    A. $750
    B. $1,000
    C. $1,025
    D. $1,250

7. Klaus Bruin purchases a 9 percent convertible bond maturing in 20 years. The bond is convertible into common stock at $50 per share. If the common stock price is at parity (57½), how much does Klaus pay for the bond?

    A. $850.00
    B. $942.50
    C. $1,057.50
    D. $1,150.00

8. If Belle Charolais owns a convertible bond for Consolidated Codfish, she is

    A. an owner
    B. a creditor
    C. both owner and creditor
    D. neither owner nor creditor

Answers & Rationale

1. **C.** Debentures represent unsecured loans to an issuer. All of the other bonds listed are backed by one form or another of collateral. (Page 31)

2. **C.** The investor in a corporate zero-coupon bond receives his return in the form of growth of the principal amount during the bond's life. The bond is purchased at a steep discount, and the discount is accrued by the investor and taxed by the government annually. (Page 31)

3. **B.** The order in a liquidation is as follows: the IRS and other government agencies, secured debt holders, unsecured debt holders and general creditors, holders of subordinated debt, preferred stockholders and, finally, common stockholders. (Page 32)

4. **A.** Coupon rates are not higher; they are lower because of the conversion feature's value. The bondholders are creditors, and if the stock price falls, the conversion feature will not influence the bond's price. (Page 34)

5. **C.** The $1,000 par value divided by the $50 conversion price equals 20 shares per bond. (Page 34)

6. **D.** The bond is convertible into 20 shares ($1,000 ÷ 50 = 20). $50 times 125 percent equals $62.50. 20 shares multiplied by $62.50 equals $1,250. (Page 34)

7. **D.** Because the bond is convertible at $50 per share, each bond can be converted into 20 shares of stock ($1,000 ÷ 50 = 20). The common stock price is now 57½. For the bond to be selling at parity, it must sell for 20 multiplied by $57.50, which equals $1,150. (Page 34)

8. **B.** A bondholder is a creditor, whether or not the bond is convertible. Only after the bond is converted to stock is she considered to be an owner. (Page 33)

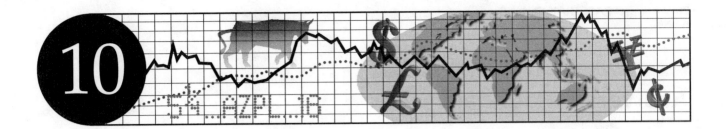

Tracking Corporate Bonds

Use the table below to answer questions 1 and 2.

Bonds	Cur Yld	Vol	Close	Net Change
Best 7 3/4's '95	7.2	5	92	− 1/2
Bzdt 7 1/2's '99	6.8	30	95 3/8	+ 3/8

1. How many Bzdt bonds were sold this day?

   A. 3
   B. 30
   C. 300
   D. 30,000

2. Best's bonds closed the day before at

   A. 91½
   B. 92
   C. 92½
   D. This cannot be determined from the information given.

Answers & Rationale

1.   **B.**   Thirty bonds, because bonds are quoted in $1,000 par value units, 30 bonds = $30,000 face amount.   (Page 35)

2.   **C.**   Today, Best closed at 92, down ½. Therefore, Best closed the day before at 92.50, or 92½.
                                                 (Page 35)

11

U.S. Government and Agency Securities

1. The holder of which of the following instruments receives no interest?

   A. Treasury STRIPS
   B. Treasury notes
   C. Treasury bonds
   D. Treasury stock

2. Which of the following maturities is available to investors in newly issued Treasury bills?

   A. One week
   B. One month
   C. Six months
   D. Nine months

3. Which of the following statements is true of a Treasury STRIPS, but not of a Treasury receipt?

   A. It may be stripped and issued by a securities broker-dealer.
   B. It is backed by the full faith and credit of the federal government.
   C. Its stripped-off interest coupons are sold separately.
   D. Investors may purchase it at a discount.

4. One of your customers would like to invest in a fairly safe security, but is not interested in regular income. Which of the following securities are offered at a discount and would meet his needs?

   A. GNMA certificates
   B. FHLB securities
   C. FNMA certificates
   D. U.S. Treasury STRIPS

5. If interest rates in general are rising, the price of new T bills SHOULD

   A. rise
   B. fall
   C. remain steady
   D. fluctuate

6. All of the following are characteristics of an investment in Treasury notes EXCEPT

   A. interest is paid semiannually
   B. they are issued in a variety of denominations
   C. they are issued with a variety of maturities
   D. they are short-term issues

7. Your customer would like to purchase a Series HH bond. He can do this by

   A. applying to the Treasury Department
   B. submitting a competitive bid
   C. trading in a T note at maturity
   D. trading in a Series EE bond at maturity

8. A client could be assured of federal government backing for an investment issued by which of the following entities?

   A. Federal National Mortgage Association
   B. Federal Home Loan Bank
   C. Government National Mortgage Association
   D. Federal Intermediate Credit Banks

9. In describing GNMAs to a potential investor, you tell him that

   A. the certificates have the full faith and credit guarantee of the U.S. government
   B. each bond is backed by a pool of uninsured mortgages
   C. interest payments the investor receives are exempt from both local and federal income taxes
   D. a GNMA can be purchased for as little as $10,000

10. CMOs are backed by which of the following?

    A. Mortgages
    B. Real estate
    C. Municipal taxes
    D. Full faith and credit of U.S. government

11. Which of the following securities is characterized by the term "tranche"?

    A. FNMA
    B. T bond
    C. CMO
    D. FHLMC

12. All of the following statements about government agency securities are true EXCEPT that

    A. they may be backed by the federal government
    B. they are often considered more risky than corporate securities
    C. interest paid is always subject to federal income tax
    D. they are authorized by Congress

Answers & Rationale

1.   **D.**   A company that has bought back its own stock and holds it in its treasury does not pay itself dividends on that stock. STRIPS (Separate Trading of Registered Interest and Principal of Securities) are T bonds with the coupons removed. Although STRIPS do not pay interest separately, they are sold at a deep discount and mature at face (par) value, which the IRS considers to be interest.   (Page 38)

2.   **C.**   Investors can acquire Treasury bills at the weekly T bill auction in denominations of $10,000 and up with maturities of 3 months, 6 months and 12 months. The U.S. government can issue 9-month certificates, but currently it does not.   (Page 36)

3.   **B.**   Treasury receipts are stripped treasuries and, as such, are issued in stripped form by an institution other than the federal government. Only direct issues of the U.S. government are backed by its full faith and credit.   (Page 38)

4.   **D.**   U.S. Treasury STRIPS (Separate Trading of Registered Interest and Principal of Securities) are direct obligations of the U.S. Treasury issued in the form of zero-coupon bonds. Zero-coupon bonds pay no interest. They are issued at a discount and appreciate in value each period until maturity.   (Page 38)

5.   **B.**   Bill prices decrease as interest rates rise.   (Page 36)

6.   **D.**   Treasury notes are intermediate-term issues; T bills are short-term issues, and T bonds are long-term issues. The other choices are characteristics of T notes.   (Page 37)

7.   **D.**   Series HH bonds can be purchased only by trading in a Series EE bond at maturity.
(Page 38)

8.   **C.**   Only the Government National Mortgage Association issues securities backed by the full faith and credit of the U.S. government. The other entities listed are considered government agencies, and although their securities are considered second only to U.S. government issues in safety, they do not have direct U.S. government backing.   (Page 39)

9.   **A.**   The certificates issued by the GNMA represent interests in government-insured mortgages pooled by mortgage brokers who guarantee the monthly cash flow, but it is the U.S. government that actually "backs" GNMA pass-through certificates. GNMA pass-throughs are issued in minimum denominations of $25,000, and all interest earned is subject to federal income tax.
(Page 39)

10.   **A.**   Collateralized mortgage obligations are collateralized by mortgages on real estate. They do not own the underlying real estate, so they are not considered to be backed by it.   (Page 41)

11.   **C.**   Collateralized mortgage obligations are divided into maturity classes called *tranches*. The tranche determines the maturity schedule and level of risk associated with a particular CMO.
(Page 41)

12.   **B.**   Corporate securities are generally considered more risky than government agency issues. Agency issues have only a slight risk of default because they are backed by revenues from taxes, fees and interest income. Agency issues include GNMAs, which are backed by the full faith and credit of the government. Some agency issues are exempt from state and local taxation, but they are not exempt from federal taxation. Congress authorizes these agencies to issue debt securities.   (Page 39)

Municipal Bonds

12

1. Which of the following sources of funds back revenue bonds?

   I. Federal revenue sharing
   II. Special taxes on tobacco and alcohol
   III. Rental payments under leaseback arrangements
   IV. Tolls and fees

   A. I and II only
   B. II, III and IV only
   C. III and IV only
   D. I, II, III and IV

2. Which of the following statements is(are) true of industrial development bonds?

   I. They are a primary obligation of the corporation.
   II. They are issued by municipalities to provide funds for local industries.
   III. The bonds' credit rating is the same as the municipality's credit rating.

   A. I and II
   B. II
   C. II and III
   D. III

3. Which of the following statements are NOT true concerning revenue bonds?

   I. They are secured by a specific pledge of property.
   II. They are a type of general obligation bond.
   III. Generally, they are not subject to the issuing jurisdiction's statutory debt limitations.
   IV. They are analyzed primarily on the project's ability to generate earnings.

   A. I and II
   B. I, II and IV
   C. II and III
   D. III and IV

4. The doctrine of tax-free reciprocity for municipal bonds originated in

   A. U.S. Supreme Court decisions
   B. state laws
   C. federal laws
   D. IRS interpretations

5. All of the following entities may issue municipal bonds EXCEPT

   A. New York/New Jersey Port Authority
   B. Holy Name Cathedral, Chicago
   C. Territory of Puerto Rico
   D. City of Little Rock

6. A taxpayer in the 28 percent bracket would net the highest after-tax income from a

   A. 5 percent municipal bond
   B. 5½ percent T bill
   C. 6 percent income bond
   D. 6½ percent corporate bond

Answers & Rationale

1.   **B.**   Typical sources of funds for revenue bonds include user charges, special taxes, payments under leaseback arrangements, lease revenues, and tolls and other fees from the facility's operation. Federal revenue sharing is not a funding source for revenue bonds.   (Page 44)

2.   **A.**   Although municipalities issue IDBs to provide funds for local industries, IDBs are a primary obligation of a corporation, not a municipality. The municipality merely acts as a conduit in issuing the bonds. Thus, the bonds' credit rating depends on the corporation's credit rating, not the municipality's.   (Page 45)

3.   **A.**   Revenue bonds are not secured by a specific pledge of property and are not a type of general obligation bond.   (Page 44)

4.   **A.**   The doctrine of reciprocal immunity, or mutual exclusion, was determined in the Supreme Court Case of *McCulloch v. Maryland*.   (Page 42)

5.   **B.**   Only U.S. territorial possessions, legally constituted taxing authorities and public authorities can issue municipal debt securities. Churches may issue bonds, but they do not offer the tax benefits of municipal bonds.   (Page 44)

6.   **A.**   Municipal bonds are exempt from federal taxation and, in most cases, from taxation by the states in which they are issued. This particular investor would be taxed at the 28 percent level. The equivalent yield on a corporate bond would be 6.94 percent (5 percent ÷ 72 percent). (Page 43)

13

The Money Market

1. Corporations issue commercial paper with maturities ranging from as little as 1 day to as long as

   A. 7 days
   B. 90 days
   C. 270 days
   D. 365 days

2. Which of the following are characteristics of negotiable CDs?

   I. Issued in amounts of $100,000 to $1 million
   II. Fully insured by the FDIC
   III. Mature in less than 270 days
   IV. Trade in the secondary market

   A. I, II and III
   B. I and IV
   C. II, III and IV
   D. III and IV

3. Which of the following are characteristics of commercial paper?

   I. Backed by money-market deposits
   II. Negotiated maturities and yields
   III. Issued by commercial banks
   IV. Exempt from registration

   A. I and II
   B. I, II and III
   C. II and IV
   D. III and IV

4. Which of the following instruments is commonly used to settle transactions involving imports and exports?

   A. ADRs
   B. Bankers' acceptances
   C. Eurodollars
   D. Foreign currencies

5. Which of the following is a money-market instrument?

   A. Short-term debt
   B. Long-term debt
   C. Short-term equity
   D. Long-term equity

6. Commercial paper is a

   A. secured note issued by a corporation
   B. guaranteed note issued by a corporation
   C. promissory note issued by a corporation
   D. promissory note issued by a broker-
      dealer

Answers & Rationale

1.   **C.**   Commercial paper with a maximum maturity of 270 days is issued by a corporation in part to avoid certain registration requirements under the act of 1933.   (Page 46)

2.   **B.**   Negotiable CDs are issued for $100,000 to $1 million and, as money-market instruments, are commonly traded in the secondary market. Most are issued with maturities of less than a year, but initial maturities of three to five years can be arranged. The FDIC insures nonnegotiable CDs up to $100,000 each.   (Page 47)

3.   **C.**   Commercial paper represents the unsecured debt obligations of corporations in need of short-term financing. Both yield and maturity are open to negotiation. Because commercial paper is issued with maturities of less than 270 days, it is exempt from registration under the act of 1933.
               (Page 46)

4.   **B.**   Corporations use BAs to settle transactions involving imports and exports of goods.
               (Page 46)

5.   **A.**   A money-market instrument is short-term debt with one year or less to maturity.
               (Page 45)

6.   **C.**   A corporation issues commercial paper as a short-term promissory note.   (Page 46)

The Underwriting Process

1. Which of the following is NOT a basic responsibility of an investment banker?

   A. Distributing large blocks of stock to the public and to institutions
   B. Providing a secondary market for securities that have been issued
   C. Advising corporations on the best way to raise long-term capital
   D. Buying previously unissued securities from an issuer and selling them to the public

2. This Can't Be Sushi (TCB) wants to offer $7 million of its common stock in its home state and in three other states. For the SEC to clear the offer for sale, TCB must file a(n)

   A. offering circular
   B. registration statement
   C. letter of notification
   D. preliminary prospectus

Answers & Rationale

1.   **B.**   An investment banker's main functions are raising intermediate and long-term capital for corporations through the distribution of securities, buying securities from an issuer and reselling them to the public, distributing large blocks of stock and advising corporations on the best way to raise long-term capital. It is not the investment banker's responsibility to provide a continuing secondary market for securities once they have been issued.   (Page 48)

2.   **B.**   TCB must file a standard registration statement.   (Page 49)

Types of Underwriting Commitments

1. Which of the following are terms for different types of underwritings?

   I. Best efforts
   II. Standby
   III. Firm commitment
   IV. Fail-to-receive

   A. I
   B. I, II and III
   C. I and III
   D. II, III and IV

2. ALFA Securities is the managing underwriter for a new issue of 1,000,000 Microscam common. It has agreed to sell as much of the stock as possible in the market, and Microscam has agreed to take back the rest unsold. This is known as what type of offering?

   A. Standby
   B. Best efforts
   C. All or none
   D. Contingency

3. ALFA Securities is the managing underwriter for a new issue of 1,000,000 Microscam common. It has agreed to sell all of the stock being offered, and has agreed to buy for its own account any stock that it cannot sell to the public. Microscam will receive the proceeds from the sale of 1,000,000 shares. This is known as what type of offering?

   A. Firm commitment
   B. Best efforts
   C. All or none
   D. Standby

4. Microscam is engaged in a stock rights offering with the help of ALFA Securities as managing underwriter. ALFA has offered to purchase any of the stock Microscam is unable to sell to current stockholders. This arrangement is known as what type of underwriting?

   A. Special
   B. Best efforts
   C. Standby
   D. All or none

Answers & Rationale

1.   **B.**   A fail-to-receive occurs when a broker-dealer does not receive the securities due it from a buy transaction. The main types of underwritings are:

- Best efforts—when an underwriter will do its best to sell the entire new issue but will not guarantee success.
- All or none—the underwriter will sell the entire issue or none will be sold.
- Firm commitment—the underwriter will guarantee to sell the entire issue.
- Standby—when a corporation will try and sell the new issue itself through a rights offering but will have an underwriter standing by to sell the unsold shares.

(Page 51)

2.   **B.**   A best efforts underwriting is one in which any stock that remains unsold is returned to the issuing corporation.   (Page 52)

3.   **A.**   A firm commitment requires the underwriter to sell the entire issue of stock or to purchase any unsold stock for its own inventory.
(Page 51)

4.   **C.**   A standby underwriting arrangement allows a corporation to sell as much of a new issue to current stockholders as possible, backed by the promise of an underwriter to take and sell any unsold shares to the public.   (Page 52)

Securities Markets and Broker-Dealers

1. An open-end investment company bought preferred utility stock from a bank through INSTINET. This trade took place in which market?

   A. Primary
   B. Secondary
   C. Third
   D. Fourth

2. A client tells you that his company regularly trades securities in the fourth market. This means that the company trades

   A. listed securities OTC
   B. unlisted securities OTC
   C. unlisted securities on an exchange
   D. all securities directly with other institutions

3. Your firm, Serendipity Discount Securities, has received an order from one of your customers to buy 300 shares of DWQ at the market. Serendipity goes into the market, buys 300 shares of DWQ from another broker-dealer, and delivers them to your customer's account. Serendipity's role in this transaction is that of a

   A. broker acting as an agent for a commission
   B. dealer acting as a principal for a profit
   C. broker acting as an agent for a profit
   D. dealer acting as a principal for a commission

4. Your firm, Serendipity Discount Securities, has received an order from one of your customers to buy 300 shares of DWQ at the market. Serendipity goes into the market and buys 300 shares of DWQ from another broker-dealer for its own inventory. It then sells those shares out of inventory to the customer's account. Serendipity's role in this transaction is that of a

   A. broker acting as an agent for a commission
   B. dealer acting as a principal for a profit
   C. broker acting as an agent for a profit
   D. dealer acting as a principal for a commission

5. Which of the following statements about transactions in the different securities markets is(are) true?

   I. Transactions in listed securities occur mainly in the exchange markets.

   II. Transactions in unlisted securities occur mainly in the OTC market.

   III. Transactions in listed securities that occur in the OTC market are said to take place in the third market.

   IV. Transactions in listed securities that occur directly between customers or institutions without broker-dealers as intermediaries are said to take place in the fourth market.

   A. I only
   B. I and II only
   C. II and III only
   D. I, II, III and IV

6. Which of the following trades occur(s) in the secondary market?

   I. Specialist on the NYSE buying stocks for his own inventory

   II. Municipal bond syndicate selling new issues to the public

   III. Registered representative buying unlisted securities for a client

   IV. Insurance company buying municipal bonds directly from another insurance company

   A. I, II and III
   B. I, III and IV
   C. II and III
   D. IV

Answers & Rationale

1.   **D.**   The fourth market consists of direct trades between institutions, pension funds, broker-dealers and others. Many of these trades use INSTINET.   (Page 53)

2.   **D.**   The fourth market (INSTINET) consists of transactions between corporations and other large institutions, such as mutual funds and pension plans, that do not involve intermediaries.
(Page 53)

3.   **A.**   Your firm acted as the customer's agent in acquiring the 300 shares of DWQ. The best way to remember the difference between brokers and dealers is through the letters BAC/DPP: "Brokers act as Agents for Commissions/Dealers act as Principals for Profits." *Profit* is another way of saying *markup*.   (Page 55)

4.   **B.**   Your firm acted as principal in first acquiring the 300 shares of DWQ for its inventory before selling them to the customer. The best way to remember the difference between brokers and dealers is through the letters BAC/DPP: "Brokers act as Agents for Commissions/Dealers act as Principals for Profits." *Profit* is another way of saying *markup*.   (Page 55)

5.   **D.**   Listed securities traded on exchanges compose the exchange market. Unlisted securities traded over the counter make up the OTC market. Listed securities traded OTC compose the third market. Securities bought and sold without the aid of a broker-dealer constitute the fourth market. INSTINET is a reporting service many institutions use to locate other parties for fourth-market equity transactions.   (Page 53)

6.   **B.**   Underwriters distribute new issues in the primary market. The secondary market is the trading market. In the trading market, a trade can take place on a stock exchange (the first market); in the unlisted or over-the-counter market (the second market); by trading listed securities in the over-the-counter market (the third market); or in a direct institution-to-institution trade without a brokerage firm's services (the fourth market).
(Page 53)

17

Brokerage Office Procedures

1. Under the Uniform Practice Code, regular way transactions settle on the

    A. same day as trade date
    B. second business day following trade date
    C. third business day following trade date
    D. fifth business day following trade date

2. The regular way ex-dividend date for stock is the

    A. second business day preceding the record date
    B. second business day following the record date
    C. second business day preceding the settlement date
    D. third business day preceding the record date

3. Settlement of securities transactions is made

    A. when the selling broker-dealer delivers the securities to the buying broker-dealer's office
    B. at either the office of the buyer or the seller, as specified at the time the parties enter into contract
    C. when the buying customer mails a check to his broker-dealer's office
    D. when the seller and the buyer meet at the transfer agent's office

4. When a client's account is frozen, the client

    A. must deposit the full purchase price no later than the settlement date for a purchase
    B. must deposit the full purchase price before a purchase order may be executed
    C. may make sales but not purchases of securities
    D. may not trade under any circumstances

5. Hugh Heifer wants to place an order to sell 200 shares of COD stock. Hugh currently has no COD shares in his account. Which of the following must a rep try to determine before accepting the order?

   A. The name of the broker from whom the stock was purchased
   B. Where the stock is currently held and whether it can be delivered in three business days
   C. The willingness of Hugh to deliver other securities from his account should he fail to deliver the COD stock
   D. Whether Hugh will pledge his other securities as collateral to secure a stock loan to effect timely delivery

Answers & Rationale

1.   **C.**   Under the Uniform Practice Code, regular way trades settle three business days after the trade date.   (Page 56)

2.   **A.**   The regular way ex-dividend date is two business days before the record date. This is the date on which the value of the stock is reduced by the dividend.   (Page 58)

3.   **A.**   Settlement of securities transactions occurs when the selling broker-dealer delivers to the buying broker-dealer.   (Page 56)

4.   **B.**   When an account is frozen, the client must deposit the full purchase price prior to any subsequent orders.   (Page 58)

5.   **B.**   The rep should ascertain the location of the stock and whether the customer can deliver within three business days, so that the firm can make timely delivery. The broker from whom the securities were purchased, and any other securities held by the customer, are immaterial.
                     (Page 56)

18

Economics

1. Arrange the following economic phases in the normal order in which they occur.

    I. Contraction
    II. Expansion
    III. Peak
    IV. Trough

    A. I, II, III, IV
    B. II, III, I, IV
    C. III, II, I, IV
    D. IV, I, III, II

2. During the past two quarters, the GDP declined by 3 percent, unemployment rose by .7 percent and the Consumer Price Index fell off by 1.3 percent. This economic condition is called

    A. inflation
    B. depression
    C. stagflation
    D. recession

3. What term do economists use to describe a downturn in the economy that lasts more than two consecutive quarters?

    A. Inflation
    B. Stagflation
    C. Depression
    D. Recession

4. The FOMC purchases T bills in the open market. Which two of the following scenarios are likely to occur?

    I. Secondary bond prices will rise.
    II. Secondary bond prices will fall.
    III. Interest rates will rise.
    IV. Interest rates will fall.

    A. I and III
    B. I and IV
    C. II and III
    D. II and IV

5. If the Federal Reserve Board decided that it was necessary to change the money supply, which of the following instruments would it NOT use?

    A. Bank reserve requirements
    B. Open market operations
    C. Tax rate
    D. Discount rate

6. Which organization or governmental unit sets fiscal policy?

    A. Federal Reserve Board
    B. Government Economic Board
    C. Congress
    D. Secretary of the Treasury

7. If the Federal Open Market Committee has decided that the rate of inflation is too high, it is MOST likely to

   I. tighten the money supply
   II. loosen the money supply
   III. lower the discount rate
   IV. raise the discount rate

   A. I and III
   B. I and IV
   C. II and III
   D. II and IV

8. An increase in the FRB's reserve requirement has which of the following effects on total bank deposits?

   I. Decrease
   II. Increase
   III. Multiplier
   IV. Logarithmic

   A. I and III
   B. I and IV
   C. II and III
   D. II and IV

Answers & Rationale

1.   **B.**   Economists consider expansion (recovery) as the beginning of the business cycle, followed by the peak (prosperity), contraction (recession or deflation) and trough.   (Page 61)

2.   **D.**   Two or more consecutive quarters of decline is termed a *recession*.   (Page 61)

3.   **D.**   An economic downturn that lasts for more than two consecutive quarters (six months) is known as a *recession*.   (Page 61)

4.   **B.**   When the Federal Open Market Committee purchases T bills in the open market, it pays for the transaction by increasing member banks' reserve accounts, the net effect of which increases the total money supply and signals a period of relatively easier credit conditions. Easier credit means interest rates will decline and the price for existing bonds will rise.   (Page 65)

5.   **C.**   The Federal Reserve Board has several tools at its disposal that it could use to change the money supply, including bank reserve requirements, open market operations (trading government securities) and the discount rate.   (Page 64)

6.   **C.**   Congress sets fiscal policy, while the FRB sets monetary policy.   (Page 63)

7.   **B.**   If the FOMC decides that it is in the economy's interest to lower the inflation rate, it can encourage this to occur by raising the discount rate, which in turn tightens the money supply.   (Page 65)

8.   **A.**   If the FRB raises the reserve requirement, total bank deposits decrease because of the multiplier effect. With a greater requirement, the banks have less money available to lend.

          (Page 64)

19

Know Your Customer

1. To open a new account, the registered representative must obtain information about the client's

   I. financial needs
   II. investment objectives
   III. financial condition

   A. I and II only
   B. I and III only
   C. II and III only
   D. I, II and III

2. Which of the following characteristics best define(s) the term "growth"?

   A. Value of the investment increasing over time
   B. Increasing principal and accumulating interest and dividends over time
   C. Investment that appreciates tax deferred
   D. All of the above

3. A person's investment decisions should be based primarily on her

   I. risk tolerance
   II. rep's recommendations
   III. investment needs

   A. I only
   B. I and III only
   C. II and III only
   D. I, II and III

4. A registered representative has a new client who has just received a $25,000 inheritance. The client wishes to use the money to purchase 8¼ percent Tallawhosits City general obligation bonds selling at an 8.45 percent yield. The $1 million bond issue is due in 15 years and is rated Ba. All of the following factors would result in your recommending *against* such a purchase EXCEPT that

   A. the client is in the 18 percent tax bracket
   B. this would be the client's only investment
   C. the client is willing to accept a moderate amount of risk
   D. the client's job is not secure

5. Randy Bear, who is 27 years old and in a low tax bracket, wants an aggressive long-term investment. His rep recommends a high-rated municipal general obligation bond. Which of the following statements is true?

   A. The rep violated the suitability requirements of NASD and MSRB rules.
   B. The rep recommended a suitable investment because GOs are good long-term investments.
   C. The rep committed a violation because municipal bonds weather the ups and downs of the markets well.
   D. The rep did not commit a violation if the customer agrees to the transaction.

6. If a customer wishes to place an order for 30 GNMAs that her registered representative feels is unsuitable for her, the rep must advise the customer of his opinion and

   A. not execute the order
   B. execute the order only with the prior approval of a senior partner of the firm
   C. execute the order only with prior MSRB approval
   D. execute the order at the customer's direction

7. Which of the following activities are a registered representative's responsibilities?

   I. Determining a customer's suitability for investing
   II. Describing the characteristics and benefits of various securities products
   III. Offering tax advice and assisting customers in completing tax returns
   IV. Personally holding a customer's securities for a future transaction

   A. I and II
   B. I and III
   C. II and IV
   D. III and IV

Answers & Rationale

1.   **D.**   All of this information is considered essential before opening an account.   (Page 67)

2.   **A.**   "Growth" refers to an increase in an investment's value over time.   (Page 70)

3.   **B.**   Understanding and acceptance of risk, along with the reasons for investing, shape a client's portfolio. A rep's recommendations should suit the client's needs—they should not be used to drive investment decisions.   (Page 68)

4.   **C.**   A Ba rating is consistent with the client's willingness to accept moderate risk. The client's tax bracket might be too low to take full advantage of the bonds' tax-exempt feature. Also, the bonds would not be very liquid because only 1,000 bonds were issued. If the client lost her job and needed cash, the bonds might be difficult to sell.   (Page 69)

5.   **A.**   In suggesting a conservative, tax-exempt investment to this customer, the rep failed to make a suitable recommendation.   (Page 71)

6.   **D.**   Under NASD/NYSE rules, even though the registered rep feels the security is unsuitable, he may execute the trade at the customer's demand.   (Page 71)

7.   **A.**   A registered rep is responsible primarily for determining customer suitability and for explaining different investments to prospective investors. A registered rep is not responsible for helping prepare tax returns, and he cannot hold customer funds or securities.   (Page 71)

20

Analyzing Financial Risks and Rewards

1. If a customer is concerned about interest rate risk, which of the following securities would a rep NOT recommend?

   A. Treasury bills
   B. Project notes
   C. 10-year corporate bonds
   D. 18-year municipal bonds

2. You have a convertible corporate bond available that has an 8 percent coupon and is yielding 7.1 percent, but may be called some time this year. Which feature of this bond would probably be LEAST attractive to your client?

   A. Convertibility
   B. Coupon yield
   C. Current yield
   D. Near-term call

3. Credit risk involves which of the following?

   A. Safety of principal
   B. Fluctuations in overall interest rates
   C. Danger of not being able to sell the investment at a fair market price
   D. Inflationary risks

4. Bondholders face the risk that the value of their bonds may fall as interest rates rise. This is known as what type of risk?

   A. Credit
   B. Reinvestment
   C. Marketability
   D. Market

5. The risk of not being able to convert an investment into cash at a time when cash is needed is known as what type of risk?

   A. Legislative
   B. Liquidity
   C. Market
   D. Reinvestment

Answers & Rationale

1. **D.** Interest rate risk is the danger that interest rates will change over the life of the debt instrument and adversely affect a bond's price. This risk is greatest for long-term bonds.
(Page 72)

2. **D.** The near-term call would mean that no matter how attractive the bond's other features, the client may not have very long to enjoy them.
(Page 73)

3. **A.** Credit risk is the risk of losing all or part of a person's invested principal due to the issuer's failure.
(Page 72)

4. **D.** Market risk is the risk of losing some or all of an investor's principal due to price volatility in the marketplace. Prices of existing bonds can fluctuate with changing interest rates. (Page 72)

5. **B.** Liquidity risk is the measure of marketability—or how quickly and easily a security can be converted to cash.
(Page 73)

21

Lesson One — Securities and Markets

1. A company may pay dividends in which of the following ways?

   I. Stock of another company
   II. Cash
   III. Stock
   IV. Product

   A. I only
   B. II and III only
   C. III only
   D. I, II, III and IV

2. Which of the following is(are) an underwriter's responsibility(ies)?

   I. Managing the distribution of large blocks of stock to the public and to institutions
   II. Selling a predetermined share of an offering to its customers
   III. Raising capital for corporations by assisting in the distribution of a corporation's new offering
   IV. Lending money to corporate clients that require debt financing

   A. I, II and III only
   B. I, II and IV only
   C. II only
   D. I, II, III and IV

3. Which of the following activities are characteristic of a primary offering?

   I. Raising additional capital for the company
   II. Selling previously issued securities
   III. Increasing the number of shares or bonds outstanding

   A. I and II only
   B. I and III only
   C. II and III only
   D. I, II and III

4. Which of the following statements describe a securities exchange?

   I. The highest bid and the lowest offer prevail.
   II. Only listed securities can be traded.
   III. Minimum prices are established.

   A. I and II only
   B. I and III only
   C. II and III only
   D. I, II and III

5. Which of the following describe stock rights, also called *subscription rights*?

    I. Short-term instruments that become worthless after the expiration date
    II. Most commonly offered in connection with debentures to sweeten the offering
    III. Issued by a corporation
    IV. Traded in the securities market

    A. I and II
    B. I and III
    C. I, III and IV
    D. II, III and IV

6. An owner of common stock has the right to

    I. determine when dividends will be issued
    II. vote at stockholders' meetings or by proxy
    III. receive a predetermined fixed portion of the corporation's profit in cash when declared
    IV. buy restricted securities before they are offered to the public

    A. I, III and IV
    B. II
    C. II, III and IV
    D. II and IV

7. Which of the following best describe warrants?

    I. Short-term instruments that become worthless after the expiration date
    II. Most commonly offered in connection with debentures to sweeten the offering
    III. Issued by a corporation
    IV. Traded in the securities market

    A. I and II
    B. I and III
    C. I, III and IV
    D. II, III and IV

8. The ex-dividend date is which of the following?

    I. Date on and after which the buyer is entitled to the dividend
    II. Date on and after which the seller is entitled to the dividend
    III. Second business day before the record date
    IV. Second business day after the record date

    A. I and III
    B. I and IV
    C. II and III
    D. II and IV

9. A common stockholder's voting rights apply to which of the following?

    I. Election of the board of directors
    II. Declaration of dividends
    III. Authorization or issue of more common shares

    A. I only
    B. I and III only
    C. II and III only
    D. I, II and III

10. Which of the following option investors are bearish?

    I. Buyer of a call
    II. Writer of a call
    III. Buyer of a put
    IV. Writer of a put

    A. I and II
    B. I and IV
    C. II and III
    D. III and IV

11. Belle tells her broker that she thinks ALF's price will go up, but she does not have the money to buy 100 shares right now. How could she use options to profit from a rise in the stock's price?

    I. Buy calls on ALF.
    II. Write calls on ALF.
    III. Buy puts on ALF.
    IV. Write puts on ALF.

    A. I and III
    B. I and IV
    C. II and III
    D. II and IV

12. Rank the following government securities according to the length of their maturities, from longest to shortest.

    I. Notes
    II. Bills
    III. Bonds

    A. I, II, III
    B. II, I, III
    C. III, I, II
    D. III, II, I

13. Which of the following statements about a bond selling above par value is(are) true?

    I. The nominal yield is lower than the current yield.
    II. The yield to maturity is lower than the nominal yield.
    III. The yield to maturity is lower than the current yield.
    IV. The nominal yield always stays the same.

    A. I and IV only
    B. II, III and IV only
    C. III only
    D. I, II, III and IV

14. The interest from which of the following bonds is exempt from federal income tax?

    I. State of California
    II. City of Anchorage
    III. Treasury
    IV. GNMA

    A. I and II only
    B. I, II and IV only
    C. III and IV only
    D. I, II, III and IV

15. Which of the following are money-market instruments?

    I. Bankers' acceptances
    II. Treasury bills
    III. Commercial paper
    IV. Treasury bonds maturing in six months

    A. I and II only
    B. I, II and III only
    C. III and IV only
    D. I, II, III and IV

16. Which of the following statements is(are) true of Treasury bonds?

    I. They are sold at a discount.
    II. They pay a fixed rate of interest semiannually.
    III. They mature in one year or less.
    IV. They mature in 10 years or more.

    A. I, II and III
    B. I and III
    C. II and IV
    D. III

17. Which of the following would NOT be considered money-market instruments?

    I. Debentures rated Aaa
    II. Treasury notes
    III. Commercial paper
    IV. Treasury bonds maturing in six months

    A. I and II only
    B. I and III only
    C. II, III and IV only
    D. I, II, III and IV

18. Which of the following statements about corporate bonds are true?

    I. They represent ownership in the corporation.
    II. They generally involve less market risk than common stock.
    III. They pay a variable rate of income.
    IV. They usually mature 10 or more years after issue.

    A. I and III only
    B. II and III only
    C. II and IV only
    D. I, II, III and IV

19. Which of the following statements about general obligation municipal bonds are true?

    I. They are second only to U.S. government bonds in safety of principal.
    II. They are backed by the municipality's taxing power.
    III. They are nonmarketable.
    IV. They pay higher interest rates than corporate debt securities.

    A. I and II
    B. I and IV
    C. II and III
    D. II, III and IV

20. Corporate bonds are considered safer than corporate stock issued by the same company because the

    I. bonds represent equity in the company
    II. company is more likely to back the original investors
    III. bonds are senior to common stock
    IV. holder of a corporate bond is a debtor to the company

    A. I and II
    B. II, III and IV
    C. III
    D. III and IV

21. Which of the following bonds qualifies as a municipal bond?

    I. General obligation bond of the City of Denver
    II. Revenue bond issued by the City of Detroit to build the Joe Louis Arena
    III. Sewer bond issued by Cook County, Illinois
    IV. Highway bond issued by the State of New Mexico

    A. I only
    B. I and II only
    C. II and III only
    D. I, II, III and IV

22. Which of the following statements is(are) true of a Treasury STRIPS?

    I. The rate of return is locked in.
    II. There is no reinvestment risk.
    III. The interest is taxed as a capital gain.
    IV. The interest is realized at maturity.

    A. I
    B. I, II and III
    C. I, II and IV
    D. IV

23. TCBS currently has earnings of $4 and pays a $.50 quarterly dividend. If TCBS's market price is $40, what is the current yield?

    A. 1.25 percent
    B. 5 percent
    C. 10 percent
    D. 15 percent

Answers & Rationale

1. **D.** A company may pay a dividend in any of the ways listed.   (Page 11)

2. **A.** An underwriter manages the offering and helps the corporation raise capital.   (Page 49)

3. **B.** A primary offering involves the sale of previously unissued securities. The issuing company receives the proceeds from the sale. Of course, once the securities are sold, more securities will be outstanding and in the hands of the public.   (Page 50)

4. **A.** An exchange is an auction market in which securities listed on that exchange are traded. No minimum price is set for securities; rather, the highest price bid and the lowest price offered prevail. The Securities Exchange Act of 1934 regulates trading activity on the exchanges as well as on the OTC market.   (Page 54)

5. **C.** A corporation issues rights that allow subscribers to purchase stock within a short period of time at a price lower than the stock's current market price. Rights need not be exercised, but may be traded in the secondary market. Warrants are commonly used as sweeteners in debenture offerings.   (Page 16)

6. **B.** The stockholder has the right to vote and the right to dividends if and when declared (although not to a fixed dividend). A restricted security has prescribed limits on resale, generally requiring registration.   (Page 5)

7. **D.** Warrants are commonly used as sweeteners in debenture offerings and carry long lives. A corporation issues rights that allow subscribers to purchase stock within a short period of time at a price lower than the stock's current market price. Warrants need not be exercised, but may be traded in the secondary market.   (Page 17)

8. **C.** Stock sold on the ex-dividend date entitles the seller to the dividend. Stock sells ex-dividend two business days before the record date.   (Page 59)

9. **B.** Common stockholders may elect the board of directors (which only indirectly influences the policy on dividend payment) and may vote on issues concerning the company's capitalization, such as the issuance of more common stock.   (Page 6)

10. **C.** Option investors in a position to sell the stock (put buyers and call writers) have bearish outlooks. Remember that diagonal positions (those positions that are total opposites, such as buys versus sells and puts versus calls) are on the same side of the market.   (Page 18)

11. **B.** The bullish strategies are buying calls and writing puts.   (Page 19)

12. **C.** Treasury bills mature in less than a year, notes mature in from 1 to 10 years and bonds mature in more than 10 years.   (Page 37)

13. **B.** Nominal yield is fixed and stays the same on all bonds. A bond selling above par is selling at a premium, so the current yield and yield to maturity are less than the nominal yield.   (Page 27)

14. **A.** Municipal bonds are exempt from federal income tax. Treasury bonds are exempt from state tax. GNMAs are subject to federal and state income tax.   (Page 42)

15. **D.** Money markets are made up of short-term, high-yield debt issues. All of the items listed here are considered short term—even the Treasury bonds, because they mature within six months.   (Page 46)

16. **C.** T bonds are sold at par and pay interest semiannually. They are issued with maturities of 10 years or more.   (Page 37)

17. **A.** Money markets are made up of short-term debt issues, such as commercial paper.

Because the Treasury bond matures in less than a year, it is considered a money-market instrument. The debenture and Treasury note are long-term instruments. (Page 46)

18. **C.** Bonds represent a creditor relationship; stock represents an ownership interest. Normally, bonds are issued with a stated rate of interest and mature in 10 or more years. Because of their steady interest payments, bond prices tend to be less volatile than stock prices. (Page 19)

19. **A.** General obligation bonds are backed by the municipal issuer's general taxing authority. As such, they are often considered very safe investments. Municipal issues are marketable and are bought and sold in the secondary marketplace. Because interest received on municipal debt is exempt from federal taxation, yields offered on municipal debt are lower than yields offered on corporate debt. (Page 44)

20. **C.** A bond represents the company's legal obligation to repay principal and interest. A corporate bondholder is a *creditor* of the company. (Page 19)

21. **D.** Any bond issued by a state, municipality or governmental unit other than the federal government is categorized as a municipal issue. (Page 44)

22. **C.** A STRIPS has no reinvestment risk because the investor receives no interest payments and, therefore, needs not worry about reinvestment. Because there is no reinvestment risk, the total rate of return is locked in or set at issuance. The interest on the bond is paid at maturity, but it is taxed as interest income over the life of the bond. (Page 38)

23. **B.** The quarterly dividend is $.50; therefore, the annual dividend is $2. $2 divided by the $40 market price equals a 5 percent annual yield (current yield). (Page 11)

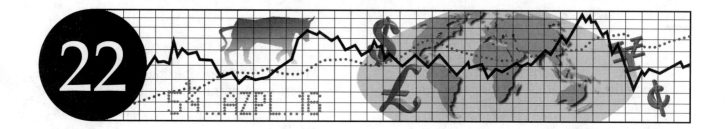

Investment Company Offerings

1. Under the Investment Company Act of 1940, any of the following could be considered a redeemable security EXCEPT a(n)

   A. security that pays out each investor's proportionate share of the company's assets
   B. security that can be sold on an exchange at the fair market price the buyers and sellers have established
   C. investment company security issued as common stock
   D. security issued by an open-end investment company

2. Under the definition of a management company, all of the following would qualify EXCEPT

   I. face-amount certificate companies
   II. unit investment trusts
   III. closed-end investment companies
   IV. open-end investment companies

   A. I
   B. I and II
   C. I, II and III
   D. III and IV

3. GEM Precious Metals Fund, a diversified open-end investment company, invested 5 percent of its total assets in Monaghan Minerals and Mining, Inc. The market soared and, because of Monaghan's phenomenal appreciation, Monaghan securities now make up 8 percent of GEM Fund's total assets. In this case, which of the following statements is true?

   A. GEM Fund must sell enough Monaghan securities to reduce its holdings in Monaghan to 5 percent of its total assets.
   B. GEM Fund must sell out its holdings in Monaghan completely.
   C. GEM Fund must sell Monaghan shares only if the 8 percent investment represents more than 10 percent of Monaghan's outstanding voting securities.
   D. GEM Fund does not have to sell Monaghan shares, but cannot buy more Monaghan shares and still advertise itself as a diversified company.

4. A face-amount certificate company can include any or all of the following conditions in its contract EXCEPT

   A. require the issuer to pay a stated sum of money on a fixed date
   B. require the purchaser to pay stated sums at fixed intervals
   C. provide a return that varies daily based on market fluctuation
   D. provide a fixed rate of return during periods of prolonged market decline

5. A typical unit investment trust has which of the following?

   A. No investment adviser
   B. Listed securities
   C. Securities representing a divided interest in a unit of specified securities
   D. Board of directors

6. An investment company that is not classified as either a unit investment trust or a face-amount certificate company would be classified as a(n)

   A. mutual fund
   B. management investment company
   C. open-end company
   D. closed-end company

7. A diversified investment company must invest at least ____ of its assets in such a way that no more than ____ of its assets are in any one company and each investment represents no more than ____ of the target company's voting securities.

   A. 50 percent; 10 percent; 5 percent
   B. 75 percent; 5 percent; 10 percent
   C. 75 percent; 10 percent; 5 percent
   D. 100 percent; 5 percent; 15 percent

8. Which of the following statements is FALSE regarding a unit investment trust?

   A. It invests according to stated objectives.
   B. It charges no management fee.
   C. Overall responsibility for the fund rests with the board of directors.
   D. The transfer agent may limit sales to current unit holders.

9. Which of the following statements are true of open-end investment companies?

   I. They may constantly issue new shares.
   II. They redeem shares at any time.
   III. They may leverage common shares by issuing bonds.

   A. I and II only
   B. I and III only
   C. II and III only
   D. I, II and III

10. According to the Investment Company Act of 1940, a diversified mutual fund may hold, at most, what percentage of a corporation's voting securities?

    A. 5 percent
    B. 10 percent
    C. 50 percent
    D. 75 percent

11. ArGood Fund, a diversified investment company, has a net asset value of $225 million. ArGood wishes to invest in General Gizmonics, Inc. GIZ stock is selling at $30 a share, and 100,000 shares are outstanding. The maximum GIZ shares that ArGood Fund could buy and still be diversified is

    A. 5,000
    B. 10,000
    C. $11,250,000 worth
    D. $12,500,000 worth

12. A regulated, diversified investment company cannot own more than what percentage of any one company's outstanding shares?

    A. 2 percent
    B. 5 percent
    C. 8 percent
    D. 10 percent

13. To be considered a diversified investment company by the SEC, the company must meet which of the following requirements?

    A. At least 25 percent of the fund's assets must be invested in one industry.
    B. The fund must be invested in at least 20 different industries.
    C. 75 percent of the fund's assets must be invested, with no more than 5 percent invested in any one company and with no investment representing more than 10 percent of a single company's stock.
    D. The fund must be invested in both stocks and bonds.

14. Closed-end investment company shares can be purchased and sold

    A. in the secondary marketplace
    B. from the closed-end company
    C. in the primary market
    D. All of the above

15. Which of the following statements describe(s) an open-end investment company?

    I. It can sell new shares in any quantity at any time.
    II. It must redeem shares in any quantity within seven days of request.
    III. It provides for mutual ownership of portfolio assets by shareholders.

    A. I and II only
    B. II only
    C. III only
    D. I, II and III

16. All of the following statements concerning investment companies are true EXCEPT

    A. a nondiversified company is any management company not classified as a diversified company
    B. to be considered a diversified investment company, the company must invest at least 75 percent of its total assets in cash or securities
    C. an investment company that invests the majority of its assets in one company or industry is considered a nondiversified company
    D. a diversified company can be an open-end investment company only

17. Which of the following statements describe an open-end investment company?

    I. The company may sell new shares in any quantity at any time.
    II. The company must sell new shares in any quantity at any time.
    III. The company may redeem shares in any quantity at any time, but may restrict the redemption of shares at the board of directors' discretion.
    IV. The company must redeem shares in any quantity at any time except that it may suspend the redemption of shares with SEC approval.

    A. I and III
    B. I and IV
    C. II and III
    D. II and IV

Answers & Rationale

1. **B.** A redeemable security is purchased from and redeemed with the security's issuer. If the security can be traded on a secondary market, it is not considered a redeemable security. Open-end shares are redeemable securities; closed-end shares are not. (Page 82)

2. **B.** As defined in the act of 1940, closed-end and open-end funds are subclassifications of management companies (actively managed portfolios). Face-amount certificate companies and unit trusts are separate investment company classifications under the act. (Page 81)

3. **D.** A fund does not lose its diversified status because of market movement. While this fund may not purchase more Monaghan shares, it need not sell off any part of its Monaghan holdings. (Page 82)

4. **C.** Face-amount certificate companies pay fixed returns. (Page 80)

5. **A.** A unit investment trust issues redeemable securities traded by the issuer only (the issuer must maintain a second market); the securities are not listed on an exchange. A UIT's shares (units) evidence an undivided interest in a portfolio of securities that is not actively managed. A UIT has neither an investment adviser nor a board of directors. (Page 80)

6. **B.** Management investment companies are the third classification of investment companies under the Investment Company Act of 1940. Open-end funds (mutual funds) and closed-end funds are subclassifications of management investment companies. (Page 81)

7. **B.** A management company must be at least 75 percent invested, and its investments must be diversified so that no more than 5 percent of its assets are in any one company and no single investment represents more than 10 percent of another company's voting securities. (Page 82)

8. **C.** A unit investment trust has no board of directors. Answers A and B are true: a UIT must follow a stated investment objective, as must any investment company, and a UIT does not charge a management fee because it is not a managed portfolio. (Page 80)

9. **A.** An open-end company must stand ready to redeem shares within seven days of receiving a customer's request and may continuously offer its shares for sale. Although an open-end company may invest in just about any security, it may issue only one class of voting stock. The company cannot issue any type of debt. (Page 82)

10. **B.** To be considered a diversified investment company, a mutual fund can own no more than 10 percent of a target company's voting securities. Additionally, no diversified investment company may invest more than 5 percent of its portfolio in a single company's securities. (Page 82)

11. **B.** A diversified investment company invests at least 75 percent of its assets so that no more than 5 percent of the assets own more than 10 percent of a company's stock. In this question, 5 percent of ArGood Fund's assets could purchase the entire General Gizmonics company. Therefore, ArGood Fund is limited to 10 percent of GIZ stock, or 10,000 shares. (Page 82)

12. **D.** To be considered a diversified investment company, the fund must invest at least 75 percent of its portfolio so that no more than 5 percent of the *assets* own no more than 10 percent of a company's outstanding *stock*. Remember: 75 percent invested, 5 percent assets, 10 percent stock. (Page 82)

13. **C.** By definition, a diversified investment company must invest at least 75 percent of its assets, concentrate no more than 5 percent of its assets in any one company and own no more than

10 percent of any single company's voting securities. (Page 82)

14. **A.** A closed-end company share is bought *and sold* in the secondary marketplace. (Page 82)

15. **D.** An open-end investment company can sell any quantity of new shares, redeem shares within seven days and provide for mutual ownership of portfolio assets by shareholders. (Page 82)

16. **D.** A diversified company could be either a closed-end company or an open-end company. (Page 82)

17. **B.** Under the Investment Company Act of 1940, an investment company selling mutual funds need not continuously offer new shares for sale; in fact, a fund often suspends sales to new investors when it grows too large to adequately meet its investment objective. The act of 1940 does require a fund to continuously offer to redeem shares, and this redemption privilege may be suspended only during nonbusiness days or with the SEC's approval. (Page 82)

Investment Company Registration

23

1. The shareholders of an investment company must vote to approve which of the following?

   I. Change from a diversified company to a nondiversified company
   II. Change from an open-end company to a closed-end company
   III. Change in operations that would cause the firm to cease business as an investment company
   IV. Change in the fund's objectives

   A. I and IV only
   B. II and III only
   C. II, III and IV only
   D. I, II, III and IV

2. To make a public offering, a registered investment company must have a minimum net worth of

   A. $100,000
   B. $1 million
   C. $10 million
   D. $100 million

3. Each of the following is considered an investment company EXCEPT a

   A. face-amount certificate company
   B. company that has invested 65 percent of its assets in securities
   C. bank investment advisory account
   D. company that issues redeemable securities

4. An investment company must register with the SEC and, in doing so, must provide all of the following information EXCEPT its

   A. intention to borrow money
   B. intended trading practices
   C. present or future plans to issue senior securities
   D. intention to concentrate its investments in a single industry

5. SEC rules and regulations regarding securities issued by investment companies prohibit

    I.   closed-end funds from issuing preferred stock
    II. open-end funds from issuing preferred stock
    III. closed-end funds from issuing bonds
    IV. open-end funds from issuing bonds

    A. I and III
    B. I and IV
    C. II and III
    D. II and IV

6. An open-end investment company may do all of the following EXCEPT

    A. continuously offer shares
    B. borrow money
    C. lend money
    D. issue bonds

7. An open-end investment company wishes to change its investment objective. It may do so only with a

    A. majority vote of the outstanding shares
    B. majority vote of the outstanding shareholders
    C. two-thirds vote of the outstanding shareholders
    D. unanimous vote of the board of directors

8. An open-end investment company must maintain what percentage of net assets to debt?

    A. 33⅓ percent
    B. 50 percent
    C. 100 percent
    D. 300 percent

9. The Investment Company Act of 1940 requires that a mutual fund

    I.   issue a statement of investment policy
    II. have $100,000 minimum capitalization
    III. ensure that 40 percent of the directors are neither officers nor investment advisers of the company

    A. I only
    B. II only
    C. II and III only
    D. I, II and III

10. Which of the following are required of investment companies under the Securities Act of 1933?

    I.   Filing a registration statement with the SEC
    II. Providing a prospectus to potential purchasers
    III. Publishing a tombstone advertisement giving the issuer's name and a brief description of the issuer's type of business
    IV. Obtaining the SEC's approval of the truthfulness of the information in the prospectus

    A. I and II only
    B. I and III only
    C. II and IV only
    D. I, II, III and IV

11. Financial information cannot be used in a prospectus if the information is aged more than

    A. 60 days
    B. 9 months
    C. 12 months
    D. 16 months

12. An investment company offering securities registered under the act of 1933 may make which of the following statements?

    I. "The SEC has passed on the merits of these securities as an investment."
    II. "The SEC has passed on the adequacy of the information in our prospectus."
    III. "The SEC has passed on the accuracy of the information in our prospectus."
    IV. "The SEC has approved these securities for retirement accounts and institutional clients."

    A. I
    B. I and II
    C. II, III and IV
    D. None of the above

13. A member firm can be sued for damages if an investor purchases an open-end fund and

    I. receives no prospectus
    II. is told an untrue statement by the member or by a person associated with the member
    III. is given a prospectus that omits a material fact
    IV. loses 20 percent or more in the investment within the first 30 days after the initial purchase

    A. I
    B. I, II and III
    C. II and III
    D. II, III and IV

14. A prospectus must be delivered to the purchaser of a unit investment trust

    A. before the purchase
    B. with the first confirmation
    C. with each confirmation
    D. between 45 days and 18 months following the initial deposit

15. All of the following would violate NASD rules EXCEPT

    A. sending a prospect a prospectus and sales literature at the same time
    B. selling a mutual fund without first distributing a prospectus
    C. selling a mutual fund with sales literature that is not a prospectus describing the fund's performance over a 10-year period
    D. sending a customer sales literature that represents a fund's performance history for five years when the fund has been in existence for 10 years

16. An investor must be provided with a statement of additional information about a mutual fund

    A. annually
    B. any time after she receives the prospectus
    C. upon request
    D. at the same time she receives the prospectus

17. In a mutual fund portfolio, it is permissible to buy all of the following securities EXCEPT

    A. index options
    B. junk bonds
    C. shares of other mutual funds
    D. stock on margin

Answers & Rationale

1.   **D.** Any substantive change in an investment company's form, structure, investment objectives or business operations must be approved by a majority vote of the outstanding shares.   (Page 86)

2.   **A.** No investment company may register an offering with the SEC unless it has a minimum net worth of $100,000 (or will have within 90 days).   (Page 84)

3.   **C.** A bank advisory account is specifically exempted from the definition of an investment company.   (Page 85)

4.   **B.** Investment companies need not outline their trading practices. However, a registration statement must describe any intent to borrow money or issue senior securities. A company's concentration of investments would be part of its required investment policy description. (Page 84)

5.   **D.** Closed-end funds can issue more than one class of securities, including debt issues and preferred stock. Open-end funds can issue only one class of voting stock; they cannot issue any senior security. Open-end funds may borrow from a bank, but they are limited to the same asset coverage requirements as closed-end funds that issue debt (300 percent).   (Page 82)

6.   **D.** A mutual fund cannot issue any senior securities, although it may purchase just about any type of security as an investment. All shares of a mutual fund must be of the same class.   (Page 82)

7.   **A.** The Investment Company Act of 1940 requires the fund to have a clearly defined investment objective. The only action that can be taken to change the investment objective is a majority vote of the outstanding shares (shares vote, not shareholders).   (Page 78)

8.   **D.** The Investment Company Act of 1940 prohibits a mutual fund from borrowing more than one-third of its net asset value. In other words, the fund must maintain at least 300 percent assets to debt.   (Page 85)

9.   **D.** The Investment Company Act of 1940 requires a mutual fund to have an initial capitalization of $100,000, at least 100 shareholders and a clearly defined investment objective. Additionally, the interlocking directorate rules state that at least 40 percent of the fund's directors must be independent from the fund's operations.   (Page 85)

10.   **A.** The Securities Act of 1933 sets forth the registration and prospectus requirements for all companies contemplating the issuance of securities. There is no requirement to publish a tombstone; and the SEC does not approve of, pass on the adequacy of, or pass on the completeness of an offering.   (Page 86)

11.   **D.** An investment company may distribute a prospectus to prospective investors if the information it contains is no more than 16 months old. The fund also must send an audited financial report to current shareholders at least annually and an unaudited report every six months.   (Page 85)

12.   **D.** The SEC neither approves nor disapproves of an issue, nor does it pass on the adequacy, accuracy or completeness of the information presented in a prospectus. (Page 86)

13.   **B.** Federal securities laws require that purchasers of newly issued securities be given a full disclosure of material information concerning the issuers and the securities. Choice I states that the purchaser received no disclosures. Choices II and III imply a measure of fraud or improper disclosure, and in each of these cases the purchaser could sue to recover damages and costs. A drop in an investment's value (choice IV) is not grounds for suit—unless the loss was directly related to improper disclosure by the company.   (Page 86)

14. **B.** A purchaser of newly issued securities must receive a prospectus no later than with receipt of the confirmation of his purchase.
(Page 85)

15. **A.** Any solicitation for sale must be preceded or accompanied by a prospectus that meets the guidelines put forth by the Securities Act of 1933. (Page 86)

16. **C.** The investor may obtain the statement of additional information upon request. The prospectus contains information on the fund's objective, investment policies, sales charges and management expenses, and services offered, as well as a 10-year history of per share capital changes. The statement of additional information typically contains the fund's consolidated financial statements, including the balance sheet, statement of operations, income statement and portfolio list at the time the statement was compiled. (Page 86)

17. **D.** Mutual funds may not purchase securities on margin because, in the event of a margin call, they have no recourse to investors' funds. A fund is not prohibited from buying options, low-quality bonds and other mutual funds. (Page 86)

24

Management of Investment Companies

1. An investment company may loan money to one of its officers in accordance with its policy

   A. if it notifies both the SEC and the NASD in writing
   B. if a majority of the voting shareholders approve the loan prior to its taking effect
   C. if the board of directors issues a statement of approval and gives the shareholders notice through a quarterly statement
   D. under no circumstances

2. When selecting a board of directors, a registered investment company must not include more than what percentage of interested persons?

   A. 10 percent
   B. 40 percent
   C. 50 percent
   D. 60 percent

3. Under the Investment Company Act of 1940, investment companies must

   I. limit the membership of their boards of directors to a maximum of 60 percent interested persons
   II. state and adhere to their investment objectives
   III. maintain adequate debt/equity diversification
   IV. have a minimum of $100,000 in capital before embarking on a public offering

   A. I
   B. I and II
   C. I, II and IV
   D. III and IV

4. Which of the following are functions of an investment company's custodian bank?

   I. Safekeeping of portfolio securities and cash
   II. Providing portfolio advice regarding transactions
   III. Maintaining books and records for accumulation plans
   IV. Safekeeping of customer securities

   A. I and III only
   B. I, III and IV only
   C. II and IV only
   D. I, II, III and IV

5. A management investment company must do all of the following EXCEPT

   A. hold all portfolio securities in a custodian bank
   B. hold all cash in a custodian bank
   C. maintain a bond for persons who have access to monies or securities
   D. investigate the employment record of the custodian bank's officers

6. A noninterested member of a board of directors would include a director

   A. whose spouse is the principal underwriter
   B. whose only involvement with the company is her role as a member of the board
   C. who is the attorney for the investment adviser
   D. who is also president of the custodian bank

7. Under the Investment Company Act of 1940, shareholders must receive financial reports

   A. monthly
   B. quarterly
   C. semiannually
   D. annually

8. CBS Investment Services charges a fee for its services in managing several mutual funds. Which of the following would be included in the services CBS supplies?

   I. Ensuring that the fund portfolio meets diversification requirements
   II. Attempting to meet the investment objectives of the fund
   III. Analyzing the market and deciding when securities in the portfolio should be bought or sold
   IV. Changing investment objectives in order to maximize potential gain for the shareholders

   A. I, II and III only
   B. I and IV only
   C. II and III only
   D. I, II, III and IV

9. Usually the fee received by the management company from an investment company depends on the

   A. net assets of the fund
   B. profits of the fund
   C. volume of new shares sold
   D. type of securities in the fund portfolio

10. The money holder of a mutual fund's account would generally be a

   A. commercial bank
   B. investment banker
   C. savings and loan association
   D. stock exchange member

11. The investment adviser in a regulated, diversified open-end investment company performs which of the following functions?

    I. Makes sure the fund invests in such a manner as to retain its diversified status
    II. Attempts to fulfill the fund's investment objective by means of careful investing
    III. Changes investment objectives as he believes is in the best interest of the investors
    IV. Investigates the tax status of potential investments

    A. I, II and III
    B. I, II and IV
    C. II and IV
    D. III and IV

12. An investment adviser of a mutual fund can liquidate shares held in the fund's portfolio

    A. only with the consent of a majority vote of the shareholders
    B. only with the consent of the board of directors
    C. as long as the liquidation is within the guidelines set forth by the fund's objective
    D. only with the consent of the board of directors and a majority vote of the shareholders

13. Mutual funds are like other types of corporations in that

    I. they may issue equity and debt
    II. the board of directors makes policy decisions
    III. shareholders have ownership rights

    A. I and III only
    B. II only
    C. II and III only
    D. I, II and III

14. The principal underwriter of an open-end investment company is also known as the

    A. sponsor
    B. dealer
    C. trustee
    D. registrar

Answers & Rationale

1.   **D.**   An investment company is not permitted to make loans to affiliated or interested persons under any circumstances. An officer is an affiliated person of an investment company.
(Page 88)

2.   **D.**   The Investment Company Act of 1940 requires that at least 40 percent of the board be independent (that is, noninterested) directors. Consequently, no more than 60 percent of the directors can be interested persons as defined by the act.
(Page 87)

3.   **C.**   According to the Investment Company Act of 1940, 40 percent of a company's directors must be independent, a company must state and follow a clearly defined investment objective (which may be changed only with a majority vote of the outstanding shares), and a company must have a minimum of $100,000 in assets before it may begin to operate.
(Page 87)

4.   **A.**   The custodian bank performs bookkeeping and clerical functions and, principally, retains the fund's cash and securities for safekeeping. The adviser offers portfolio advice and management services. The custodian does not provide for safekeeping of investors' securities.
(Page 89)

5.   **D.**   The investment company is not required (and would probably find it difficult) to investigate the employment records of the officers of its custodian bank. The Investment Company Act of 1940 requires only that investment companies keep all cash and securities with a custodian bank and maintain a bond.
(Page 89)

6.   **B.**   A director who holds no other position in the fund is exempt from the interested person definition. However, a director associated with or employed in another capacity with the fund is considered interested. The act of 1940 requires that at least 40 percent of the directors are independent (that is, noninterested persons).(Page 87)

7.   **C.**   Investment company shareholders must receive financial reports at least semiannually (that is, every six months).
(Page 91)

8.   **A.**   The objective of the fund may be changed by a majority vote of the outstanding shares only. The fund manager is assigned the day-to-day management responsibilities of the fund. Duties would include attempting to meet the objective as set out by the fund and buying and selling securities to be held in the portfolio.
(Page 89)

9.   **A.**   The management company usually receives a fee based on the average annual net assets of the fund managed.
(Page 89)

10.   **A.**   The money holder of a mutual fund is its custodian. In most instances, the custodian will be a commercial bank.
(Page 89)

11.   **B.**   The investment adviser is responsible for making investments according to the objective stipulated by the fund. The fund's objective may be changed only with a majority vote of the outstanding shares.
(Page 88)

12.   **C.**   A mutual fund investment adviser is given authority to select and make investments in the fund portfolio. The fund must follow the adviser's advice.
(Page 88)

13.   **C.**   Mutual funds may issue only one class of voting stock. Like corporate stockholders, mutual fund shareholders have various rights, one of which is the right to elect the board of directors, which sets policies for the fund.   (Page 87)

14.   **A.**   The term "sponsor" is synonymous with the term "underwriter."
(Page 90)

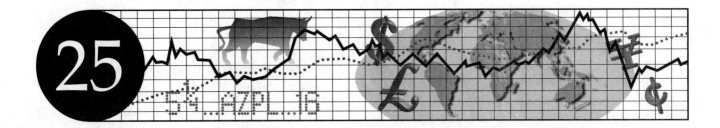

Characteristics of Mutual Funds

1. The ZBest Invest Fund is a mutual fund that has as its primary objective the payment of dividends, regardless of the current state of the market; preservation of capital and capital growth are secondary objectives. Which of the following industry groups would be appropriate for the ZBest Invest Fund's portfolio?

    A. Aerospace
    B. Public utilities
    C. Computer technology
    D. Consumer appliances

2. All of the following statements are true of money-market funds EXCEPT that

    A. investors pay a management fee
    B. interest is computed daily and credited to the investor's account monthly
    C. investors can buy and sell shares quickly and easily
    D. high interest rates are guaranteed

3. Mutual fund shares represent an undivided interest in the fund, which means that

    A. investors can purchase full shares only
    B. the fund can hold securities of only certain companies
    C. the number of shares outstanding is limited to a predetermined maximum
    D. each investor owns a proportional part of every security in the portfolio

4. Lotta Leveridge owns 150 shares of American Conservative Equity Fund. Which of the following statements are true?

    I. When a dividend is declared by the fund, she will receive or reinvest a cash dividend for each share owned.
    II. She will have difficulty liquidating her shares.
    III. The amount of her dividend will reflect her proportional interest in the value of the fund portfolio on the record date.
    IV. She will receive dividends from only 150 shares of stock held in the fund portfolio.

    A. I, II and IV
    B. I and III
    C. II and III
    D. II, III and IV

5. Max Leveridge believes that the electronics industry will be very successful in the next ten years. If he wants to invest in the industry but does not want to limit his investments to only a few companies, he should invest in what type of fund?

   A. Bond
   B. Money market
   C. Hedge
   D. Specialized

6. Last year the bond market was very profitable, and ZBest Invest Fund had 70 percent of its assets in bonds. Next year the fund's managers expect the stock market to do well, and they adjust the fund's portfolio so that 60 percent will be invested in stock. ZBest Invest is probably what type of fund?

   A. Balanced
   B. Hedge
   C. Specialized
   D. Aggressive growth

7. ZBest Invest Fund pays regular dividends, offers a high degree of safety of principal and especially appeals to investors seeking tax advantages. ZBest Invest is a(n)

   A. corporate bond fund
   B. money-market fund
   C. aggressive growth fund
   D. municipal bond fund

8. Your client asks whether he should invest in a particular investment company. You should tell him to check the investment company's

   I. investment policy
   II. track record
   III. portfolio
   IV. sales load

   A. I, II and III only
   B. I and IV only
   C. III only
   D. I, II, III and IV

9. An investor who owns shares of a mutual fund in fact owns

   A. an undivided interest in the fund's debt capitalization
   B. specific shares of stock in the fund's portfolio
   C. an undivided interest in the fund's portfolio
   D. certain unspecified securities among those owned by the fund

10. A balanced fund is one that at all times invests

    A. a portion of its portfolio in both debt and equity instruments
    B. equal amounts of its portfolio in common stock and corporate bonds
    C. equal amounts of its portfolio in common and preferred stock
    D. a portion of its portfolio in both common stock and government securities

11. All the following are advantages of mutual fund investment EXCEPT

    A. the investor retains personal control of her investment in the mutual fund portfolio
    B. exchange privileges within a family of funds managed by the same management company
    C. the ability to invest almost any amount at any time
    D. the ability to qualify for reduced sales loads based on accumulation of investment within the fund

12. Which of the following is(are) characteristics of money-market funds?

    I. Portfolio of short-term debt instruments
    II. High beta
    III. Offered without a sales load
    IV. Fixed NAV

    A. I
    B. I, II and IV
    C. I, III and IV
    D. II, III and IV

13. A mutual fund's expense ratio is its expenses divided by

    A. average net assets
    B. public offering price
    C. income
    D. dividends

14. Although alternatives are available to a mutual fund issuer regarding the details of redemption procedures, by law the issuer must

    A. make payment for shares within seven days of tender
    B. inform the investor of his loss or profit
    C. redeem shares at the public offering price
    D. redeem shares at the net asset value minus the sales charge

15. A tax-exempt bond fund may invest in

    A. corporate bonds
    B. short-term money-market instruments
    C. common stock
    D. municipal bonds

16. An elderly widower explains to his rep that he requires his investments to provide high current income. The rep should recommend

    A. a growth fund
    B. a zero-coupon bond
    C. a mutual fund that matches the investor's stated objective
    D. the ZBest Widow Fund, a fund structured specifically for this type of investor

Answers & Rationale

1.   B.   Utilities belong to the *defensive industries*, as compared to the other groups mentioned. They produce dividends more consistently, although relative growth potential is limited.   (Page 93)

2.   D.   Money-market instruments earn high interest rates but the rates are not guaranteed. Money-market funds are typically no-load funds with no redemption fee, but investors do pay a management fee. The interest earned on an investor's shares is computed every day and credited to the account at month end. An advantage of money-market funds is the ease with which shares can be purchased and sold.   (Page 95)

3.   D.   A mutual fund shareholder owns an undivided interest in the investment company's portfolio. Because each share represents one class of voting stock, the investor's interest in the fund reflects the number of shares owned.   (Page 92)

4.   B.   A mutual fund share represents an undivided interest in the fund's portfolio. If a dividend is declared, the shareholder receives a dividend for each mutual fund share held. Dividends are paid in cash unless the investor elects to reinvest the cash distribution by purchasing more fund shares.   (Page 92)

5.   D.   A specialized or sector fund invests all of its assets in a particular type of security or a particular industry.   (Page 94)

6.   A.   This fund is invested in both stock and bonds; it is likely to be a balanced fund. The percentage invested in the two types of securities is adjusted to maximize the yield obtained. The percentages are seldom fixed.   (Page 94)

7.   D.   Municipal bonds are considered second only to U.S. government securities in terms of safety. Also, interest received from the bonds is exempt from federal income tax.   (Page 95)

8.   D.   All of these elements should be checked when assessing a fund.   (Page 96)

9.   C.   Each shareholder owns an undivided (mutual) interest in the fund portfolio.   (Page 92)

10.   A.   Balanced funds carry both equity and debt issues, not necessarily in equal amounts.   (Page 94)

11.   A.   Control of the investment is given over to the investment manager. All of the other items mentioned are considered advantages.   (Page 82)

12.   C.   Money-market mutual funds invest in a portfolio of short-term debt instruments such as T bills, commercial paper and repos. They are offered without a sales load or charge. The principal objective of the fund is to generate current interest income, and generally the NAV does not appreciate.   (Page 96)

13.   A.   Calculate a mutual fund's expense ratio by dividing its expenses by its average net assets.   (Page 97)

14.   A.   The Investment Company Act of 1940 requires an open-end investment company to redeem shares upon request within seven days from receipt of the request.   (Page 106)

15.   D.   The fund will distribute taxable income or dividends unless it invests in municipal bonds. Because the fund's stated investment objective is to provide tax-exempt income, it must invest in instruments that enable it to achieve this objective.   (Page 95)

16.   C.   Investors should be careful not to be misled by a mutual fund's name. Although the name of a fund should bear a resemblance to its objective, the investor and the rep should read the fund's prospectus carefully to be sure that the fund's objective matches the investor's objective. Growth funds and zero-coupon bonds are not designed to meet the requirement of providing maximum current income.   (Page 96)

26

Mutual Fund Marketing and Pricing

1. A registered representative is seeking to sell shares in an investment company to a client. Which of the following statements would be accurate and permissible for him to say regarding his recommendation?

   I. "When you redeem your shares, you will not know immediately their dollar value."
   II. "If you purchase the shares of two or more funds in the same family of funds, you may be entitled to a reduced sales charge."
   III. "If you invest just before the dividend distribution, you can benefit by receiving the added value of that dividend."

   A. I and II only
   B. I and III only
   C. II and III only
   D. I, II and III

2. What services must a mutual fund sponsor offer to be permitted to charge the maximum allowable sales charge for the fund shares?

   I. Rights of accumulation
   II. Privilege to reinvest dividend distributions at no sales charge
   III. Price breakpoints offering reduced commissions for larger purchases

   A. I and II only
   B. I and III only
   C. II and III only
   D. I, II and III

3. Lotta Leveridge signed a letter of intent stating that she would purchase $25,000 worth of ACE Fund over the next 9 months. After 13 months, she had invested only $12,000. What effect will her actions have?

   A. Her entire investment will be charged an 8½ percent sales charge.
   B. She qualifies for the second breakpoint only and will be charged 8 percent.
   C. The entire amount is still due because she signed a binding contract when she signed the letter of intent.
   D. Her actions will have no effect; she will be charged whatever sales charge she is entitled to for the actual amount she invested.

4. Minnie Leveridge is explaining mutual funds to a prospective investor. Which of the following statements could she use?

   I. "Mutual fund shares are liquid, so you can use them as either short-term or long-term investments."

   II. "Mutual funds always redeem shares at NAV, so you have very little chance of a financial loss."

   III. "Mutual fund shares' redemption value fluctuates according to the value of a fund's portfolio."

   IV. "Because mutual funds must make payment within seven days of redemption, you will always receive a return of your original investment."

   A. I, II and IV
   B. I and III
   C. III
   D. III and IV

5. An investment company share purchased at its net asset value that can be redeemed later at the then-current net asset value is a share issued by a(n)

   A. open-end investment company
   B. closed-end investment company
   C. front-end load company
   D. no-load open-end investment company

6. The NASD allows sales charges up to a maximum of

   A. 9 percent on mutual funds and variable annuities
   B. 9 percent on mutual funds and contractual plans
   C. 8½ percent on mutual funds and contractual plans
   D. 8½ percent on mutual funds and variable annuities

7. In general, the NASD Rules of Fair Practice permit selling concessions and discounts

   A. as consideration for services rendered by nonmember broker-dealers in obtaining business
   B. to member broker-dealers engaged in the investment banking or securities business
   C. to anyone that deals in securities transactions
   D. within certain percentage limits

8. The maximum sales load may be charged on the purchase of shares from an open-end investment company that offers

   I. dividend reinvestment
   II. rights of accumulation
   III. quantity discounts
   IV. exchange privileges

   A. I and II only
   B. I, II and III only
   C. III and IV only
   D. I, II, III and IV

9. A purchase or redemption order for investment company shares must be executed at a price based on the

   A. net asset value next computed after the fund receives the order
   B. net asset value last computed before the fund receives the order
   C. net asset value computed at the close of trading on the NYSE the day before the fund receives the order
   D. best net asset value computed the same day the fund receives the order

10. Which of the following describe a qualified investor eligible for a quantity discount?

    I. Pension plan trustee
    II. Investor in an individual retirement account
    III. Investment club
    IV. Woman and her husband in a joint account

    A. I and II only
    B. I, II and IV only
    C. III and IV only
    D. I, II, III and IV

11. For purposes of rights of accumulation, the quantity of securities an investor owns could be based on the

    I. current net asset value of the securities
    II. current public offering price of the securities
    III. total purchases of shares at the actual offering prices
    IV. current value of all redeemable securities the investor owns within the same family of funds

    A. I and III only
    B. II only
    C. III only
    D. I, II, III and IV

12. Letters of intent can be backdated up to how many days?

    A. 30
    B. 60
    C. 90
    D. 120

13. A member can allow reduced sales charges for purchases by nonmembers under certain circumstances, including

    I. the customer signing a letter of intent
    II. a lump-sum purchase that qualifies for a breakpoint
    III. additional purchases that qualify for breakpoints under rights of accumulation
    IV. special level access charges

    A. I
    B. I, II and III
    C. I and IV
    D. II and III

14. "Sales load" is defined as the

    A. difference between the public offering price and the net asset value
    B. commissions paid on the purchase or sale of securities
    C. fee paid to the investment adviser
    D. concessions allowed on the purchase or sale of securities

15. Selling mutual fund shares at a total dollar amount immediately below the price stated in the prospectus that would qualify an investor to receive a reduced sales charge is called

    A. breakpoint selling
    B. conditional orders
    C. selling dividends
    D. freeriding and withholding

16. An investor redeems 200 shares in ACE Fund. The current POP is $12.50, and the NAV is $11.50. The investor receives

    A. $2,200
    B. $2,300
    C. $2,400
    D. $2,500

17. If the value of securities held in a fund's portfolio increases and the amount of liabilities stays the same, the fund's net assets

    A. increase
    B. decrease
    C. stay the same
    D. are more liquid

18. A customer wishes to redeem 1,000 shares of a mutual fund. The NAV and POP is 11–11.58. A ½ percent redemption fee will be charged. How much will the customer receive?

    A. $10,945
    B. $11,000
    C. $11,522
    D. $11,580

19. A client deposits $2,200 in an open-end investment company. After 60 days, he signs a letter of intent for the $10,000 breakpoint. Six months later, he deposits $11,000. In this case, which of the following statements is true?

    A. He will receive a reduced load on $1,000 worth of the shares.
    B. He will receive a reduced load on $8,800 worth of the shares.
    C. He will receive the beneficial effect of a reduced load on $13,200 worth of the shares.
    D. He will not receive any break in the sales load.

20. The exchange privilege offered by open-end investment companies allows investors to

    A. exchange personally owned securities for investment company shares
    B. exchange shares of one open-end fund for those of another fund in the same company on a net asset value basis
    C. purchase new fund shares from dividends
    D. delay payment of taxes

21. A letter of intent for a mutual fund does NOT contain which of the following provisions?

    A. The time limit is 13 months.
    B. The letter can be backdated 90 days to include a previous deposit.
    C. The fund can halt redemption during the period of time the letter of intent is in effect.
    D. The fund might keep some of the initially issued shares in an escrow account to ensure payment of the full spread.

22. Class A shares of a mutual fund have a

    A. back-end load
    B. level load
    C. front-end load
    D. asset-based fee

23. If a mutual fund collects 12b-1 fees, which of the following statements are true?

    I. The fund may use the money to pay for mailing sales literature.
    II. Advertising materials may state that the fund is no-load.
    III. The fund may use the money to pay for commissions on securities transactions.
    IV. The fund's prospectus must disclose the fee.

    A. I and II only
    B. I and IV only
    C. II and III only
    D. I, II, III and IV

24. Under a letter of intent, the sales charge is deducted from purchases of mutual fund shares

    A. monthly
    B. annually
    C. when each purchase is made
    D. when each letter of intent is completed

Answers & Rationale

1. **A.** Purchase of two funds in the same family of funds may qualify an investor for combination privileges. At redemption, he will receive the next price calculated (forward pricing), which is not yet known. Purchase of a mutual fund just before a dividend distribution is a detriment: the distribution about to be paid is included in the purchase price and, when the investor receives it, is treated as ordinary income—even though he is essentially being returned a portion of his investment. (Page 105)

2. **D.** NASD rules prohibit sales charges exceeding 8½ percent on mutual fund purchases by public customers. Unless a mutual fund grants its shareholders certain privileges, the amount charged must be *lower* than 8½ percent. To qualify for the maximum 8½ percent sales charge, the fund must extend *all* of the following privileges to its shareholders:

   - rights of accumulation
   - dividend reinvestment at net asset value
   - quantity discounts (breakpoints)

   (Page 103)

3. **D.** An LOI is not a binding contract, so the customer is not required to deposit the rest of the money. She will be entitled to whatever breakpoint her $12,000 investment qualifies for. (Page 104)

4. **C.** Mutual funds are very marketable, but because of the sales charge, they are recommended for long-term investments. Shares are redeemed at NAV. However, the NAV fluctuates, and upon redemption the investor may have more or less money than originally invested. (Page 100)

5. **D.** A share purchased at its NAV and sold at its NAV is a no-load fund. NAV plus the sales charge equals the POP; if there is no sales charge, the NAV equals the POP. (Page 99)

6. **D.** The NASD's maximum allowable sales charges are as follows: contractual plans (periodic pay unit trusts), 9 percent; mutual funds, 8½ percent; variable annuities, 8½ percent. (Page 100)

7. **B.** NASD Rules of Fair Practice permit member broker-dealers to allow concessions and discounts only to other members. Exceptions include dealings in exempt securities or with foreign nonmembers. (Page 102)

8. **B.** Investment companies may charge the maximum sales load if they offer all of the following benefits: dividend reinvestment, rights of accumulation and quantity discounts (also known as *breakpoints*). If a member offers none of these services, it cannot assess a sales charge of more than 6.25 percent. (Page 103)

9. **A.** Purchase or redemption of mutual fund shares may occur at the net asset value next calculated after the fund receives the order. This is known as *forward pricing*. (Page 106)

10. **B.** The NASD defines "person" as any individual; a joint account held by any combination of an individual, a spouse or children; or a trustee purchasing for a single account. It allows quantity discounts to any of these. Investment clubs do not qualify under the definition, nor do groups of individuals who form a business or an organization for the sole purpose of investment. (Page 103)

11. **D.** All of the methods listed are permitted. The choice is left to the investment company; however, it must disclose the method it chooses. (Generally, the greater of choices I or III is the option offered.) (Page 105)

12. **C.** The time limit for a letter of intent (LOI) is 13 months, but the letter can be backdated by up to 90 days from the date it was filed. (Page 104)

13. **B.** Reduced sales charges are allowed for purchases made under a letter of intent, large purchases that have reached breakpoints and pur-

chases made under a customer's rights of accumulation. (Page 103)

14. **A.** A sales load is the difference between the public offering price and the amount actually added to the investment company's portfolio at the current NAV. Commissions, concessions and allowances are part of the sales load. (Page 101)

15. **A.** The term "breakpoint sale" refers to a sale made just below a breakpoint (that point at which an investor would qualify for a quantity discount) for the sole purpose of earning a higher commission. (Page 104)

16. **B.** Shares are redeemed at NAV. If the investor redeems 200 shares at an NAV of $11.50, he receives $2,300 (200 × $11.50). (Page 106)

17. **A.** An appreciation in value of fund assets without an attendant increase in liabilities leads to an increase in the fund's net asset value (Assets − Liabilities = NAV). (Page 91)

18. **A.** Always redeem at NAV (bid): 1,000 shares times 11 equals $11,000. Next, determine the redemption fee: $11,000 times .005 (a ½ percent redemption fee) equals $55. Finally, subtract the fee from the gross redemption proceeds: $11,000 minus $55 equals $10,945. A shortcut alternative to the last two steps is to multiply the gross redemption proceeds by the complement of the redemption fee: $11,000 times .995 equals $10,945. (Page 82)

19. **C.** An investor signing a letter of intent has 13 months to contribute funds to reach the reduced load. The investor may also backdate the letter within 90 days to include an amount previously deposited. (Page 104)

20. **B.** Exchange privileges allow investors to move from fund to fund within a family of funds without paying an additional sales charge. (Page 105)

21. **C.** A letter of intent is not binding on the client in any way. Should the client decide to liquidate the account before completing the letter, the company may reduce the redemption only by the amount of shares held in escrow. (Page 104)

22. **C.** Class A shares have a front-end load; Class B shares have a back-end load; and Class C shares have a level load that is an asset-based fee. (Page 102)

23. **B.** 12b-1 fees may be used only to cover promotional expenses for funds that act as distributors of their own shares. The amount of the fee must be disclosed in the prospectus, and the fund may not use the term "no-load" in any communications with the public. (Page 101)

24. **C.** When the customer makes her first investment under a letter of intent, the reduced sales charge applies immediately. At the time each additional investment is made, the same reduced charge is deducted. If the investor does not invest the amount stated in the letter, the full sales load applies retroactively to the total investment. (Page 104)

Mutual Fund Distributions and Taxation

1. Investment companies cannot distribute capital gains to their shareholders more frequently than

   A. monthly
   B. quarterly
   C. semiannually
   D. annually

2. When calculating net investment income, an investment company includes

   A. only dividends
   B. only interest
   C. both dividends and interest
   D. both dividends and interest, minus operating expenses

3. Three months after you purchase 100 shares of an open-end investment company, the company pays a $.32-per-share capital gain distribution. On your tax return, you do which of the following?

   A. Report the distribution as ordinary income
   B. Report the distribution as a capital gain
   C. Claim the distribution under your $200 dividend exclusion if you itemize
   D. Report your registered rep for selling dividends

4. Which of the following statements is permitted under the Rules of Fair Practice?

   I. "This fund distributed a $.30 dividend from investment income and $.70 from realized security profits, for a total yield of 7 percent on its current price of $13.58."
   II. "This fund distributed a $.30 dividend from investment income and $.70 from realized security profits, for a 5.1 percent yield on its current price of $13.58."
   III. "This fund distributed a $.30 dividend from investment income and $.70 from realized security profits, for a 2.2 percent return on its current price of $13.58."
   IV. "You would be advised to purchase this fund at this time to benefit from the already announced and pending capital gain distribution."

   A. I and II
   B. I and III
   C. III
   D. IV

5. An investor purchased 200 shares of ACE Fund when the POP was $11.60 and the NAV was $10.60. ACE Fund's current POP is $12.50, and current NAV is $11.50. If the investor liquidates her 200 shares now, she will have a

   A. loss of $200
   B. loss of $20
   C. gain of $20
   D. gain of $200

6. Three years ago, Bea Kuhl purchased 300 shares of ACE Fund. She sold the shares on August 15, for a loss of $400. On September 4 of the same year, she repurchased the shares. How would she record the loss for tax purposes?

   A. 40 percent of the loss is deductible.
   B. 50 percent of the loss is deductible.
   C. 60 percent of the loss is deductible.
   D. The loss is not deductible.

7. If you invest in a regulated investment company, any dividend you receive from that investment is taxed

   A. as a long-term capital gain
   B. as a long-term or short-term capital gain, depending on how long you have been an investor
   C. to you as ordinary income, but is not taxed at the fund's level
   D. to you as capital gains, but is not taxed at the corporate level

8. Which of the following fees cannot be deducted as an expense from an open-end investment company's investment income?

   A. Custodial
   B. Auditing
   C. Advertising
   D. Accounting

9. As the owner of mutual fund shares, you pay no tax on

   A. dividends that you reinvest in the fund
   B. unrealized capital gains
   C. capital gains issued as additional shares
   D. dividends that do not qualify for the $100 dividend exclusion

10. Randy Bear buys ACE Growth Fund and enjoys a substantial paper capital gain. When Randy believes the market has reached its peak, he switches into ACE Income Fund within the ACE family of funds. He incurs a small service fee, but is not charged an additional sales charge. What is the tax effect?

   A. Any gain or loss is deferred until he liquidates the ACE Income Fund.
   B. The tax basis of ACE Income Fund is adjusted to reflect the gain in ACE Growth Fund.
   C. It is a tax-free exchange.
   D. Any gain in ACE Growth Fund is taxable because the switch is treated as a sale and a purchase.

11. Your client has asked about the automatic dividend reinvestment ACE Fund offers. In describing the differences between dividend reinvestment and receiving distributions in cash, you can say which of the following?

    I. "One benefit of dividend reinvestment is that distributions reinvested are tax deferred, whereas dividends received in cash are taxable in the year received."

    II. "The taxation of dividend distributions is not affected by your choice to reinvest or receive the dividends in cash."

    III. "Your proportionate ownership in ACE Fund will decline if you elect to receive dividend distributions in cash."

    IV. "Your proportionate ownership in ACE Fund is guaranteed to increase if you elect dividend reinvestment."

    A. I and III
    B. I and IV
    C. II and III
    D. II and IV

Answers & Rationale

1.   **D.**   Under the act of 1940, investment companies cannot distribute capital gains more frequently than once per year. This does not require gains to be distributed, as the fund may retain gains for reinvestment.   (Page 107)

2.   **D.**   Net investment income equals gross investment income minus operating expenses. Gross investment income is interest and dividends received from securities in the investment company's portfolio. Capital gains are not included in investment income.   (Page 107)

3.   **B.**   If a fund makes a capital gains distribution, shareholders must report it as capital gain on their individual tax returns (the investment company provides both the shareholders and the IRS with 1099B forms reflecting the distribution).   (Page 107)

4.   **C.**   While a fund can advertise both capital gains and dividend distributions, the two amounts cannot be calculated as one figure and represented as the fund's yield. The dividend distribution of $.30 divided by $13.58 equals the yield. Choice IV describes the practice of selling dividends, which also violates the Rules of Fair Practice.   (Page 107)

5.   **B.**   The investor's cost base in the shares is $11.60. If she liquidates, she will receive the net asset value of $11.50, resulting in a loss of $.10 per share. Liquidating 200 shares, therefore, results in a total loss of $20 (200 × $.10).   (Page 109)

6.   **D.**   The customer repurchased the shares within 30 days of the loss transaction, and the loss is disallowed (a wash sale).   (Page 111)

7.   **C.**   A mutual fund qualifying as a regulated investment company distributes at least 90 percent of its net investment income as a dividend to shareholders. Because the company has qualified, the fund pays no tax on the income distributed. However, shareholders are taxed at their ordinary income tax rates on the distribution.   (Page 107)

8.   **C.**   Advertising costs are an underwriting expense paid from the sales charge collected on the sale of investment company shares.   (Page 107)

9.   **B.**   A gain is not taxable until it is realized or sold.   (Page 107)

10.   **D.**   The exchange is treated as a sale, regardless of the holding period and the fact that it does not involve a new sales charge. The gain or loss on ACE Growth Fund is determined by comparing the cost basis with the net asset value of the shares at the time of exchange. Any difference is a capital gain or loss.   (Page 111)

11.   **C.**   Dividend reinvestment does not defer the distribution's taxation. Whether the dividend is received in cash or reinvested, the distribution is taxable in the year paid. An investor electing to receive distributions in cash will see his interest in the fund decline if others are reinvesting. However, reinvestment of distributions does not guarantee an investor will increase his proportionate interest in the fund.   (Page 107)

28

New Accounts

1. Joe Kuhl wants to open a cash account with you. To open this account, you must do all of the following EXCEPT

   A. get Joe's signature on the new account form
   B. ascertain that Joe is of legal age
   C. get Joe's Social Security number
   D. learn Joe's occupation

2. A lawyer with power of attorney over one of your customer's accounts trades for the account because the customer currently resides in the Near East. The lawyer requests that all statements and trade confirmations be sent to his office. Which of the following statements is true?

   A. The lawyer needs NYSE approval for such a discretionary account.
   B. You must continue to send statements and trade confirmations to the customer's official permanent residence.
   C. You must follow the lawyer's orders because he has power of attorney.
   D. The customer must approve each trade, regardless of where he currently resides.

3. August Polar wishes to open a cash account with you. You are the registered rep, and Mr. Kuhl is your office's branch manager. Who must sign the new account form to open this account?

   A. Mr. Polar only
   B. You only
   C. Mr. Kuhl and you only
   D. Mr. Polar, Mr. Kuhl and you

4. A registered rep must follow special rules when opening an account for

   A. the six-year-old child of a clerical employee of a competitive brokerage firm
   B. the wife of an operations manager at another brokerage firm
   C. a registered rep at an affiliated brokerage firm owned by the same financial holding company
   D. any of the above

5. A customer wishes to open a new account, but declines to provide all of the financial information the member firm requests. In this case, the member firm may

    I. not open an account
   II. open the account if it determines by other means that the customer has the financial resources to carry the account and determines that trading is suitable
  III. not recommend any transactions unless they are suitable for the customer

    A. I
    B. II
    C. II and III
    D. III

6. A change in which of the following should be indicated in a customer's file?

    I. Name or address
   II. Marital status
  III. Objectives

    A. I only
    B. I and II only
    C. III only
    D. I, II and III

7. If a partner of an NASD member firm wishes to open an account with another member firm, which of the following statements is(are) true?

    I. The account may not be opened under any circumstances due to the privileged information to which the partner has access.
   II. The account may be opened, but the partner may not engage in any transactions in securities his own firm recommends.
  III. The member firm opening the account must send duplicate confirmations or statements to the employing member firm, if requested to do so.
  IV. The member firm opening the account must give notice to the employing member firm.

    A. I
    B. II and III
    C. II and IV
    D. III and IV

8. A person wishing to give a broker the right to make investment decisions for him does so by

    A. providing a letter from an attorney
    B. providing a letter giving discretionary powers
    C. calling the broker each time such an order is to be placed
    D. calling the broker once to advise her to use her own judgment in investment decisions

9. A woman wishes to open a cash account in her name only and allow her husband to make purchases and receive checks in his name only. She must instruct her broker-dealer to open a

    A. margin account
    B. cash account with limited power of attorney
    C. cash account with full power of attorney
    D. cash account

10. Which of the following is(are) a discretionary order(s) under the Rules of Fair Practice?

    I. A customer sends a check for $25,000 to a registered representative and instructs the rep to purchase bank and insurance company stocks when the price appears favorable.
    II. A customer instructs a registered representative to buy 1,000 shares of Acme Sweatsocks at a time and price that the representative determines.
    III. A customer instructs a registered representative to purchase as many shares of Quantum Rapid Search as the rep deems appropriate.
    IV. A customer instructs a registered representative to sell 300 shares of Greater Health, Inc., that are long in the account when the rep thinks the time and price appropriate.

    A. I and III only
    B. II and IV only
    C. III only
    D. I, II, III and IV

11. For which of the following pairs of customers could a registered rep open a joint account?

    I. Max Leveridge and his 13-year-old son Tiny
    II. Bea Kuhl and June Polar, two adult college roommates
    III. Randy Bear and Adam Grizzly, friends and partners in business for more than 20 years
    IV. Belle Charolais and her minor nephew Klaus Bruin, for whom she is guardian

    A. I and III only
    B. II and III only
    C. II and IV only
    D. I, II, III and IV

12. A woman wishes to make a gift of securities to her niece's account under the Uniform Gifts to Minors Act. The niece's guardian is opposed to the gift. Under these circumstances, the woman may give the securities

    A. only if the niece approves
    B. as she desires
    C. only with the guardian's written approval
    D. only after obtaining the court's permission

13. Under the Uniform Gifts to Minors Act, which of the following is allowable?

    A. Gift from one donor to one child, with both parents named as custodians
    B. Gift from two donors to more than one child jointly
    C. Gift from one donor to more than one child jointly
    D. Gift from one donor to one child

14. Under the Uniform Gifts to Minors Act, a person can do which of the following?

    I. Give an unlimited amount of cash
    II. Give securities
    III. Give up to $10,000 cash
    IV. Revoke a gift

    A. I
    B. I and II
    C. I, II and IV
    D. II and III

15. A gift given to a minor may be revoked under UGMA

    A. at any time before the minor reaches the age of majority
    B. if the minor dies before reaching the age of majority
    C. if the custodian dies before the minor reaches the age of majority
    D. under no circumstances

16. Under the Uniform Gifts to Minors Act, a custodian may invest in all of the following EXCEPT

    A. variable annuities
    B. commodity futures
    C. blue chip stocks
    D. corporate bonds

17. A woman acting as custodian has given securities to her 10-year-old niece under the Uniform Gifts to Minors Act. The aunt may do which of the following?

    I. Pay for the niece's support and education out of the niece's funds
    II. Donate bearer securities to the account
    III. Buy and sell securities in the custodian account
    IV. Withhold a reasonable amount of dividends and interest earned in the account as reimbursement for expenses

    A. I and II
    B. I, II and III
    C. II and III
    D. III and IV

Answers & Rationale

1. **A.** In opening a cash account, you do not need the customer's signature. You do need to ascertain whether he is of legal age and to obtain other information, including his Social Security number and his occupation. (Page 114)

2. **B.** A rep must continue to send statements and confirms to a customer's official permanent residence unless the customer instructs the rep in writing to discontinue this service. (Page 114)

3. **C.** The customer's signature is not required to open a cash account. To open a margin account, the customer's signature must be obtained on the margin agreement. For any other account, the registered rep must sign the new account form, indicating that the information on the form is true and complete. The branch manager serves as the principal and must review and accept the new account by signing the form before opening the account. (Page 114)

4. **D.** The NYSE, NASD and MSRB all have rules that require broker-dealers to give special attention to accounts opened by certain individuals. This special attention typically involves permission from, or written notification to, some other broker-dealer regarding the establishment of an account. (Page 116)

5. **C.** If a customer refuses to provide financial information, the member firm must use whatever information it has available to decide whether to open the account. Any recommendation made to a customer must be suitable, taking into account the customer's investment objectives, financial situation and any other relevant information. (Page 114)

6. **D.** All information that could affect recommendations or a customer's financial situation must be noted immediately in the file. (Page 114)

7. **D.** The member firm at which the account is being opened must give notice to the employing firm, and the employing firm must receive duplicate copies of all trade confirmations if it requests them. (Page 116)

8. **B.** A discretionary account always requires prior written authorization from the customer in the form of a limited power of attorney. (Page 118)

9. **C.** For a person other than the person in whose name an account is held to enter trades and withdraw assets, a full power of attorney is required. A limited power of attorney enables someone other than the account owner to enter trades, but not to withdraw assets. (Page 118)

10. **A.** Discretion is given when the rep chooses the stock, the number of shares or whether to buy or sell. Discretionary authority must be given to an individual; it may not be given to a firm. Time and price are not considered discretionary decisions. (Page 118)

11. **B.** An account owner is the person who can control investments within an account and request distributions of cash or securities from the account. A joint account can be opened only for account owners who can legally exercise such control over the account. Minors cannot legally exercise such control; thus, a joint account could not be opened if a minor would be one of the owners. (Page 116)

12. **B.** In a custodian account, any adult, whether related or unrelated, can make gifts. All gifts, however, are irrevocable. (Page 119)

13. **D.** Under UGMA, a donor may give an unlimited amount of money or number of securities to *one child* with *one* entity named as *custodian*. (Page 119)

14. **B.** Under an UGMA account, the size of a gift that may be transferred is unlimited. Gifts under UGMA are irrevocable and may consist of cash and securities. (Page 119)

15. **D.** The Uniform Gifts to Minors Act states that all gifts to minors are irrevocable. (Page 119)

16. **B.** Commodity futures cannot be purchased in a custodial account because they are purchased on margin. Margin transactions are prohibited in a custodial account. (Page 121)

17. **B.** A custodian may use custodial property for the minor's support, education and general use and benefit. A custodian is empowered to collect, hold, manage, sell, exchange or dispose of the property as she deems advisable. However, a donor may not designate herself custodian of bearer securities unless the gift is accompanied by a deed of gift. A custodian may be compensated for reasonable services and reimbursed for necessary expenses if she is not the donor. (Page 120)

29

Mutual Fund Purchase and Withdrawal Plans

1. An advantage of dollar cost averaging during a bull market is that it results in an average cost per share that is *less* than the stock's cost on any given day, assuming that

    I. the price of the underlying shares fluctuates
    II. a set number of shares is purchased regularly
    III. a set dollar amount is invested regularly
    IV. a set dollar amount of investments is maintained

    A. I and II
    B. I and III
    C. II and III
    D. III and IV

2. Under the spread-load plan provision of the 1970 amendments to the Investment Company Act of 1940, an investor may have no more than what percentage deducted from any one payment?

    A. 8½ percent
    B. 9 percent
    C. 16 percent
    D. 20 percent

3. A customer canceling a contractual plan will have all of his sales charge refunded if he cancels the plan within

    A. 15 days of receiving the notice from the custodian bank
    B. 30 days of the mailing of the notice by the custodian bank
    C. 45 days of the mailing of the notice by the custodian bank
    D. 18 months of receiving the notice from the custodian bank

4. The average sales charge on a spread-load contractual plan over the plan's first four years can be no more than

    A. 9 percent
    B. 16 percent
    C. 20 percent
    D. 50 percent

5. A customer purchased a front-end load periodic payment plan last year. The investment company stopped receiving payments from her after six months. Because she hasn't been heard from for the last four months, the investment company does which of the following?

   A. Recalculates the deposits, retains its 50 percent sales charge and returns the balance from the escrow account
   B. Sends a notice to the customer informing her of both the account's value and the refund to which she is entitled if she decides to cancel the plan
   C. Refunds all sales charges exceeding 15 percent of the deposits and returns her investment's net asset value
   D. Sues the customer for the past due payment(s)

6. A subscriber to a front-end load contractual plan that has a 10-year life is expected to make payments totaling $12,000 over that period of time. Instead, he cancels after the 10th month and spends the remaining amount on health club dues. How much of the sales charge already paid will be refunded to him?

   A. $0
   B. $350
   C. $425
   D. $500

7. Periodic payment plan certificates represent what type of interest in the underlying securities?

   A. Divided
   B. Undivided
   C. Personal
   D. Fractional

8. The maximum sales charge on a unit investment trust using mutual funds for its underlying investment is

   A. 7 percent
   B. 8 percent
   C. 8½ percent
   D. 9 percent

9. One risk of a withdrawal plan is that the

   A. sales charge for the service is high
   B. cost basis of the shares is high
   C. plan is illegal in many states
   D. principal value fluctuates

10. June Polar signs up for a mutual fund contractual plan with a 50 percent front-end load and $300 monthly payments. She decides to cancel the plan after her second payment, but within 45 days. If her current NAV is $340, how much will she get back from the plan?

    A. $340
    B. $550
    C. $600
    D. $640

11. An investor in a spread-load plan wants to withdraw after investing $150 a month for eight months. The plan has taken $240 in sales charges. If the NAV has not changed, how much refund will the investor receive?

    A. $600
    B. $960
    C. $1,020
    D. $1,200

12. June Polar has just invested a lump sum in ACE Fund. If she wishes to purchase additional shares by reinvesting all dividends and capital gains, she can set up what type of plan?

    A. Accumulation
    B. Regular
    C. Dollar cost averaging
    D. Lump-sum

13. Which of the following characteristics describe a contractual planholder?

 I. Receives a plan certificate
 II. Owns a specific portion of the underlying mutual fund shares
 III. Owns specific shares in the underlying portfolio
 IV. Must complete the contractual plan

 A. I and II
 B. I and III
 C. II and IV
 D. III and IV

14. Klaus Bruin has decided to terminate his contractual plan one month after opening it. At the time he opened the account, the NAV was $11.50, and it is now $11.80. He has acquired 212 shares and has paid sales charges of $930. What will Klaus's refund be?

 A. Total NAV for his shares at the time of their purchase plus 50 percent of the sales charges
 B. Current NAV of his shares plus all sales charges
 C. Only the current NAV of his shares
 D. Current NAV of his shares plus sales charges that exceed 15 percent of gross payments

15. An investor has requested a withdrawal plan from his mutual fund and currently receives $600 per month. This is an example of what type of plan?

 A. Contractual
 B. Fixed-share periodic withdrawal
 C. Fixed-dollar periodic withdrawal
 D. Fixed-percentage withdrawal

16. June Polar owns $24,000 worth of ZBest Invest Fund shares. She chooses to have the money forwarded to her, using a 10-year fixed-time withdrawal. She receives which of the following?

 A. Fixed number of dollars for a variable amount of time
 B. Variable number of dollars for a fixed amount of time
 C. Fixed number of dollars for a fixed amount of time
 D. Variable number of dollars for a variable amount of time

17. A customer has a contractual plan. The customer's daughter is in college and needs money for expenses. The customer has been investing $150 per month into the contractual plan. What would you recommend she do to provide her daughter with expense money?

 A. Give the daughter $100 per month and invest $50 per month instead of $150 per month into the contractual plan
 B. Liquidate the plan
 C. Continue to invest and make periodic withdrawals from the plan
 D. Set up a systematic withdrawal plan and continue to make investments

18. A customer canceling a front-end load contractual plan will have all or part of his sales charge refunded if he cancels the plan within how many months?

 A. 8
 B. 18
 C. 28
 D. 38

Answers & Rationale

1.   **B.**   Dollar cost averaging results in a lower average cost per share as long as the shares' price fluctuates, the general trend of the stock price is up and the same number of dollars is invested during each interval.   (Page 122)

2.   **D.**   Under the Investment Company Act Amendments of 1970, a spread-load plan cannot take more than 20 percent of any plan payment in the first year as a sales charge. Therefore, total sales charges cannot exceed 20 percent in the first year and cannot average more than 16 percent over the plan's first four years. A maximum sales charge of 9 percent is permitted over the life of the plan; 8½ percent is the maximum sales charge the NASD permits for single pay unit trusts and investment company open accounts.   (Page 124)

3.   **C.**   Under the Investment Company Act of 1940, a contractual planholder must be allowed a full refund if he returns his shares within 45 days of the mailing of the notice by the custodian bank.   (Page 125)

4.   **B.**   The Investment Company Act Amendments of 1970 state that a spread-load plan cannot take more than 20 percent of any plan payment as a sales charge and the sales charge cannot exceed an average of more than 16 percent over the first four years of the plan investment.   (Page 124)

5.   **B.**   A purchase of a front-end load plan has surrender rights for 18 months after the initial investment. The purchaser must be notified officially of these rights if she misses any three payments within the first 15 months or misses one or more payments between the 15th and the 18th month. Under these rights, the purchaser will be refunded some (but not all) of the sales charges as well as the account's current value.   (Page 124)

6.   **B.**   Under the act of 1940, the subscriber would receive the sales charge of $500 (one half of the $1,000 in premiums already paid) less 15 percent of $1,000 ($150). Therefore, $500 minus $150 equals $350.   (Page 124)

7.   **B.**   Periodic payment plan certificates represent an undivided interest in a pool of underlying securities. Typically, the pool is composed of open-end investment company shares. (Page 123)

8.   **D.**   A UIT investing in mutual fund shares is most likely a contractual plan operating under the Investment Company Act of 1940 or the 1970 act amendments. The maximum sales load permissible under either type of plan (front-end load or spread-load) is 9 percent over the life of the plan.   (Page 124)

9.   **D.**   Withdrawal plans have no guarantee of payment. The investor's account value is at the mercy of market fluctuations.   (Page 126)

10.   **D.**   Under the Investment Company Act of 1940, an investor terminating a plan within 45 days is entitled to a refund of all sales charges plus the account's current value. Because the customer has made two payments of $300 each, she invested a total of $600. From that $600, 50 percent ($300) was deducted as a sales charge. The account's current value is $340, so the customer will receive $640 as a refund.   (Page 125)

11.   **B.**   A refund from a spread-load plan that has been in effect for more than 45 days is limited to a return of net asset value only. The investor would receive the difference between the amount invested (NAV remains the same) and the sales charges deducted. In this case, a total investment of $1,200 minus the sales charge of $240 equals a refund of $960.   (Page 125)

12.   **A.**   The customer can elect to reinvest fund distributions through an accumulation plan.   (Page 123)

13.   **A.**   A contractual planholder receives a certificate evidencing ownership of shares the plan company holds in trust. Remember, plan companies are unit investment trusts that invest in mutual fund shares. The plan participant holds

units in the trust, not specific mutual fund shares. (Page 123)

14. **B.** Termination of a contractual plan within 45 days results in a refund of all sales charges plus the account's current value. (Page 125)

15. **C.** If the investor receives $600 a month, the withdrawal's dollar amount is fixed; this must be a fixed-dollar plan. (Page 125)

16. **B.** Under a fixed-time withdrawal plan, only the distribution's time period is fixed. The amount of money received each month or the number of shares liquidated varies. (Page 125)

17. **A.** The best choice is to reduce the contractual plan payments to $50 per month and give the daughter $100 per month (most plans allow this).

By doing so, the contractual plan remains intact, although the time necessary to accumulate the plan's stated investment is extended. By liquidating or withdrawing from the plan, the customer uses money that has been subject to heavy sales charges (50 percent or 20 percent loads). Clearly, using money reduced by heavy sales charges is not in the customer's best interest. (Page 123)

18. **B.** Purchasers of front-end load plans have surrender rights for 18 months after their initial investments. Under the Investment Company Act of 1940, an investor terminating a plan within 18 months is entitled to a refund of all sales charges exceeding 15 percent of the total (gross) payments made to date, plus the investment's current value, which is liquidated at current NAV and may result in a profit or loss. (Page 124)

30

Tracking Investment Company Securities

1. ATF Fund has an NAV of $5.84 and a POP of $6.05. ATF Fund is MOST likely a(n)

    A. closed-end investment company
    B. face-amount certificate company
    C. open-end investment company
    D. no-load mutual fund

2. GEM Fund has an NAV of $8.50 and a POP of $8.20. GEM Fund is MOST likely a(n)

    A. closed-end investment company
    B. face-amount certificate company
    C. open-end investment company
    D. no-load mutual fund

3. ACE Fund has an NAV of $10.10 and a POP of $10.10. ACE Fund is MOST likely a(n)

    A. closed-end investment company
    B. face-amount certificate company
    C. open-end investment company
    D. no-load mutual fund

Answers & Rationale

1.   **C.**   ATF Fund is most likely an open-end investment company because the offering price is higher than the NAV.   (Page 126)

2.   **A.**   GEM Fund must be a closed-end investment company because the offering price is less than the NAV. GEM Fund is selling at a discount from its NAV.   (Page 126)

3.   **D.**   ACE Fund is a no-load fund because the NAV and the offering price are the same, indicating that no sales charge is applied.   (Page 126)

31

Lesson Two — Investment Companies

1. Which of the following statements about open-end investment companies are true?

   I. They may constantly issue new shares.
   II. They redeem shares at any time.
   III. They may leverage common shares by issuing bonds.

   A. I and II only
   B. I and III only
   C. II and III only
   D. I, II and III

2. Lotta Leveridge owns 150 shares of ArGood Mutual Fund. Which of the following statements are true?

   I. When the fund declares a dividend, she will receive a cash dividend for each share owned.
   II. She will have difficulty liquidating her shares.
   III. The amount of her dividend will reflect her proportional interest in the value of the fund portfolio on the record date.
   IV. She will receive dividends from only 150 shares of stock held in the fund portfolio.

   A. I, II and IV
   B. I and III
   C. II and III
   D. II, III and IV

3. Mutual funds are like other types of corporations in that

   I. they may issue equity and debt
   II. their boards of directors make policy decisions
   III. shareholders have ownership rights

   A. I and III only
   B. II only
   C. II and III only
   D. I, II and III

4. ALFA Financial Services charges a fee for managing a mutual fund. Which of the following would be included in the services ALFA supplies?

   I. Ensuring that the fund portfolio meets diversification requirements
   II. Attempting to meet the fund's investment objectives
   III. Analyzing the market and deciding when securities in the portfolio should be bought or sold
   IV. Changing investment objectives to maximize potential gain for shareholders

   A. I, II and III only
   B. I and III only
   C. II and III only
   D. I, II, III and IV

5. June Polar is explaining mutual funds to a prospective investor. Which of the following statements may she use in her conversation with the client?

I. "Mutual fund shares are liquid, so an investor can use them as either short-term or long-term investments."
II. "Mutual funds always redeem shares at NAV, so you have very little chance of a financial loss."
III. "The redemption value of mutual fund shares fluctuates according to the value of the fund's portfolio."
IV. "Because mutual funds must make payment within seven days of redemption, you will always be able to receive a return of your original investment."

A. I, II and IV
B. I and III
C. III
D. III and IV

6. Which of the following would PROBABLY be found in a money-market fund's portfolio?

I. T bills
II. T bonds with a short time to maturity
III. Bank certificates of deposit
IV. Common stock

A. I
B. I and II
C. I, II and III
D. II, III and IV

7. Which of the following would be classified as an investment company?

I. Closed-end company
II. Open-end company
III. Qualified plan company
IV. Fixed-annuity company

A. I and II
B. I, II and IV
C. II
D. III and IV

8. According to the Investment Company Act of 1940, which of the following are required of investment companies?

I. Investment company registration statement filed with the SEC
II. Minimum net worth of $100,000 before the offer of shares to the public
III. Statement of investment policies and diversification status

A. I and II only
B. I and III only
C. II and III only
D. I, II and III

9. If Joe Kuhl fails to pay for XYZ Mutual Fund shares within the required amount of time, the broker-dealer could

I. cancel the order
II. fine Joe based on the dollar amount of the sale
III. sell the securities and charge Joe for any loss

A. I and II only
B. I and III only
C. III only
D. I, II and III

10. Which of the following statements is true of unrealized gain in a mutual fund portfolio?

I. It affects the mutual fund shares' value.
II. It is the growth in market value of securities held in the portfolio.
III. It is realized by shareholders only when they redeem their shares.

A. I and II only
B. I and III only
C. II and III only
D. I, II and III

11. Under the conduit theory of taxation, which of the following statements are true?

    I. A fund is not taxed on earnings it distributes.
    II. Retained earnings are taxed as regular corporate income.
    III. Earnings distributed by a regulated mutual fund are taxed twice.

    A. I and II only
    B. I and III only
    C. II and III only
    D. I, II and III

12. Which of the following statements are true of a mutual fund dividend distribution?

    I. The fund pays dividends from net income.
    II. A single taxpayer may exclude $100 worth of dividend income from taxes annually.
    III. An investor is liable for taxes on the distribution, whether it is a cash distribution or it is reinvested in the fund.
    IV. An investor is liable for taxes only if she receives the distribution in cash.

    A. I and II
    B. I, II and III
    C. I and III
    D. II and IV

13. Clara Bullock and Klaus Bruin each has an open account in ArGood Mutual Fund. Clara has decided to receive all distributions in cash, while Klaus automatically reinvests all distributions. How do their decisions affect their investments?

    I. Cash distributions may reduce Clara's proportional interest in the fund.
    II. Clara may use the cash distributions to purchase shares later at NAV.
    III. Klaus's reinvestments purchase additional shares at NAV rather than at the offering price.

    A. I and II only
    B. I and III only
    C. II and III only
    D. I, II and III

14. Which of the following statements describe contractual plans?

    I. They cannot be sold in certain states.
    II. They do not obligate a planholder to complete the contracted number of payments.
    III. They have predetermined fixed schedules of sales charges.

    A. I and II only
    B. I and III only
    C. II and III only
    D. I, II and III

15. If a mutual fund offers a fixed-time withdrawal plan, which of the following statements is true?

    I. The amount the client receives each month may vary.
    II. A fixed number of shares are liquidated each month.
    III. Not all funds offer this type of withdrawal.
    IV. This plan is self-exhausting.

    A. I
    B. I and II
    C. I, III and IV
    D. II, III and IV

16. Which of the following withdrawal plans offered by ArGood Mutual Fund pay(s) the client a fixed monthly amount?

    I. Fixed-dollar withdrawal
    II. Fixed-percentage withdrawal
    III. Fixed-share withdrawal
    IV. Liquidation over a fixed period of time

    A. I only
    B. II and III only
    C. II, III and IV only
    D. I, II, III and IV

17. In a mutual fund, a shareholder who elects not to receive share certificates can liquidate all or a portion of his holdings and receive payment from the fund if the fund receives which of the following from the shareholder?

    I. Written request
    II. Signed stock power
    III. Signature guarantee

    A. I
    B. I and II
    C. I and III
    D. II and III

18. Which of the following are characteristic of a mutual fund voluntary accumulation plan?

    I. Minimum initial purchase
    II. Minimum optional additional purchases
    III. Declining sales charges on new investment as money accumulates
    IV. Obligatory purchase goal

    A. I and II only
    B. I, II and III only
    C. II and IV only
    D. I, II, III and IV

19. Which of the following characteristics describe(s) a contractual planholder?

    I. He receives unit trust certificates.
    II. He owns an undivided interest in the mutual fund shares underlying the plan.
    III. He owns an undivided interest in the underlying mutual fund's portfolio.

    A. I and II
    B. I and III
    C. II and III
    D. III

20. A customer opens a new cash account. Which of the following signatures is(are) required before orders can be executed?

    I. Customer
    II. Registered representative
    III. Registered principal

    A. I only
    B. I and II only
    C. II and III only
    D. I, II and III

21. A change in which of the following should be indicated in a customer's file?

    I. Name or address
    II. Marital status
    III. Objectives

    A. I only
    B. I and II only
    C. III only
    D. I, II and III

22. The investment adviser in a regulated, diversified open-end investment company performs which of the following functions?

    I. Makes sure the fund invests in such a manner as to retain its diversified status
    II. Attempts to fulfill the fund's investment objective through careful investing
    III. Changes investment objectives as he believes is in the investors' best interest
    IV. Investigates the tax status of potential investments

    A. I, II and III
    B. I, II and IV
    C. II and IV
    D. III and IV

23. June Polar wants to buy $1,000 worth of an open-end investment company. She may buy shares through

    I. the fund's sponsor
    II. a brokerage firm
    III. the fund's custodian
    IV. a bank acting as dealer

    A. I and II
    B. I, II and IV
    C. II
    D. III and IV

24. ACE Fund experienced an unrealized loss last month that will

    I. result in a lower NAV per share
    II. mean lower dividend payments to shareholders
    III. reduce the proceeds payable to shareholders who liquidate their shares

    A. I and II only
    B. I and III only
    C. II and III only
    D. I, II and III

25. You notice that the total assets of ALFA, a regulated open-end investment company, went down 28 percent last year. You also note that the stock in which ALFA deposited its capital did very well. Lastly, you learn that ALFA holds a large number of bonds. Which two of the following most likely occurred?

    I. ALFA was holding too much cash.
    II. Interest rates went up.
    III. ALFA paid huge commissions to agents for their extra sales efforts.
    IV. A large number of ALFA shares were redeemed.

    A. I and II
    B. I and III
    C. II and III
    D. II and IV

26. Which of the following statements about sales charges is(are) true?

    I. Under NASD rules, mutual fund sales charges may not exceed 8.5 percent of the offering price.
    II. Under NASD rules, mutual fund sales charges may not exceed 8.5 percent of the share's net asset value.
    III. An investment company must offer rights of accumulation, breakpoints and reinvestment of dividends at NAV to charge an 8.5 percent sales charge.
    IV. Under the Investment Company Act of 1940, the maximum sales charge for purchases of mutual fund shares under a contractual plan is 9 percent.

    A. I
    B. I and III
    C. I, III and IV
    D. II, III and IV

27. ACE Fund's offering price is $9, and its net asset value is $9.40. GEM Fund's offering price is $23.80, and its net asset value is $19.45. From these quotes you know that

    I. ACE is an open-end fund
    II. ACE is a closed-end fund
    III. GEM is an open-end fund
    IV. GEM is a closed-end fund

    A. I and III
    B. I and IV
    C. II and III
    D. II and IV

28. Which of the following statements is(are) true regarding an open-end investment company's NAV?

    I. It is calculated seven days a week.
    II. It is calculated as stipulated in the prospectus.
    III. It takes into account cash the fund holds, but has not invested.
    IV. When divided by the number of shares outstanding, it equals the net asset value per share.

    A. I and IV
    B. II, III and IV
    C. II and IV
    D. III

29. Which of the following characteristics describe the net asset value per share?

    I. Increases if the fund's assets appreciate in value
    II. Decreases if the fund distributes a dividend to shareholders
    III. Decreases when shares are redeemed
    IV. Increases if shareholders reinvest dividend and capital gains distributions

    A. I and II
    B. I and III
    C. II and III
    D. II and IV

30. Under what circumstances could a mutual fund temporarily suspend the redemption provision?

    I. If the New York Stock Exchange is closed on days other than customary weekends and holidays
    II. If the SEC permits it
    III. If an emergency condition exists and then only with SEC approval
    IV. At the discretion of the investment company management

    A. I, II and III only
    B. II and III only
    C. II, III and IV only
    D. I, II, III and IV

31. For a registered investment company to implement a 12b-1 plan, the plan must be approved by a majority of the

    I. outstanding voting shares of the company
    II. board of directors
    III. uninterested members of the board of directors
    IV. investment advisory board

    A. I
    B. I and II
    C. I, II and III
    D. II, III and IV

32. To qualify for the quantity discount, which of the following could NOT be joined under the definition of "any person"?

    I. Father and his 35-year-old son investing in separate accounts
    II. Husband and wife investing in a joint account
    III. Husband and wife investing in a separate account
    IV. Trust officer working on behalf of a single trust account

    A. I
    B. II, III and IV
    C. II and IV
    D. III and IV

33. A fund seeks high current yield accompanied by reasonable risk. It invests most of its portfolio in corporate bonds having one of the top three ratings according to Moody's and Standard & Poor's. It seeks to reduce the risk associated with interest rate fluctuations by investing a portion of its assets in short-term corporate debt. This information describes which of the following mutual funds?

    A. ZBEST Government Income Fund
    B. NavCo Tax-free Municipal Bond Fund
    C. ArGood Investment-grade Bond Fund
    D. ArGood Balanced Fund

34. A fund seeks to preserve capital, to generate current income and to provide long-term growth. Its strategy is to invest 60 percent of its portfolio in common stocks and 40 percent in bonds and fixed-income securities. Through diversification, the fund intends to provide protection against downturns in the market. In its endeavors to produce positive returns during market declines, the fund may not participate fully in rising stock markets. This information describes which of the following mutual funds?

    A. ATF Capital Appreciation Fund
    B. ATF Overseas Opportunities Fund
    C. ATF Biotechnology Fund
    D. ArGood Balanced Fund

35. A fund aims for consistent total returns. The management is empowered to shift assets among stocks, bonds and short-term fixed-income securities in accordance with its projections of future market conditions. Because of its ability to diversify among many investment instruments, the fund has the potential to provide maximum returns while reducing volatility. This information describes which of the following mutual funds?

    A. ZBEST Government Income Fund
    B. ZBEST Asset Allocation Fund
    C. ArGood Stock Index Fund
    D. ATF Capital Appreciation Fund

36. A fund seeks primarily current income, with secondary objectives of capital growth and growth of income. Its portfolio is composed of common stock, preferred stock and convertible securities of large, well-established companies with histories of paying high dividends. Its equity concentration can help protect against the loss of purchasing power owing to inflation. This information describes which of the following mutual funds?

    A. ACE Equity Income Fund
    B. NavCo Cash Reserves Money-Market Fund
    C. NavCo Tax-free Municipal Bond Fund
    D. ZBEST Government Income Fund

Answers & Rationale

1.   **A.**   An open-end company must stand ready to redeem shares within seven days of receiving a customer's request and may continuously offer its shares for sale. Although an open-end company may invest in just about any security, it may issue only one class of voting stock. The company cannot issue any type of debt.
(Page 82)

2.   **B.**   A mutual fund share represents an undivided interest in the fund's portfolio. If a dividend is declared, the shareholder receives a dividend for each mutual fund share held. Dividends are paid in cash unless the shareholder elects to reinvest the cash distribution for the purchase of more fund shares.
(Page 107)

3.   **C.**   Mutual funds may issue only one class of voting stock. Like corporate stockholders, mutual fund shareholders have various rights, one of which is the right to elect the board of directors, which sets policies for the fund.   (Page 92)

4.   **A.**   The mutual fund's objective may be changed only by a majority vote of the outstanding shares. The fund manager is assigned the day-to-day management responsibilities of the fund. Duties include attempting to meet the objective as set out by the fund and buying and selling securities to be held in the portfolio.
(Page 89)

5.   **C.**   Mutual funds are very marketable, but because of the sales charge, they are recommended for long-term investments. Shares are redeemed at NAV; however, the NAV fluctuates, and upon redemption the investor may have more or less money than originally invested. (Page 100)

6.   **C.**   Money-market instruments are considered short-term, very liquid debt instruments. Because common stock is equity, it would not be found in a money-market fund.
(Page 96)

7.   **A.**   Open- and closed-end funds are classified as investment companies. Plan companies offer plans in which an investment company may be selected as an investment vehicle, but they are not investment companies themselves. Only insurance companies offer fixed annuities.
(Page 82)

8.   **D.**   The Investment Company Act of 1940 requires registration of funds, a minimum initial net worth of $100,000, at least 100 shareholders and a specifically defined investment objective.
(Page 84)

9.   **C.**   If Joe fails to pay for the shares within five business days, the broker-dealer must sell the shares to pay for the transaction. Any gain or loss is settled between the broker-dealer and Joe. The order has taken place and cannot be canceled.
(Page 92)

10.   **D.**   Unrealized gains in portfolio securities result from the assets' appreciation in value. This appreciation in value is reflected in an appreciation of the mutual fund shares themselves. A shareholder wanting to cash in on this appreciation can do so only by selling the shares and realizing the gain.
(Page 108)

11.   **D.**   By qualifying as a regulated investment company (the conduit, or pipeline, tax theory), the fund is liable for taxes only on the income retained. The investor benefits because the income is taxed only twice (at the corporate level and at the individual level) and not three times (also at the fund level).
(Page 107)

12.   **C.**   Funds pay dividends from net income, and an investor is liable for taxes on all distributions. The $100 annual exclusion was eliminated with the new tax code.   (Page 109)

13.   **B.**   By electing to receive distributions in cash while others purchase shares through reinvestment, Clara lowers her proportional interest in the fund. Most funds allow reinvestment of dividends at net asset value. Cash invested is considered a new purchase, and the shares are pur-

chased at the public offering price, not NAV.
(Page 108)

14. **D.** The contractual plan is not legal in several states; the contract is unilateral (only the company is bound); and the prospectus details the specific charges to be deducted from each payment over the life of the plan.   (Page 123)

15. **C.** A fixed-time withdrawal plan is considered self-liquidating. Only the time is fixed; the number of shares liquidated, the amount of money received and the percentage of the account liquidated vary from period to period. Funds may or may not offer withdrawal plans. If they do, the prospectuses contain information concerning the plans.   (Page 125)

16. **A.** In a withdrawal plan, if one variable is fixed, such as the dollar amount, all other aspects of the payment vary. If a client receives a fixed-dollar payment, the plan must be a fixed-dollar plan.   (Page 125)

17. **C.** An order for redemption without a certificate being issued requires a written request and signature guarantee.   (Page 106)

18. **B.** A voluntary accumulation plan is voluntary, not binding. The company may require that the initial investment meet a certain minimum dollar amount. It may also specify that any additions meet set minimums (for example, $50). The sales charge is level, and the plan may qualify for breakpoints based on the accumulated value.   (Page 122)

19. **A.** A contractual plan buys mutual fund shares, to hold in trust. The planholder then owns an undivided interest in the mutual fund shares, as evidenced by the unit trust certificate(s).   (Page 123)

20. **C.** When a customer opens a new account, the card is signed by the registered rep introducing the customer to the firm and by the principal, who accepts the customer for the firm. The customer need not sign the new account card. The

customer's signature is required only on a margin account.   (Page 114)

21. **D.** All information that affects a registered rep's recommendations or a customer's financial situation must be noted immediately in the file.   (Page 114)

22. **B.** The investment adviser is responsible for making investments according to the objective stipulated by the fund. The fund's objective may be changed only with a majority vote of the outstanding shares.   (Page 89)

23. **A.** The custodian does not sell the shares, but holds them for safekeeping. A bank cannot be a member of the NASD and, therefore, cannot act as a dealer (although subsidiaries independent of the bank may be set up as broker-dealers).   (Page 90)

24. **B.** An unrealized loss is the same as a depreciation in asset value, which results in a lower NAV per share. A shareholder would receive less at redemption than he would have received if redemption took place before the asset's depreciation.   (Page 100)

25. **D.** Because ALFA has a portfolio composed of bonds, if interest rates increase, the bond's value declines. If shares are redeemed, the portfolio's value declines as the money is paid out. Commissions are paid from sales charges collected; they are not an expense of the fund.   (Page 100)

26. **C.** The NASD limits sales charges to 8.5 percent of the POP as a maximum. If the fund does not allow for breakpoints, reinvestment of dividends at net, or rights of accumulation, the maximum is less than 8.5 percent. Under the Investment Company Act of 1940, the maximum sales charge on mutual funds is deferred to the NASD rules, while a contractual plan specifically may charge 9 percent over the life of the plan.   (Page 103)

27. **D.** ACE Fund is selling below its net asset value, so it must be a closed-end fund. GEM is selling above its NAV by more than the

8½ percent sales load allowed, so it also must be a closed-end fund.   (Page 82)

28. **B.**   NAV must be calculated at least every business day, but not on weekends or holidays. It takes into account all of the fund's assets and is arrived at by totaling the assets and dividing that amount by the number of shares outstanding.
(Page 100)

29. **A.**   Share prices increase when assets in the portfolio increase in value. Share prices decrease when the fund distributes a dividend, as shareholders receive either cash or additional shares. Redeeming or purchasing shares does not affect share prices, only total assets. Reinvesting dividends or capital gains has no effect on share prices either.   (Page 100)

30. **A.**   The seven-day redemption guideline is law and may be suspended only with SEC permission or if the NYSE is closed on a day other than customary holidays and weekends.   (Page 106)

31. **C.**   A 12b-1 plan must be approved by a majority vote of the shareholders, board of directors and uninterested members of the board of directors. The fee must be reapproved annually.
(Page 101)

32. **A.**   For the purpose of qualifying for breakpoints, the definition of "person" includes family units—but only minor children, not someone 35 years old.   (Page 103)

33. **C.**   Investment-grade bond funds invest in corporate bonds having one of the top three ratings according to Moody's and Standard & Poor's.   (Page 95)

34. **D.**   Balanced funds invest in both common stocks and bonds to preserve capital, generate current income and provide long-term growth.
(Page 94)

35. **B.**   Asset allocation funds shift assets among stocks, bonds and short-term fixed-income securities in accordance with projections of future market conditions.   (Page 95)

36. **A.**   Equity income funds invest in common stock, preferred stock and convertible securities for current income and capital growth. (Page 94)

Annuity Plans

32

1. Which of the following represent rights of investors who have purchased variable annuities?

   I. Right to vote on proposed changes in investment policy
   II. Right to approve changes in the plan portfolio
   III. Right to vote for the investment adviser
   IV. Right to make additional purchases at no sales charge

   A. I and III
   B. I and IV
   C. II and III
   D. II and IV

2. Ms. Charolais invests in a variable annuity. At age 65, she chooses to annuitize. Under these circumstances, which of the following statements are true?

   I. She will receive the annuity's entire value in a lump-sum payment.
   II. She may choose to receive monthly payments for the rest of her life.
   III. The accumulation unit's value is used to calculate the total number of annuity units.
   IV. The accumulation unit's value is used to calculate the annuity unit's value.

   A. I and III
   B. I and IV
   C. II and III
   D. II and IV

3. For a retiring investor, which of the following is the MOST important factor in determining a variable annuity investment's suitability?

   A. Fact that the annuity payment may go up or down
   B. Whether the investor is married
   C. Whether the investor has concerns about taxes
   D. Fact that the periodic payments into the contract may go up or down

4. Ms. Charolais purchases a nonqualified annuity at age 60. Before the contract is annuitized, she withdraws some of her funds. What are the consequences?

 A. 10 percent penalty plus payment of ordinary income on all funds withdrawn

 B. 10 percent penalty plus payment of ordinary income on all funds withdrawn in excess of basis

 C. Capital gains tax on earnings in excess of basis

 D. Ordinary income tax on earnings in excess of basis

5. Once a variable annuity has been annuitized, which of the following statements is true?

 A. Each annuity unit's value varies, but the number of annuity units is fixed.

 B. Each annuity unit's value is fixed, but the number of annuity units varies.

 C. The number of accumulation units is fixed, but the value per unit varies.

 D. Each annuity unit's value and the number of annuity units vary.

6. Under the Tax Reform Act of 1986, all of the following investments offer either full or partially tax-deductible contributions to individuals who meet eligibility requirements EXCEPT

 A. IRAs
 B. Keogh plans
 C. variable annuities
 D. defined contribution plans

7. Holders of variable annuities receive the largest monthly payments under which of the following payout options?

 A. Life annuity
 B. Life annuity with period certain
 C. Joint and last survivor annuity
 D. All of the above options offer the same payout.

8. Changes in payments on a variable annuity correspond MOST closely to fluctuations in the

 A. cost of living
 B. Dow Jones Industrial Average
 C. value of underlying securities held in the separate account
 D. prime rate

9. The difference between a fixed annuity and a variable annuity is that the variable annuity

 I. offers a guaranteed return
 II. offers a payment that may vary in amount
 III. always pays out more money than a fixed annuity
 IV. attempts to offer the annuitant protection from inflation

 A. I and III
 B. I and IV
 C. II and III
 D. II and IV

10. When an investor begins to receive the payout on a variable annuity, which of the following statements is true?

 A. Accumulation units are converted to annuity units.

 B. Annuity units are converted to accumulation units.

 C. The annuity unit's value is fixed.

 D. The amount of each payment is fixed.

11. Which of the following describe a joint life with last survivor annuity?

    I. Covers more than one person
    II. Continues payments as long as one annuitant is alive
    III. Continues payments as long as all annuitants are alive
    IV. Guarantees payments for a certain period of time

    A. I and II
    B. I and III
    C. I and IV
    D. II and IV

12. Which of the following statements about variable annuities is FALSE?

    A. The value of the underlying portfolio determines the rate of return.
    B. These annuities are designed to combat inflation risk.
    C. The AIR guarantees a minimum rate of return.
    D. The number of annuity units becomes fixed when the contract is annuitized.

13. Distributions from both an IRA and a variable annuity are subject to which of the following forms of taxation?

    A. Short-term capital gains
    B. Long-term capital gains
    C. Ordinary income
    D. No tax is due.

Answers & Rationale

1.   **A.**   Owners of variable annuities, like owners of mutual fund shares, have the right to vote on changes in investment policy and the right to vote for the investment adviser every two years. They also have the benefit of enjoying reduced sales charges for large dollar purchases.
(Page 135)

2.   **C.**   When a variable contract is annuitized, the number of accumulation units is multiplied by the unit value to arrive at the total current value. An annuity factor is taken from the annuity table, which considers the investor's sex and age, for example. This factor is used to establish the dollar amount of the first annuity payment. Future annuity payments will vary according to the separate account's value.   (Page 141)

3.   **A.**   The most important consideration in purchasing a variable annuity is that benefit payments fluctuate with the separate account's investment performance. Choice D is not a consideration because normally the payments into an annuity are level or in a lump sum.   (Page 136)

4.   **D.**   Contributions to a nonqualified variable annuity are made with after-tax dollars. This is in contrast to tax-qualified retirement vehicles such as IRAs or Keoghs, in which contributions are made with pretax dollars. Distributions from a tax-qualified plan are considered to be 100 percent taxable ordinary income because the original contributions were never subject to tax. Distributions from a nonqualified plan represent both a return of the original investment made in the plan with after-tax dollars (a nontaxable return of capital) and the income from that investment. Because the income was deferred from tax over the plan's life, it is taxable as ordinary income once it is distributed.   (Page 143)

5.   **A.**   The annuity period of a variable annuity is the payout period that occurs after the contract has been annuitized. Payments are based on a fixed number of annuity units established when the contract was annuitized. This number of annuity units is multiplied by an annuity unit's value (which can vary) to arrive at the payment for the period. Accumulation units relate to the accumulation phase of a variable annuity, when owners make payments to the contract.
(Page 141)

6.   **C.**   Contributions to a variable annuity are not tax deductible. Contributions to an IRA or a Keogh may be tax deductible, depending on the individual's earnings and his access to company-sponsored retirement plans.   (Page 143)

7.   **A.**   A life simple annuity provides the investor with the largest payments when the contract is annuitized.   (Page 141)

8.   **C.**   Payments from a variable annuity depend on the value of the securities in the separate account's underlying investment portfolio.
(Page 136)

9.   **D.**   Variable annuities differ from fixed because the payments vary and because they were designed to offer annuitants protection against inflation.   (Page 136)

10.   **A.**   To determine the payment amount, accumulation units are converted to annuity units. In a variable annuity, neither the annuity unit's value nor the monthly payment amount can be fixed.   (Page 140)

11.   **A.**   A joint life with last survivor contract covers multiple annuitants and ceases payments at the death of the last surviving annuitant. A period certain contract guarantees payments for a certain amount of time.   (Page 140)

12.   **C.**   The assumed interest rate provides an earnings target for the annuity contract, not a guarantee. A variable annuity provides a rate of return based on the performance of the separate account, which is generally invested in growth instruments with the intention of keeping pace with inflation. At the time the investor begins

receiving payments, accumulation units are converted to annuity units.   (Page 141)

13. **C.**   All retirement account distributions exceeding cost basis are subject to taxation at the owner's then-current ordinary tax rate. The advantage of most retirement accounts is that withdrawals usually begin after an account owner has dropped into a lower tax bracket (i.e., upon retirement).   (Page 143)

Variable Life Insurance

1. A variable life insurance policy is defined as any policy that provides for a death benefit that varies according to the

   A. investment experience of the life insurance company's general account
   B. amount of the premium invested into the insurance company's general account
   C. investment experience of the life insurance company's separate account
   D. investment experience of the variable annuity set up to provide for retirement benefits

2. Which of the following statements can an agent use to describe the scheduled-premium VLI product his life insurance company offers?

   A. "The variable life policy is a life insurance policy providing for a variable death benefit, cash values and premium payments depending on the performance of investments held in an insurance company's separate account."
   B. "The variable life policy is a fixed-premium life insurance policy providing for a variable death benefit and cash values depending on the performance of investments held in an insurance company's separate account."
   C. "The variable life policy is a fixed-premium life insurance policy providing for a fixed death benefit and cash values that fluctuate depending on the performance of investments held in the insurance company's separate account."
   D. The agent can use none of the above statements.

3. A distinguishing characteristic of scheduled-premium VLI is that an increase or a decrease in the value of the separate account used to fund the VLI contract leads to an increase or a decrease in the

   I. annual premium payable
   II. death benefit payable exclusive of the minimum guaranteed in the contract
   III. cash value
   IV. number of individuals the insured can name as beneficiaries of the contract

   A. I, II and III only
   B. I and IV only
   C. II and III only
   D. I, II, III and IV

4. The maximum amount a variable life insurance contract may deduct for mortality and expense fees is

   A. .5 percent
   B. .75 percent
   C. the maximum stated in the contract
   D. dependent on the insurance company's mortality experience

5. Which of the following fees and expenses may be deducted from the gross premium paid in a variable life insurance contract?

   I. Mortality risk fee
   II. Administrative fees
   III. Mortality insurance
   IV. Sales expenses, including commissions paid to agents

   A. I and II
   B. II and III
   C. II and IV
   D. III and IV

6. The separate account of a variable life insurance contract has an assumed interest rate of 4 percent. Its performance in the past six months has been 3 percent. The account is now earning 8 percent. Based on this information, which of the following statements is true?

   A. The death benefit will increase immediately.
   B. The death benefit will increase at the next valuation.
   C. The death benefit will increase only if the earnings offset the negative performance of the previous months.
   D. The death benefit is fixed at the guaranteed rate.

7. If the assumed interest rate of a variable life insurance policy is 4 percent and the separate account earns 6 percent, the policyholder would expect the

   I. cash value to increase
   II. cash value to decrease
   III. death benefit to increase
   IV. death benefit to decrease

   A. I and III
   B. I and IV
   C. II and III
   D. II and IV

8. An individual purchases a flexible-premium policy, and the separate account earns 3 percent. Assuming the individual has paid enough premiums to fund the contract's face amount and expenses, the contract's cash value would

   A. increase
   B. decrease
   C. stay the same
   D. not be affected by separate account performance

9. After three years, an insurer must offer a policy loan provision allowing a variable life contract holder to borrow what minimum percentage of cash value?

   A. 75 percent
   B. 90 percent
   C. 100 percent
   D. A variable life contract permits no policy loan.

10. Klaus Bruin purchases a variable life insurance contract on July 3, 1992. On July 29, 1995, Klaus decides to exchange his contract for a fixed-benefit policy offered by the same insurance company. As his agent, you tell Klaus that

    A. his new policy will have the same contract date and age as his VLI policy
    B. his new policy will include the same riders as his VLI policy
    C. he will not require new evidence of insurability
    D. None of the above statements is true.

11. According to federal law, an insurance company must allow a variable life policyholder how long to convert the policy into a whole life contract?

    A. 45 days
    B. 12 months
    C. 18 months
    D. 24 months

12. The maximum sales charge that can be deducted on a variable life contract is limited to 9 percent of

    A. the first year's premium
    B. each premium collected
    C. the payments to be made over the life of the contract
    D. the policyholder's life expectancy

13. An investor purchases a fixed-premium variable life contract on July 1. Four days after receiving notification of his free-look right, he cancels the policy. The investor receives which of the following?

    A. Full refund of all money paid to date
    B. All money invested in the separate account and 30 percent of the sales charges
    C. 30 percent of the money invested in the separate account plus all sales charges
    D. No refund of the premium paid

14. If, within two years, a variable life contract holder terminates the policy, she must receive as a refund the contract's current cash value plus

    A. nothing more
    B. 10 percent of the sales charges deducted
    C. 30 percent of the sales charges deducted
    D. all sales charges deducted exceeding 30 percent of the premium in the first year and 10 percent of the premium in the second year

Answers & Rationale

1. **C.**   Variable life is any policy providing insurance protection that varies according to the investment performance of one or more separate accounts.   (Page 148)

2. **B.**   Scheduled-premium VLI is a fixed-premium contract providing for a minimum guaranteed death benefit. Cash values and the death benefit may increase or decrease depending on the investment performance of the separate account. Cash values may decline to zero, but the death benefit may never decline below the minimum guaranteed.   (Page 146)

3. **C.**   The separate account performance affects the cash value or death benefit only. Premiums are fixed and level.   (Page 147)

4. **C.**   The contract states the maximum fee that may be charged for expenses and mortality costs. The fee charged may be more or less than the actual costs the insurance company incurred during the contract period.   (Page 147)

5. **C.**   Sales load, administrative fees and a charge for state premium taxes are deducted from the gross premium; expense and mortality risk fees, investment management fees and the cost of insurance are deducted from the separate account.   (Page 147)

6. **C.**   The account must earn enough to offset previous negative earnings before an increase in the death benefit can occur.   (Page 147)

7. **A.**   If the separate account earns at a rate greater than the rate assumed, the extra earnings may lead to an increase in the death benefit and cash value.   (Page 147)

8. **A.**   With a flexible-premium policy, account performance affects the contract directly. Cash value equals the net premium invested, increased or decreased by the change in separate account assets, less charges and expenses. Cash value reflects the separate account's actual performance. If the account earned 3 percent, cash value would increase, although by very little.   (Page 147)

9. **A.**   The minimum that must be available in a VLI contract is 75 percent of cash value.   (Page 147)

10. **D.**   The investor has had the VLI contract for more than 24 months; the exchange privilege option has expired. As a result, he would be required to purchase a new contract if he wanted the new policy, although this is not recommended.   (Page 148)

11. **D.**   Although state law may allow for periods other than 24 months, federal law requires a two-year conversion privilege.   (Page 148)

12. **C.**   The maximum sales charge is limited to 9 percent of the contract's life (actual life expectancy or 20 years, whichever is less).   (Page 148)

13. **A.**   According to the act of 1940, if the investor cancels the plan within the free-look period, he receives all monies paid.   (Page 148)

14. **D.**   The law requires a full refund of cash value plus a return of sales charges exceeding 30 percent in year one and 10 percent in year two. After two years, only cash value need be refunded.   (Page 149)

34

Nonqualified Corporate Retirement Plans

1. Each of the following is an example of a qualified retirement plan EXCEPT a(n)

   A. deferred compensation plan
   B. individual retirement account
   C. pension and profit-sharing plan
   D. defined benefit plan

2. Which of the following statements is(are) true of deferred compensation plans?

   I. They are available to a limited number of select employees.
   II. They must be nondiscriminatory.
   III. They cannot include corporate officers.
   IV. They cannot include members of the board of directors.

   A. I
   B. I and IV
   C. II
   D. III and IV

3. Deferred compensation plans need the prior approval of the

   A. employer
   B. plan trustee
   C. IRS
   D. Keogh committee

4. Acme Zootech begins a nonqualified retirement plan. Which of the following statements is true?

   A. Employee contributions are tax deductible.
   B. Employer contributions are tax deductible.
   C. Employee contributions grow tax deferred if they are invested in an annuity.
   D. The employer must abide by all ERISA requirements.

Answers & Rationale

1. **A.** A deferred compensation plan is considered a nonqualified plan because no IRS approval is required to initiate a deferred compensation plan for employees. Only qualified retirement plans need IRS approval.   (Page 150)

2. **B.** Deferred compensation plans can be offered to select employees; however, directors are not considered employees.   (Page 151)

3. **A.** Deferred compensation plans do not require IRS approval (only qualified plans need that); there is no plan funding (which eliminates a plan trustee); and there is no such thing as a Keogh committee. Deferred compensation plans are an arrangement between an employer and an employee.   (Page 151)

4. **C.** Earnings accumulate tax deferred if the plan is funded by an investment vehicle that offers tax deferral, such as an annuity contract. Tax is paid on all amounts contributed to the plan by the employees and by the employer. Nonqualified plans do not have to comply with all of the ERISA requirements.   (Page 151)

Individual Retirement Accounts

35

1. Which of the following would be the MOST suitable investment for the IRAs of a young couple with a combined annual income of $42,000?

   A. Stock in a growth fund
   B. Initial public offerings of small companies
   C. Options on blue chip common stock
   D. Partnership interests in an oil and gas drilling program

2. Lotta Leveridge makes $65,000 a year as an advertising executive, and her husband Tiny makes $40,000 a year as Lotta's assistant. How much can the Leveridges contribute to IRAs?

   A. They cannot contribute because their combined income is too high.
   B. They can contribute up to $2,250 split over both accounts, with no more than $2,000 in either account.
   C. They can each contribute $2,000 to an IRA.
   D. They can each contribute $2,500 to an IRA.

3. Lotta and Tiny Leveridge, both in their 20s, have been married only a few years. When they ask for your recommendation as to an investment for their IRAs, you suggest

   A. growth-oriented mutual funds
   B. penny precious metals stocks
   C. oil and gas exploration limited partnerships
   D. index options

4. Your client, who is 50 years of age, wants to withdraw funds from her IRA. She asks you about the tax implications of early withdrawal. You tell her that the withdrawal will be taxed as

   A. ordinary income
   B. ordinary income plus a 10 percent penalty
   C. capital gains
   D. capital gains plus a 10 percent penalty

5. A customer has just started an IRA. She will be vested

   A. immediately
   B. in two years
   C. in five years
   D. at age 70½

6. Under IRS rules, IRA distributions upon retirement can go to the

   I. employee only
   II. employee jointly with the employee's spouse
   III. employee and, at the employee's death, to a designated beneficiary
   IV. employee's designated beneficiary

   A. I only
   B. I, II and III only
   C. IV only
   D. I, II, III and IV

7. Excess IRA contributions are subject to a penalty of what percentage annually until they are used up or withdrawn?

   A. 6 percent
   B. 10 percent
   C. 12 percent
   D. 15 percent

8. An employee not covered under his company's pension plan has been contributing to an IRA for five years. He now leaves his old job, starts a new job and is covered under the new corporation's pension plan. Based on this information, which of the following statements is true?

   A. His IRA must be closed.
   B. Nondeductible contributions to his IRA may continue.
   C. The money in his IRA must be combined with any money he will receive from the pension plan.
   D. Contributions to his IRA must stop; the money in the account will be frozen, but interest and dividends can accrue tax free until he retires.

9. Which of the following can be rolled over into an IRA?

   I. Another IRA
   II. Corporate pension plan
   III. Corporate profit-sharing plan
   IV. Keogh plan

   A. I and IV only
   B. II and III only
   C. II, III and IV only
   D. I, II, III and IV

10. The maximum contribution allowed under an IRA is 100 percent of annual earnings

    A. before taxes or $2,000, whichever is greater
    B. before taxes or $2,000, whichever is less
    C. after taxes or $2,000, whichever is greater
    D. after taxes or $2,000, whichever is less

11. An employee makes a withdrawal from her IRA at age 52. She pays no penalty tax if she

    A. has retired
    B. is disabled
    C. had no earned income that year
    D. transferred her account to another custodian

12. You work for the Tippecanoe Ferry Co. and participate in its 401(k) plan. How much can you invest in an IRA?

    A. $0
    B. $2,000
    C. $2,250
    D. Up to 25 percent of annual compensation

13. Which of the following securities would a registered rep recommend to a customer who wants to set up an IRA?

    A. Municipal bond fund shares
    B. Term insurance contract
    C. Growth stock
    D. Put options

14. Chip Bullock received a lump-sum distribution from a 401(k) plan when he left his job. He now may do which of the following?

    I. Roll over his account within 60 days
    II. Transfer his account without taking possession of the money
    III. Keep the funds and pay ordinary income tax
    IV. Invest in a tax-exempt municipal bond fund to avoid paying tax

    A. I and II
    B. I and III
    C. II and IV
    D. III and IV

15. Which of the following statements about SEP-IRAs is true?

    A. They are used primarily by large corporations.
    B. They are used primarily by small businesses.
    C. They are set up by employees.
    D. They cannot be set up by self-employed persons.

16. Which of the following is required to establish a SEP?

    A. 50 percent of the eligible employees must have an IRA.
    B. 75 percent of the eligible employees must have an IRA.
    C. 100 percent of the eligible employees must have an IRA.
    D. The employer must establish a separate IRA for each eligible employee.

17. June Polar works for a small business and would like to participate in a SEP. Which of the following statements is true?

    A. June may not participate in a SEP because she has been employed by this company for only five years.
    B. The maximum SEP contribution is higher than the maximum IRA contribution.
    C. June's employer must match her contributions.
    D. Contributions exceeding $2,000 are not tax deductible.

18. Which of the following statements is true of both traditional IRAs and Roth IRAs?

    A. Contributions are deductible.
    B. Withdrawals at retirement are tax free.
    C. Earnings on investments are not taxed.
    D. Distributions must begin the year after the year the owner reaches age 70½.

19. What is the maximum amount that may be invested in an education IRA in one year?

    A. $500 per parent
    B. $500 per child
    C. $500 per couple
    D. $2,000 per couple

Answers & Rationale

1. **A.** This couple's IRA should be established with an eye toward long-term appreciation. Choices B and C are risky and are generally considered inappropriate for IRAs. The DPP is inappropriate because tax losses in an IRA cannot be used to offset gains. (Page 155)

2. **C.** No matter how much an individual or a couple make, they can contribute to their IRAs. Each spouse is entitled to contribute 100 percent of earned income up to $2,000 (if both spouses are working). (Page 154)

3. **A.** A growth mutual fund is appropriate for a young couple's IRA. All other answers bear a high risk that is not appropriate for a retirement account. (Page 155)

4. **B.** An early withdrawal from an IRA is taxed as ordinary income plus a 10 percent penalty. (Page 143)

5. **A.** Investors are always vested immediately in their IRAs. (Page 154)

6. **D.** Under IRS rules, when an employee retires IRA payments can be made to the employee or jointly to the employee and his spouse. In the event that the account owner dies, payments may continue to be made to a designated beneficiary; a person's rights to accumulated IRA benefits do not stop at that person's death. (Page 156)

7. **A.** Excess IRA contributions are subject to a yearly penalty of 6 percent until they are withdrawn or applied to the following year's contribution limit. (Page 155)

8. **B.** An employee covered under a qualified retirement plan may continue to own and contribute to an IRA. The contributions may not be fully tax deductible, depending on the amount of compensation earned, but the employee benefits from the tax deferral of IRA earnings. (Page 154)

9. **D.** Assets from any qualified corporate plan or from another IRA may be rolled over into an IRA. (Page 156)

10. **B.** The maximum annual contribution to an IRA plan is 100 percent of earnings before taxes or $2,000, whichever is less. (Page 154)

11. **B.** An IRA account holder may withdraw money before the age of 59½ without incurring a penalty tax only in the case of death or disability. A transfer between custodians does not constitute a withdrawal from the account. (Page 154)

12. **B.** The maximum annual contribution to an IRA is $2,000 whether or not the account owner participates in a qualified retirement plan. The full amount of the contribution may not be tax deductible, but all earnings in the account are tax deferred. (Page 154)

13. **C.** Although a municipal bond fund is permissible, earnings on IRA accounts are always tax deferred, so the tax advantage of municipal investments is not a benefit. Insurance contracts are ineligible IRA investments, and option investments are generally inappropriate for retirement accounts owing to their high risk. (Page 154)

14. **B.** If the investor does not roll over the money into an IRA account, it is taxed as ordinary income. Because he has already received the lump sum, he cannot transfer the account to a new custodian. Any amount he does not roll over is taxed as income even if he invests it in tax-exempt bonds. (Page 156)

15. **B.** Primarily, small businesses and self-employed persons use SEP-IRAs because they are much easier and less expensive than other plans for an employer to set up and administer. (Page 156)

16. **C.** For a small business to establish a SEP, each eligible employee must have an IRA. If an employee refuses to establish an IRA, the

employer *must* open an IRA in that employee's name. (Page 157)

17. **B.** The contribution limit is 15 percent of earned income up to $30,000 for a SEP retirement plan, compared to just $2,000 for a regular IRA, and the entire amount is tax deductible. Full-time employees who have been employed for at least three of the immediately preceding five years are automatically eligible to participate. The entire amount of the employer's contribution up to the maximum contribution is tax deductible.
(Page 157)

18. **C.** The common factor for both traditional and Roth IRAs is that investment earnings are not taxed when earned. Traditional IRAs offer tax-deductible contributions, but withdrawals are taxed. Roth IRAs do not offer tax-deductible contributions, but qualified withdrawals are tax free. Traditional IRAs require distributions to begin in the year after the year an owner reaches age 70½, but this is not true for Roth IRAs. (Page 152)

19. **B.** Only $500 may be invested in each child's education IRA every year. If a couple has three children, they may invest $1,500 in total, or $500 for each child. (Page 152)

36

Keogh (HR-10) Plans

1. Your client, who is 40 years of age, wants to withdraw funds from her Keogh. She asks you about the tax implications of early withdrawal. You should tell her the withdrawal will be taxed as

   A. ordinary income
   B. ordinary income plus a 10 percent penalty
   C. capital gains
   D. capital gains plus a 10 percent penalty

2. Hugh Heifer has a salaried, full-time position, but his employer does not offer a company retirement plan. Hugh also has his own clock repair business, which earns less than his salaried position. He wants to invest for his retirement. Which of the following investments is an option for him?

   A. IRA, if he does not have a Keogh plan
   B. Keogh plan, if he does not have an IRA
   C. Both an IRA and a Keogh plan
   D. IRA, but not a Keogh plan because his self-employment is not his main source of income

3. Under a Keogh plan, which of the following would be an acceptable investment(s)?

   A. Unit investment trust
   B. Variable annuity
   C. U.S. government bond
   D. All of the above

4. An employee covered under a Keogh plan will become fully vested

   A. depending on the vesting schedule the employer has chosen
   B. after one year
   C. after two years
   D. after three years

5. Which of the following people would NOT be eligible to start her own Keogh, but WOULD be eligible to open an IRA?

   A. College professor who makes $10,000 on the sale of a book and several articles
   B. Corporate officer who earns $40,000 plus an additional $10,000 as a part-time speaker
   C. Doctor who receives $10,000 from a restaurant she owns
   D. Corporate officer who receives a $5,000 bonus

6. Which of the following individuals is(are) entitled to participate in a Keogh plan?

    I. Doctor
    II. Security analyst who makes $2,000 giving lectures
    III. Engineer of a corporation who earns $5,000 making public speeches
    IV. Executive of a corporation who receives $5,000 in stock options from his company

    A. I
    B. I and II
    C. I, II and III
    D. IV

7. An individual earned $75,000 in royalties from his writings; $5,000 from interest and dividends; $2,000 from long-term capital gains in the stock market; and $3,000 from rents on two cottages. He could contribute to his Keogh plan

    A. $12,570
    B. $12,750
    C. $15,000
    D. $18,750

8. A nurse had been participating in her employer's Keogh plan. Upon leaving the clinic, she may roll over the distributed Keogh assets into an IRA and defer taxes on these assets if she completes the transaction within

    A. 30 days
    B. 60 days
    C. 90 days
    D. 6 months

9. Max Leveridge earned $100,000 this year and would like to make a large contribution toward his retirement. Because he is self-employed, you should recommend that he contribute to a(n)

    A. IRA
    B. Keogh account
    C. 401(k) plan
    D. TSA

Answers & Rationale

1. **B.** An early withdrawal from a Keogh is taxed in the same way as an early withdrawal from an IRA—as ordinary income plus a 10 percent penalty. (Page 159)

2. **C.** The investor can start an IRA, assuming that he is younger than age 70½. How much of his IRA contributions are deductible depends on his income level. He is also eligible to invest in a Keogh plan because he is self-employed, regardless of how much or how little he earns from his self-employment or how those earnings compare to his salary. Investment in an IRA does not affect his eligibility for a Keogh plan. (Page 157)

3. **D.** The only investments that are not permitted in Keoghs are commodities, term life insurance, collectibles and antiques, precious metals (other than U.S.–issued gold and silver coins) and uncovered options. (Page 159)

4. **A.** Benefits vest to an employee according to the schedule the employer chooses, usually over five or seven years. (Page 158)

5. **D.** Anyone can open an IRA; the tax deductibility of a person's contributions depends on the availability of an employer-sponsored qualified retirement plan and on the person's income. Each of the listed individuals had income earned from self-employment except for the corporate officer receiving a bonus. (Page 157)

6. **C.** Stock options, dividends, capital gains and interest are not considered income earned from self-employment. (Page 157)

7. **C.** Only the royalties count as self-employment income; therefore, 20 percent of $75,000 equals $15,000. (Page 157)

8. **B.** Rollovers may take place once a year and must occur within a 60-day period. Direct transfers of retirement assets are not limited. (Page 159)

9. **B.** Keogh plans allow contributions of 25 percent of earned income up to $30,000 in a single tax year, while contributions to IRAs are limited to $2,000. Both TSAs and 401(k) plans are administered by employing companies, so this investor could not participate. (Page 158)

37

Tax-Sheltered Annuities

1. Adam Grizzly invests in a tax-qualified variable annuity. What is the tax treatment of the distributions he receives?

   A. Partially tax free; partially ordinary income
   B. Partially tax free; partially capital gains
   C. All ordinary income
   D. All capital gains

2. Which of the following would be ineligible for a tax-sheltered 403(b) annuity?

   A. Professor at a land grant college
   B. Custodian at a municipal public school
   C. Student at a private college
   D. Employee of a county high school

3. Your customer works as a nurse in a public school. He wants to know more about participating in his school's TSA plan. You tell him which of the following?

   I. Contributions are made with before-tax dollars.
   II. He is not eligible to participate.
   III. Distributions before age 59½ are normally subject to penalty tax.
   IV. Mutual funds and CDs are available investment vehicles.

   A. I, II and III
   B. I and III
   C. I, III and IV
   D. II

4. Of the following statements describing IRAs, which one is NOT true of TSA qualified plans?

   A. A self-employed person may participate.
   B. Contributions are tax deferred.
   C. Distributions must begin by age 70½.
   D. Distributions after age 59½ are taxed as ordinary income.

Answers & Rationale

1.   **C.**   In a tax-qualified annuity, the annuitant has no basis unless the annuitant made voluntary after-tax contributions. Such after-tax contributions are the exception and are not mentioned in this question. Because the annuitant has no basis, all payments are considered ordinary income. In a nonqualified annuity, contributions are made with after-tax dollars, which establish the annuitant's basis. Annuity payments from nonqualified annuities are treated as ordinary income to the extent that they exceed the basis.   (Page 162)

2.   **C.**   All of the individuals listed meet the requirement of being an employee of a school system except for the student.   (Page 160)

3.   **C.**   Because he is employed by a public school system, your customer is eligible to participate in the tax-sheltered annuity plan. Employee contributions to a TSA plan are excluded from gross income in the year in which they are made. As in other retirement plans, a penalty tax is assessed on distributions received before age 59½. A TSA plan may invest in various instruments, including mutual funds, stocks, bonds and CDs, in addition to annuity contracts.   (Page 160)

4.   **A.**   Only employees of schools, church organizations and nonprofit organizations are eligible to participate in 403(b) TSA plans. The provisions for contributions and distributions are the same for IRAs and TSA qualified plans.   (Page 160)

38

Corporate Retirement Plans

1. Which of the following statements is true of a defined benefit plan?

   A. All employees receive the same monthly payment at retirement.
   B. All participating employees are immediately vested.
   C. High-income employees near retirement benefit the most.
   D. The same amount must be contributed for each eligible employee.

2. A qualified profit-sharing plan has all of the following features EXCEPT the

   A. contribution is tax deductible to the employee
   B. employee reports the contribution
   C. contribution is taxable upon payment at retirement
   D. beneficiary may average out the income upon retirement

3. The amount paid into a defined contribution plan is set by the

   A. ERISA–defined contribution requirements
   B. trust agreement
   C. employer's age
   D. employer's profits

4. Which of the following statements is true when an employee's voluntary contribution to an employer-sponsored qualified pension plan is distributed to the employee?

   A. It is returned tax free.
   B. It is taxed at a reduced rate.
   C. It is taxed at the beneficiary's ordinary tax rate.
   D. It is taxed at the current capital gains rate.

5. When Angus Bullwether retires, he will receive a retirement income that equals a percentage of the average of his last three years of compensation. In which kind of plan is Angus MOST likely participating?

   A. Keogh
   B. Defined contribution
   C. Defined benefit
   D. TSA

Answers & Rationale

1.   **C.**   The rules regarding the maximum amount of contributions differ for defined contribution plans and defined benefit plans. Defined benefit plans set the amount of retirement benefits that a retiree will receive as a percentage of the previous several years' salaries. For the highly paid individual nearing retirement, the defined benefit plan allows a larger contribution in a shorter period of time. Answer D describes a defined contribution plan rather than a defined benefit plan.   (Page 163)

2.   **A.**   Qualified retirement plans are tax deductible to the employer, not to the employee.
(Page 163)

3.   **B.**   A defined contribution plan's trust agreement contains a section explaining the formula(s) used to determine the contributions to the retirement plan.   (Page 163)

4.   **A.**   All voluntary employee contributions to a qualified retirement plan are made with after-tax dollars. Therefore, because the employee already paid taxes on the money, it is returned tax free. All earnings attributable to employee contributions as well as all employer-contributed money are taxed at the employee's ordinary income rate at the time of distribution. (Page 163)

5.   **C.**   A defined benefit plan specifies the amount of money to be paid to employees upon retirement. The maximum benefit is 100 percent of an employee's average compensation for the final three years of employment. Keogh plans, defined contribution plans and tax-sheltered annuity plans all specify the amount of money to be contributed to the plans.   (Page 163)

39

Employee Retirement Income Security Act

1. What was the primary purpose for creating ERISA?

   A. To establish a retirement fund for government employees
   B. To establish a means for self-employed persons to provide for their own retirements
   C. To protect employees from the mishandling of retirement funds by corporations and unions
   D. To provide all employees, both government and nongovernment, with an additional source of retirement income in the event that the Social Security system defaults

2. The requirements of the Employee Retirement Income Security Act apply to pension plans established by which of the following?

   A. Self-employed individuals with no employees
   B. Only public entities, such as the City of New York
   C. Only private organizations, such as Exxon
   D. Both public and private organizations

3. Regulations regarding how contributions are made to tax-qualified plans relate to which of the following ERISA requirements?

   A. Vesting
   B. Funding
   C. Nondiscrimination
   D. Reporting and disclosure

Answers & Rationale

1.   **C.**   ERISA was created originally to protect the retirement funds of union members and employees of large corporations. ERISA has set guidelines stating that all qualified retirement plans must be in writing; must not be discriminatory; must segregate funds from corporate or union assets; must invest in prudent investments; and must report to the participants annually. All of these activities are audited under ERISA.

(Page 164)

2.   **C.**   ERISA was established to protect the retirement funds of employees working in the private sector only. It does not apply to self-employed persons or public organizations.

(Page 164)

3.   **B.**   "Vesting" describes how quickly rights to a retirement account turn over to an employee. "Nondiscrimination" refers to employee coverage by the plan. All retirement plans must meet ERISA's fiduciary reporting and disclosure requirements. Only "funding" covers how an employer contributes to or funds a plan.

(Page 164)

40

Lesson Three —
Variable Contracts
and Retirement Plans

1. Which of the following information must be included in a prospectus describing variable life insurance to clients?

   I. Summary explanation in nontechnical terms of the policy's principal features
   II. Statement of the separate account's investment policy
   III. Statement of the separate account's net investment return for the past 10 years
   IV. Statement of the deductions and charges against the gross premium, including all commissions paid to agents for each policy year the commissions are to be paid

   A. I and II only
   B. I, II and III only
   C. III and IV only
   D. I, II, III and IV

2. If a variable annuity has an assumed investment rate of 5 percent and the separate account's annualized return is 4 percent, which of the following statements are true?

   I. The accumulation unit's value will rise.
   II. The annuity unit's value will rise.
   III. The accumulation unit's value will fall.
   IV. The annuity unit's value will fall.

   A. I and II
   B. I and IV
   C. II and III
   D. III and IV

3. Which of the following statements about a straight-life variable annuity is(are) true?

   I. The number of annuity units a client redeems never changes.
   II. The number of accumulation units a client owns never changes.
   III. If a client dies during the annuity period, the remaining funds are distributed to the beneficiary.
   IV. The monthly payout is fixed to the Consumer Price Index.

   A. I only
   B. I and II only
   C. II and III only
   D. I, II, III and IV

4. Which of the following factors may determine the amount of payout from a variable annuity?

    I. Company's mortality experience
    II. Annuitant's age and sex
    III. Annuitant's insurability
    IV. Separate account's rate of return

    A. I, II and IV only
    B. II only
    C. III and IV only
    D. I, II, III and IV

5. An annuity may be purchased under which of the following methods?

    I. Single payment deferred annuity
    II. Single payment immediate annuity
    III. Periodic payment deferred annuity
    IV. Periodic payment immediate annuity

    A. I and II only
    B. I, II and III only
    C. III and IV only
    D. I, II, III and IV

6. June Polar purchased a variable annuity with an immediate payout plan. In the first month, she received a payment of $328. Which of the following statements about June's investment is(are) true?

    I. Her next payment is guaranteed to be $328.
    II. She made a lump-sum investment.
    III. She purchased the variable annuity from a registered representative.

    A. II only
    B. II and III only
    C. III only
    D. I, II and III

7. Joe Kuhl has just purchased an immediate variable annuity. Which of the following statements describe Joe's investment?

    I. It was a lump-sum purchase.
    II. Distribution of dividends occurs during the accumulation period.
    III. Accumulation and payment of dividends occur during the payout period.

    A. I and II only
    B. I and III only
    C. II and III only
    D. I, II and III

8. Which of the following statements about deferred variable annuities are true?

    I. Purchase payments can be either lump sum or periodic.
    II. Contract holders are guaranteed a rate of return.
    III. Earnings accumulate in a contract holder's account during the prepayment period.

    A. I and II only
    B. I and III only
    C. II and III only
    D. I, II and III

9. A variable annuity contract guarantees a

    I. rate of return
    II. fixed mortality expense
    III. fixed administrative expense

    A. I and II only
    B. I and III only
    C. II and III only
    D. I, II and III

10. Separate accounts are similar to mutual funds in that both

    I. may have diversified portfolios of common stock
    II. are managed by full-time professionals
    III. give investors voting rights

    A. I and II only
    B. I and III only
    C. II and III only
    D. I, II and III

11. Klaus Bruin's annuity has a portfolio that contains mostly common stocks. What does this mean for Klaus?

    I. In a rising market, the value of Klaus's account may rise.
    II. In a rising market, the value of an accumulation unit may rise.
    III. Klaus is protected from loss.

    A. I and II only
    B. I and III only
    C. II and III only
    D. I, II and III

12. At retirement, Angus Bullwether decides to annuitize his variable annuity contract. After his final purchase payment, he has 1,857 accumulation units. What factors will be considered when determining the amount of payout he will receive?

    I. Value of one annuity unit
    II. Conversion value shown in the company's annuity table
    III. Value of Angus's share of the separate account

    A. I and II only
    B. I and III only
    C. II and III only
    D. I, II and III

13. An investor owning which of the following variable annuity contracts would hold accumulation units?

    I. Periodic payment deferred annuity
    II. Single payment deferred annuity
    III. Immediate life annuity
    IV. Immediate life annuity with 10-year certain

    A. I and II only
    B. I, III and IV only
    C. IV only
    D. I, II, III and IV

14. Which of the following investors are eligible to establish an IRA?

    I. Independently wealthy individual whose sole source of income is $125,000 per year in dividends and interest
    II. Law student who earned $1,200 in a part-time job
    III. Woman who earned $3,500 last year selling cosmetics, but whose spouse is covered by a company profit-sharing plan

    A. I and II only
    B. I and III only
    C. II and III only
    D. I, II and III

15. Joe Kuhl earned $34,000 this year, and his wife Bea earned $46,000. Which of the following statements is(are) true?

    I. Joe may contribute $2,250 to his IRA.
    II. Bea may contribute $2,250 to her IRA.
    III. Bea and Joe may each contribute $2,000 to separate IRAs.
    IV. Bea and Joe may contribute a total of $4,000 to an IRA.

    A. I and IV only
    B. II and IV only
    C. III only
    D. I, II, III and IV

16. Which of the following individuals are eligible to participate in a tax-deferred annuity?

   I. Maintenance engineer at a state university
   II. Teacher in a public school system
   III. Minister

   A. I and II only
   B. I and III only
   C. II and III only
   D. I, II and III

Answers & Rationale

1. **D.** All of the information listed here must be presented in the prospectus distributed to clients. (Page 146)

2. **B.** The accumulation unit will increase in value because the portfolio earned 4 percent; however, the annuity unit's value will decrease because the portfolio's actual return of 4 percent was less than the assumed interest rate of 5 percent necessary to maintain payments. (Page 141)

3. **A.** Annuity units are fixed; their current value when cashed in determines the payout amount. A life-only annuity ceases payments at the client's death. The company keeps any undistributed payments. Accumulation units fluctuate in value and number during the accumulation period. (Page 140)

4. **A.** Mortality experience, age, sex and rate of return all have a bearing on the size of payout. The annuitant's insurability has no bearing. (Page 142)

5. **B.** A periodic payment immediate annuity would be rather difficult to provide. As the annuitant is contributing, he would also be receiving. (Page 139)

6. **B.** A variable annuity does not guarantee the amount of monthly payments. June's next monthly payment may be more than, less than or the same as her initial payment. Because June's payments began immediately, she must have made a single lump-sum investment to the company. Finally, because a variable annuity is a security, the salesperson must be a registered representative. (Page 141)

7. **B.** An immediate annuity has no accumulation period. A single lump-sum investment is made, and payments begin immediately. During payout, the principal and earnings are distributed. (Page 139)

8. **B.** A variable annuity has no guaranteed earnings rate. A deferred annuity can be purchased either with a lump-sum investment or with periodic payments. During the accumulation period, separate account earnings (losses) are credited to (subtracted from) the value of the contract holder's account. (Page 139)

9. **C.** A variable annuity does not guarantee an earnings rate; however, it does guarantee payments for life (mortality) and normally guarantees that expenses will not increase above a specified level. (Page 142)

10. **D.** Separate accounts as well as mutual funds may contain diversified portfolios of securities and be managed by professional investment advisers. Voting rights for policy and management elections are available. (Page 138)

11. **A.** Klaus assumes the investment risk of the contract, including both upward and downward movements. If the market rises, the separate account's value increases, which is reflected in an increase in accumulation unit value and, ultimately, in Klaus's account value. (Page 136)

12. **C.** To calculate the value of the first payment when annuitizing a contract, the company multiplies Angus's account value by a factor summarizing age, sex, option and AIR. This value is then used to purchase annuity units, the current value of which determines subsequent payments. (Page 142)

13. **A.** Accumulation units represent units of ownership in a life insurance company's separate account while the contract is in the deferral stage. Annuity units are the units of ownership while the contract is in the payout stage (annuitized). Immediate annuities purchase annuity units directly. (Page 139)

14. **C.** An individual may contribute 100 percent of earned income up to a maximum of

$2,000. Interest and dividend income is passive income, not earned income.   (Page 152)

15.   **C.**   Both Joe and Bea can contribute the $2,000 maximum to separate IRAs. The $4,000 limitation is for married couples with one nonworking spouse. Still, the $4,000 must be split between two accounts, with no more than $2,000 contributed in one account.   (Page 154)

16.   **D.**   Employees of 501(c)3 and 403(b) organizations, which include charities, religious groups, sports organizations and school systems, qualify for tax-deferred annuities (TDAs).   (Page 161)

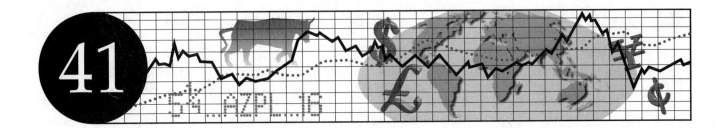

The Regulation of New Issues

1. Which of the following will NOT be found in a final prospectus?

   A. Underwriting agreements and the underwriters' compensation
   B. Business plan
   C. Date and offering price
   D. Statement that the SEC neither approves nor disapproves of the issue

2. Which of the following statements about a red herring is FALSE?

   A. A red herring is used to obtain indications of interest from investors.
   B. The final offering price does not appear in a red herring.
   C. Additional information may be added to a red herring at a later date.
   D. A registered rep may send a copy of the company's research report with it.

3. Which of the following is NOT required in a preliminary prospectus?

   A. Written statement in red that the prospectus may be subject to change and amendment and that a final prospectus will be issued
   B. Purpose for which the funds being raised will be used
   C. Final offering price
   D. Financial status and history of the company

4. Microscam must do all of the following if it intends to offer stock EXCEPT

   A. publish a tombstone
   B. issue a prospectus
   C. file a registration statement
   D. register the securities with the SEC

5. If the SEC has cleared an issue, which of the following statements is true?

   A. The SEC has guaranteed the issue.
   B. The underwriter has filed a standard registration statement.
   C. The SEC has endorsed the issue.
   D. The SEC has guaranteed the accuracy of the information in the prospectus.

6. To which securities market does the Securities Act of 1933 apply?

   A. Primary
   B. Secondary
   C. Third
   D. Fourth

7. Which of the following requires full disclosure of all material information about securities offered for the first time to the public?

   A. Securities Act of 1933
   B. Securities Exchange Act of 1934
   C. Trust Indenture Act of 1939
   D. Securities Investor Protection Act of 1970

8. "Freeriding and withholding" is defined by the

   A. Securities Act of 1933
   B. NASD Rules of Fair Practice
   C. Securities Exchange Act of 1934
   D. SEC Statement of Policy

9. Which of the following individuals may NOT purchase a hot issue under normal circumstances?

   I. Principal of an NASD member firm
   II. Officer, director or employee of an NASD member firm
   III. Family members of a member firm employee
   IV. Employee involved in the allocation of the issue

   A. I only
   B. I and II only
   C. II and III only
   D. I, II, III and IV

10. NASD freeriding and withholding rules apply to the purchase of public offering stock that

    A. immediately trades at a discount to the offering price in the secondary market
    B. immediately trades at a premium to the offering price in the secondary market
    C. is being distributed to the general public
    D. The rules apply to none of the above.

11. If a registered representative or another associated person wishes to buy a hot issue for his personal account, the NASD Rules of Fair Practice require which of the following?

    I. The order cannot be filled under any circumstances.
    II. The order cannot be filled for the rep's own account, but can be billed to a joint account between the rep and the rep's spouse or a supported relative.
    III. The order can be filled for the rep's account provided he has a history of buying hot issues.
    IV. The order can be filled for the rep's account if the amount of stock sold is insubstantial and not disproportionate to the amount allocated to filling public orders and if the rep has a history of buying hot issues.

    A. I
    B. II and IV
    C. III
    D. IV

12. Freeriding and withholding applies to

    A. new issues that sell at a discount
    B. new issues that sell at a premium
    C. all over-the-counter securities
    D. all of the above

13. Bea Kuhl's brother is a registered representative with Dewey, Cheatham & Howe, one of the member firms underwriting a hot issue of securities. Bea receives material financial support from her brother. Under which of the following conditions may she purchase hot issue shares?

    A. The transaction is consistent with her normal investment practice.
    B. She has never before bought a new issue security.
    C. She does not place the order through Dewey, Cheatham & Howe.
    D. She may not buy hot issues under any circumstances.

Answers & Rationale

1. **A.** The underwriting agreements, also known as the *agreement among underwriters*, are separate documents and are not included in a prospectus. (Page 173)

2. **D.** A registered rep cannot send a research report with either a preliminary or a final prospectus. During the first 90 days of a new issue, printed information discussing the new issue or the company cannot be circulated. (Page 173)

3. **C.** A preliminary prospectus is issued before the price is established, and it does not include the eventual offering date or the spread. (Page 173)

4. **A.** A tombstone advertisement is never required. Tombstones are advertisements often placed in the business newspapers to publicize new issues. (Page 174)

5. **B.** The SEC does not approve of endorse or guarantee a registration statement's accuracy. (Page 174)

6. **A.** The Securities Act of 1933 covers the registration and disclosure requirements regarding new issues. The new issue market is the primary market. The trading markets are covered under the Securities Exchange Act of 1934. (Page 176)

7. **A.** The Securities Act of 1933 regulates new issues of corporate securities sold to the public. (Page 176)

8. **B.** Rules regarding freeriding and withholding in conjunction with hot issues are set under the NASD Rules of Fair Practice. (Page 175)

9. **D.** Under normal circumstances, none of the persons listed may purchase a hot issue. All are considered restricted persons. (Page 175)

10. **B.** Freeriding and withholding applies to hot issues only. A hot issue is one that trades at an immediate premium in the secondary market, also called the *new issue aftermarket*. (Page 175)

11. **A.** A registered representative may never purchase a hot issue. (Page 175)

12. **B.** Freeriding and withholding rules apply to hot issues only. (Page 175)

13. **D.** Because she is supported by an associated person of a member firm, the customer may not purchase hot issue shares. In the NASD's view, a supported family member faces exactly the same restrictions as an associated person when seeking to buy hot issues. (Page 175)

42

The Regulation of Trading

1. The Securities Exchange Act of 1934 regulates or mandates which of the following?

    I. Full and fair disclosure on new offerings
    II. Creation of the SEC
    III. Manipulation of the market
    IV. Margin requirements on securities

    A. I
    B. I, II and III
    C. II
    D. II, III and IV

2. Which of the following acts requires corporations to issue annual reports?

    A. Securities Act of 1933
    B. Securities Exchange Act of 1934
    C. Trust Indenture Act of 1939
    D. Investment Company Act of 1940

3. The Securities Exchange Act of 1934 covers which of the following?

    I. Trading of government securities
    II. Trading of corporate securities
    III. Issuance of financial reports by corporations
    IV. Issuance of government securities

    A. I, II and III
    B. I, II and IV
    C. I and III
    D. II and IV

4. Under the Securities Exchange Act of 1934, the SEC does which of the following?

    I. Regulates the securities exchanges
    II. Requires the registration of brokers and dealers
    III. Prohibits inequitable and unfair trade practices
    IV. Regulates the over-the-counter markets

    A. I and II only
    B. I and IV only
    C. II, III and IV only
    D. I, II, III and IV

5. Which of the following brokerage house staff members are NOT subject to the mandatory fingerprinting rule?

   A. Associated persons employed as sales representatives
   B. Auditors and accountants in charge of the firm's money and securities accounting records
   C. Officers or partners who supervise the firm's cashiering and accounting departments in sales production
   D. Associated persons engaged exclusively in securities research

6. If a member firm suspends a registered representative, the member firm must report the suspension to

   A. its designated examining authority
   B. the state securities commissioner
   C. the SEC
   D. the news media

Answers & Rationale

1. **D.** The Securities Exchange Act of 1934 set up the SEC and regulates the market. The Securities Act of 1933 requires full and fair disclosure.

(Page 176)

2. **B.** The Securities Exchange Act of 1934 mandates that companies file annual reports with the SEC.

(Page 176)

3. **A.** The Securities Exchange Act of 1934 regulates secondary trading or trading markets, while the Securities Act of 1933 regulates the primary, or new issue, market. Trading of corporates and governments, therefore, falls under the 1934 act, as does corporate financial reporting. The 1933 act covers the issuance of new securities. Governments are exempt securities under the 1933 act.

(Page 176)

4. **D.** The Securities Exchange Act of 1934, which has greater breadth than the act of 1933, addresses the following:

- creation of the SEC
- regulation of exchanges
- regulation of credit by the FRB
- registration of broker-dealers
- regulation of insider transactions
- short sales and proxies
- regulation of trading activities
- regulation of client accounts
- customer protection rule
- regulation of the OTC market
- net capital rule

(Page 176)

5. **D.** The SEC requires that all officers and employees of a broker-dealer organization be fingerprinted if they (1) engage in the sale of securities, (2) have access to physical securities, cash or accounting records or (3) directly supervise employees who handle securities, cash or accounting records.

(Page 177)

6. **A.** If a member firm suspends a registered representative, the firm must report the suspension to its designated examining authority (DEA)—typically the NASD or exchanges where the firm is a member. Each DEA is a self-regulatory organization.

(Page 186)

43

Securities Investor Protection Corporation

1. In the event of a broker-dealer's bankruptcy, the Securities Investor Protection Corporation covers

   A. $100,000 per separate customer
   B. $100,000 per account
   C. $500,000 per separate customer
   D. $500,000 per account

2. The determination of a broker-dealer's financial failure is made under the provisions of the

   A. Securities Act of 1933
   B. Securities Exchange Act of 1934
   C. Securities Investor Protection Act of 1970
   D. determination is made at the SEC's discretion

3. Client coverage under SIPC is $500,000 for

   A. securities losses only
   B. cash and securities losses
   C. securities losses and $500,000 for cash losses
   D. cash and securities losses, of which no more than $100,000 may be for cash losses

4. A client has a special cash account with stock valued at $460,000 and $40,000 in cash. The same client also has a joint account with a spouse that has a market value of $320,000 and $180,000 in cash. SIPC coverage would be

   A. $460,000 for the special cash account and $320,000 for the joint account
   B. $500,000 for the special cash account and $420,000 for the joint account
   C. $500,000 for the special cash account and $500,000 for the joint account
   D. a total of $1 million for both accounts

5. If a brokerage firm goes bankrupt, the dollar amount of insurance coverage applicable to a customer's special cash account with a balance of $100,000 is

   A. $0
   B. $100,000
   C. $200,000
   D. $500,000

Answers & Rationale

1.   **C.**   Coverage under SIPC amounts to $500,000 per separate customer account, with no more than $100,000 of that amount going to cover cash and cash equivalents.   (Page 179)

2.   **C.**   The determination of financial failure is made under the Securities Investor Protection Act of 1970.   (Page 178)

3.   **D.**   SIPC coverage for each separate customer account is $500,000, with cash coverage not to exceed $100,000.   (Page 179)

4.   **B.**   SIPC coverage is $500,000 per separate customer account, with cash not to exceed $100,000. Thus, in the single-name account, SIPC provides full coverage, while in the joint account SIPC covers the full value of the securities, but only $100,000 of the $180,000 in cash. The remaining $80,000 becomes a general debt of the bankrupt broker-dealer.   (Page 179)

5.   **B.**   Coverage is $500,000 maximum, with cash not to exceed $100,000. An individual with $100,000 worth of securities in a special cash account is covered for $100,000.   (Page 179)

Insider Trading Act of 1988

1. Under the Securities Exchange Act of 1934, insiders include which of the following?

   I. Attorney who wrote the offering circular for the company
   II. Bookkeeper in the company's accounting department
   III. Wife of the company's president
   IV. Brother of the company's president

   A. I only
   B. II only
   C. II, III and IV only
   D. I, II, III and IV

2. Tex Longhorn possesses material inside information about General Gizmonics, Inc. He may communicate this information to a customer under what circumstances?

   A. Only if the customer knows it's inside information
   B. Only on the day before the information is made public
   C. Only if the customer enters an unsolicited order
   D. Under no circumstances

3. Which of the following statements is NOT true regarding the civil penalties that may be imposed for insider trading violations under the Securities Exchange Act of 1934?

   A. A civil penalty may be imposed only on a person who is registered under a securities act.
   B. The violation for which the penalty may be imposed is defined as "buying or selling securities while in possession of material, nonpublic information."
   C. The SEC may ask a court to impose a penalty of up to three times the loss avoided or profit gained on an illegal transaction.
   D. Improper supervision may cause an investment advisory firm to be liable to pay a penalty if one of its representatives commits an insider trading violation.

Answers & Rationale

1.   **D.**   While the act of 1934 defines an insider as an officer, a director or a 10 percent stockholder of the company, the courts have broadened the definition to include anyone who has inside information.   (Page 180)

2.   **D.**   Inside information may never be discussed until it is made public, at which point it is no longer inside information. Violations may be punished with civil penalties as well as prison sentences.   (Page 180)

3.   **A.**   The penalty may be imposed on anyone who trades on inside information, not just persons registered under the act. The other statements are correct: choice B defines "insider trading"; the penalty is up to three times the profit gained or loss avoided (choice C); and an advisory firm may face a penalty for the actions of its representatives (choice D).   (Page 180)

45

NASD Bylaws

1. A statutory disqualification applies to an employee or official of a broker-dealer who, within the past 10 years, has

   A. been charged with assaulting a police officer
   B. been convicted of a misdemeanor in the securities industry
   C. been convicted of breaking a car window at a dealership that sold him a lemon
   D. not paid income taxes

2. It is ethical for a broker-dealer to pay commissions under a continuing commission contract to which of the following?

   I. Retired employee or his widow, for continuing business
   II. Broker-dealership you purchased for that broker-dealer's continuing business
   III. Retired employee who refers an old neighbor to the broker-dealer
   IV. Retired employee who, in the course of his travels, acquires new business for the broker-dealer

   A. I and II only
   B. II and III only
   C. III and IV only
   D. I, II, III and IV

3. Which of the following individuals must register as principals with the NASD?

   I. Any person soliciting orders from the public who is a partner of a member firm
   II. Manager of an office of supervisory jurisdiction
   III. Director who is actively engaged in a member firm's securities business
   IV. Assistant vice president who trains registered reps for a member firm

   A. I and II only
   B. II and IV only
   C. III and IV only
   D. I, II, III and IV

4. The NASD Uniform Practice Code was established to

   A. require that practices in the investment banking and securities industry be just, reasonable and nondiscriminatory between investors
   B. eliminate advertising and sales literature that the SEC considers to violate standards
   C. provide a procedure for handling trade complaints from investors
   D. maintain similarity of business practices among member organizations in the securities industry

5. Blue-sky laws pertain to all of the following EXCEPT

   A. registration of securities within a state
   B. regulation of securities trading in other countries
   C. regulation of securities trading in a state
   D. registration of securities salespeople in a state

6. Most blue-sky laws have provisions for all of the following EXCEPT

   A. revoking a registration or license when a state securities division determines that a broker-dealer or salesperson has violated any part of the blue-sky laws
   B. registering all broker-dealers and their salespeople in each state in which they do business
   C. selling securities issued in other states
   D. comparably compensating salespeople registered in more than one state

7. A registered representative left her firm a year ago to write a screenplay. She is ready to return to the industry. Which of the following statements is FALSE?

   A. Her registration was terminated.
   B. She must requalify by examination.
   C. Her old firm filed a U-5 form.
   D. Her new firm must file a U-4 form.

8. A registered representative is convicted of a felony involving the sale of a security. For how many years will she be disqualified from associating with an NASD member firm?

   A. One
   B. Three
   C. Seven
   D. Ten

9. According to the rules that established SROs, these organizations are

   I. accountable to the SEC for supervising securities practices within their assigned jurisdictions
   II. supervised by government agencies
   III. permitted to issue securities
   IV. responsible for either over-the-counter or exchange trading

   A. I and II
   B. I and III
   C. I and IV
   D. II and IV

Answers & Rationale

1. **B.** Anyone who has been convicted within the past 10 years of a misdemeanor involving securities or of any felony is subject to the NASD's statutory disqualification rules. A member firm may hire someone who has a record of convictions for misdemeanors outside the industry, although the Association will review that person's application for registration before approval. (Page 186)

2. **A.** A member firm may continue to pay commissions either to a retired employee (or to a retired employee's spouse) or to a broker-dealer purchased by the firm for continuing business, provided that a prior written contract exists. (Page 183)

3. **D.** Any person actively engaged in managing a member's business (including supervising, soliciting or training other persons for such functions) must be registered with the NASD as a principal. (Page 186)

4. **D.** The Uniform Practice Code is designed to standardize the customs, practices and trading techniques used in the investment banking and securities business. (Page 182)

5. **B.** Blue-sky laws are developed within a state for control of securities trading within that state. (Page 172)

6. **D.** Typical blue-sky laws have provisions for revoking the license of a broker-dealer or salesperson. Provisions also require the registration of all broker-dealers and salespeople. Other provisions cover the sale of securities issued in other states (they must be registered in those states). Blue-sky laws do not tell brokerage firms how to compensate salespeople. (Page 172)

7. **B.** Only after a leave of absence of two years or more must registered reps requalify. When the rep left the old firm, her registration was terminated and the firm filed a U-5 form. When she is employed by a new firm, she must reapply for registration on a U-4 form. (Page 183)

8. **D.** A felony conviction within the 10 years preceding application for registration is considered a statutory disqualification. The same restriction applies to convictions for misdemeanors if they involve securities or money-related offenses. (Page 186)

9. **C.** Self-regulatory organizations were established to ensure compliance with SEC regulation in particular jurisdictions. Some SROs, such as the NYSE and the CBOE, are responsible for exchange trading; others, such as the NASD, supervise OTC trading. Because all SROs are independent membership corporations, they may not issue capital stock. (Page 181)

46

Communications with the Public

1. A testimonial used by a member firm must state

   A. the qualifications of the person giving the testimonial if a specialized or an experienced opinion is implied
   B. that past performance does not indicate future performance and that other investors may not obtain comparable results
   C. the fact that compensation was paid to the person giving the testimonial if such compensation was paid
   D. all of the above

2. Which of the following is NOT considered either advertising or sales literature?

   A. Radio advertisement that describes the range of services a firm offers
   B. Advertisement for a firm published in the telephone directory
   C. Press release sent to national newspapers stating an analyst's view of the economy
   D. Market letters sent to a firm's customers

3. With respect to recruiting advertising by NASD member firms, which of the following statements is(are) correct?

   I. Recruiting advertising is not subject to NASD filing rules.
   II. Recruiting advertising may not contain exaggerated claims about opportunities in the securities business.
   III. Recruiting advertising is not permitted.
   IV. Recruiting advertising for the firm's first year of business must be filed with the NASD.

   A. I
   B. I and II
   C. II and IV
   D. III

4. Advertising and sales literature concerning which of the following investment product lines must be filed with the NASD's advertising department within 10 days of first use?

   A. New issue equity securities
   B. Corporate straight debt securities
   C. Open-end investment company securities
   D. Closed-end investment company securities

5. Which of the following forms of written communication must a branch officer or manager approve before its use?

   A. Letter to a customer confirming an annual account review appointment
   B. Letter sent to 30 customers offering advice about a stock
   C. Interoffice memorandum
   D. Preliminary prospectus

6. Which of the following statements is true of a registered rep's recommendations to a customer?

   A. They must be approved in advance by a principal and must be suitable based on the facts disclosed by the customer regarding her other holdings and financial situations.
   B. They must be suitable based on the facts disclosed by the customer regarding her other holdings and financial situation.
   C. They must be approved in advance by a principal.
   D. They are not covered by NASD rules.

7. In recommending securities to customers, a member firm must do which of the following?

   I. Make no guarantees as to future performance
   II. Have a suitable basis for the recommendations
   III. Disclose or offer to disclose supporting documentation

   A. I only
   B. I and II only
   C. II only
   D. I, II and III

8. Which of the following activities is(are) likely to lead to a charge of rule violation by the NASD or the SEC?

   I. A featured columnist for a nationally distributed financial newspaper writes a favorable report on a certain company and is invited on an all-expenses-paid vacation sponsored by a market maker in the company's securities.
   II. A broker-dealer places in a local newspaper a paid advertisement publicizing the range of investment banking services the firm has provided for locally based corporations.
   III. A broker-dealer agrees to fund a major portion of the circulation expenses the sponsor or publisher of a monthly investment newsletter incurs in exchange for priority placements of news items and research opinions at the broker-dealer's direction.
   IV. A broker-dealer offers sales incentives in the form of higher selling concessions to registered representatives, but only on buy orders for a select list of equity securities in which the firm makes markets.

   A. I
   B. I and III
   C. I, III and IV
   D. II, III and IV

9. Which of the following are included under the terms "advertising" and "sales literature" with respect to mutual funds?

   I. Commercial messages broadcast on radio and television
   II. "Sales ideas" and marketing literature issuers send to broker-dealers to be used as internal sales development materials
   III. Sales aids and product literature a fund's principal underwriter distributes to broker-dealers, such materials to be sent to prospective buyers or displayed for their viewing
   IV. Written communications such as direct mail pieces sent to the general public

   A. I and II only
   B. I, III and IV only
   C. III and IV only
   D. I, II, III and IV

10. If ArGood Mutual Fund uses performance charts and return on investment statistics in its sales literature, which of the following NASD policy statements apply?

   I. Performance charts and similar financial information displays should cover a minimum of 10 years (or the life of the fund, if shorter); periods exceeding 10 years can be reported in 5-year increments.
   II. All earnings and total return figures should provide a separate accounting of dividends and capital gains.
   III. In computing and reporting historical yields and return on investment, the shares' maximum offering price should be used.
   IV. Current yield figures must be based on the fund's income distributions only.

   A. I and III only
   B. II and IV only
   C. III and IV only
   D. I, II, III and IV

11. All of the following are considered advertising or sales literature EXCEPT

   A. market letters
   B. research reports
   C. prospectuses
   D. telephone directory listings

12. Which of the following parties are covered under the Telephone Consumer Protection Act of 1991?

   A. University survey group
   B. Nonprofit organization
   C. Church group
   D. Registered representative

13. Which of the following must a rep do when making cold calls?

   I. Immediately record the names and phone numbers of customers who ask to not be called again
   II. Inform each customer of the firm's name and phone number or address
   III. Limit calls to between the hours of 8:00 a.m. and 9:00 p.m. of the time zone in which the customer is located
   IV. Call no customers who make do-not-call requests

   A. I and II only
   B. I and IV only
   C. II and III only
   D. I, II, III and IV

14. Max Leveridge receives a telephone solicitation from a registered rep at Stern, Sterner, Sternest. Under which of the following conditions is this solicitation exempt from the Telephone Consumer Protection Act of 1991?

    I. Max asked the rep to call him with any investment recommendations.
    II. Max is an active trader with an account at Stern, Sterner, Sternest.
    III. Max is an active trader with an account at another firm.
    IV. The rep received permission from a principal of the firm.

    A. I and II
    B. I, II and III
    C. II
    D. IV

Answers & Rationale

1. **D.** Each testimonial must state whether the testimonial giver was paid, that the giver's experience may not represent other investors' experience, and the giver's qualifications if a specialized or an experienced opinion is implied. (Page 194)

2. **C.** Publications of a general nature (that is, not recommending securities or promoting a firm) are not considered advertising. (Page 188)

3. **C.** All advertising during a firm's first year of business must be filed with the NASD 10 days before use. Recruiting advertising may not contain exaggerated claims about brokerage business opportunities. (Page 196)

4. **C.** Although NASD rules require that an officer or a designee of a member firm closely monitors all advertising and sales literature and approves such material before first use or publication, only certain investment products are subject to the 10-day filing requirement. Chief among these products are registered investment company securities, including mutual funds, variable annuity contracts and unit investment trusts. Closed-end investment company securities are treated as corporate equity securities and are not subject to filing under this rule. (Page 191)

5. **B.** Form letters fall into the category of sales literature and must be approved by a principal or manager before use. (Page 189)

6. **B.** Recommendations made to a customer must be suitable for that customer. (Page 192)

7. **D.** Choices I through III apply to customer recommendations. (Page 192)

8. **C.** The Securities Exchange Act of 1934 and the NASD's Rules of Fair Practice both prohibit the activities and inducements described in all of the choices except choice II. The rules permit pro-

motional materials that are clearly distinguishable as paid advertising. (Page 189)

9. **B.** The terms "advertising" and "sales literature" refer only to materials prepared for publication or broadcast to a mass audience or investors in general. Materials intended for internal use within a broker-dealer's organization are not considered advertising or sales literature— assuming, of course, that the firm keeps them away from customers. (Page 188)

10. **D.** Performance charts should cover enough years to allow prospective buyers to evaluate a mutual fund's performance during good times as well as bad, which is why the NASD approves of 10-year performance histories. The NASD also believes that prospective buyers should be alerted as to whether a fund's performance is based on reinvestment of capital gains only or on reinvestment of both capital gains and dividends. Furthermore, for purposes of reporting fairness and statistical consistency, yield and total return figures should be based on the maximum offering price during the period covered. (Page 193)

11. **C.** Advertising is any communication to the general public. Three answers fit this definition. Prospectuses are not considered advertising. (Page 188)

12. **D.** The Telephone Consumer Protection Act of 1991 covers all registered reps. Each firm must have a do-not-call list that every registered rep must check before soliciting any person. The act applies to commercial solicitation and does not include a university survey group or nonprofit organization. (Page 197)

13. **D.** All are requirements of the Telephone Consumer Protection Act of 1991. (Page 197)

14. **A.** The Telephone Consumer Protection Act of 1991 exempts calls made to established customers and calls made at the invitation of prospective customers. A registered principal does not have the authority to exempt certain calls from the act's provisions. (Page 198)

47

Ethics in the Securities Industry

1. The term "churning" refers to

   A. excessive trading in a customer's account for the express purpose of generating commissions
   B. the practice of freeriding in more than one customer's account at a time
   C. a firm's manipulation of market prices
   D. making false or misleading statements to a customer for the purpose of inducing the customer to purchase or sell a security

2. Which of the following defines the term "selling dividends"?

   A. Encouraging mutual fund customers to sell their holdings just before the fund declares a dividend payment
   B. Enticing customers to buy mutual fund shares just before a dividend payment
   C. Withdrawing dividends rather than reinvesting these amounts in additional shares
   D. Encouraging investors to postpone purchases of mutual fund shares until after the ex-date for a dividend distribution

3. Encouraging a customer to purchase mutual fund shares in an amount just below the next dollar volume bracket, which entitles the customer to a reduction in sales charges, is called

   A. a breakpoint sale
   B. boiler room selling
   C. double-dip selling
   D. a low-ball sale

4. According to the Rules of Fair Practice, a member organization must do which of the following?

   A. Grant an extension of the settlement date for a purchase made in a special cash account
   B. Repurchase from a client any securities the client offers for sale
   C. Quote a quantity discount on lots of more than 100 shares
   D. Authorize in writing a registered representative's request to share in a client's profits or losses

5. A rep signs an agreement to borrow money from a customer. This is permitted under what circumstances?

   A. Only with written permission from his firm
   B. Only with written permission from the NASD
   C. Only if the customer is a bank
   D. Under no circumstances

6. An associated person of Dullard Securities owns a vacation home. She is permitted to rent it out under what circumstances?

   A. Only with prior written approval of Dullard Securities
   B. Only after notifying Dullard Securities
   C. Without restriction
   D. Under no circumstances

7. When regulators determine whether a registered representative is churning an account, they take into account which of the following?

   I. Frequency of trades
   II. Motive of rep
   III. Rating of securities traded
   IV. Size of positions traded

   A. I
   B. I, II and IV
   C. I and III
   D. III and IV

8. A registered representative hired to be a guest speaker will be paid a fee. Therefore, the representative must

   A. register as an investment adviser
   B. be a certified financial planner
   C. receive permission from the NASD
   D. notify her firm in writing

Answers & Rationale

1.   **A.**   "Churning" describes trading that is excessive in light of a particular customer's circumstances or trading more excessive than what would normally be considered suitable. This is equally true for both discretionary and nondiscretionary accounts.   (Page 201)

2.   **B.**   Selling dividends is an unethical sales practice in which a seller intentionally or unintentionally misleads customers into believing they will be getting the equivalent of a rebate on their investments because the fund will soon be paying a distribution. The customers suffer out-of-pocket losses because the cash immediately coming back is dividend income, subject to tax.   (Page 202)

3.   **A.**   In a breakpoint sale, a customer unknowingly buys investment company shares in an amount just below a dollar bracket amount that would qualify the customer's investment for a reduction in sales charges. As a result, the customer pays a higher dollar amount in sales charges, which reduces the number of shares purchased and results in a higher cost basis per share.   (Page 202)

4.   **D.**   According to the NASD Rules of Fair Practice, members and persons associated with them are forbidden to guarantee that a customer will not sustain a loss; or share in the profits or losses of a customer's account unless an associated person has obtained the firm's prior written approval and the person shares only to the extent of his proportionate contribution to the account. (Note that accounts of the associated person's immediate family are exempt from the proportionate share limitation.)   (Page 203)

5.   **C.**   The prohibition against borrowing money from customers does not include customers in the business of lending money. Otherwise, borrowing money or securities from customers is strictly prohibited.   (Page 202)

6.   **C.**   Receiving payment for rent of a vacation home does not constitute a private securities transaction, so no approval or notification is required.   (Page 199)

7.   **B.**   Excessive trading, whether in terms of size or frequency, in a customer's account is a prohibited practice known as *churning*. When regulators investigate allegations of churning in an account, they take into consideration the registered rep's possible motivation.   (Page 201)

8.   **D.**   If a registered representative will receive income from a source other than the employing firm, she must notify the employing firm. Registration as an investment adviser is not necessary if the rep gives advice within the scope of her employment with the broker-dealer.   (Page 200)

Code of Procedure and Code of Arbitration Procedure

48

1. The Code of Procedure was designed for all of the following purposes EXCEPT settling

   A. when-, as- and if-issued securities transactions between member firms
   B. complaints between members
   C. complaints between registered reps and members
   D. complaints made by customers against members

2. The NASD may take which of the following actions against members who violate the Rules of Fair Practice?

   I. Expulsion
   II. Censure
   III. Fine
   IV. Suspension

   A. I, II and IV only
   B. I and IV only
   C. II and III only
   D. I, II, III and IV

3. Which of the following describes findings under the NASD Code of Arbitration Procedure?

   A. Binding on members, but not on customers
   B. Binding on all parties involved in a dispute
   C. May be appealed to the NASD's Board of Governors
   D. May be appealed to the SEC

4. Arbitration under the NASD Code of Arbitration Procedure may be used to resolve which of the following disputes?

   I. Member against a person associated with a member
   II. Member against another member
   III. Member against a public customer
   IV. Public customer against a member

   A. I only
   B. I, II and IV only
   C. II only
   D. I, II, III and IV

5. The Code of Arbitration is mandatory in disputes between a broker-dealer and

   A. the Securities and Exchange Commission
   B. another broker-dealer
   C. the general public
   D. the National Association of Securities Dealers

6. Which of the following statements apply to the Code of Procedure?

   I. The Board of Governors may review the findings of the District Business Conduct Committee within 45 days.
   II. All answers by respondents must be in writing and must be submitted to the District Business Conduct Committee within 20 calendar days.
   III. All complaints must be in writing.
   IV. The SEC will approve or disapprove of the penalty assessed within 60 days.

   A. I and II only
   B. I, II and III only
   C. III and IV only
   D. I, II, III and IV

7. How long does a client have in which to submit a claim against a registered representative or a member firm under the Code of Arbitration?

   A. 6 months
   B. 1 year
   C. 6 years
   D. 10 years

8. The maximum fine in a summary complaint proceeding is

   A. $1,000
   B. $2,500
   C. $5,000
   D. $10,000

9. How are disputes settled between NASD members regarding delivery and payment for securities transactions?

   A. By the SEC
   B. Under the provisions of the Code of Arbitration
   C. By the Board of Governors
   D. By the District Business Conduct Committee

10. Which of the following may assess the penalties on a firm or registered representative or suspend or expel the firm or rep from NASD membership?

    I. District Business Conduct Committee
    II. NASD Board of Governors
    III. Uniform Practice Committee

    A. I and II
    B. II
    C. II and III
    D. III

11. In settling disputes between member firms, arbitration is preferable to litigation because arbitration

    A. is not binding on both parties
    B. is less costly
    C. does not allow for arguments from parties outside the industry
    D. allows more time to prepare arguments

12. A matter involving a $50,000 discrepancy is brought to arbitration. The panel hearing this dispute will consist of

    A. not fewer than three or more than five arbitrators
    B. five arbitrators
    C. seven arbitrators
    D. a number of arbitrators determined by the arbitration committee

13. What is(are) a respondent's responsibil-
    ity(ies) when the party learns that it is
    involved in a customer complaint
    procedure?

    I. The respondent must file the appropri-
       ate forms with the Director of Arbitra-
       tion within 20 calendar days of the
       receipt of service.
    II. In its answer, the respondent must put
        forth all defenses to the statement of
        claim.
    III. The respondent may set forth a counter-
         claim, if any, against the initiating party
         or a third party.

    A. I only
    B. I and II only
    C. III only
    D. I, II and III

Answers & Rationale

1.   A.   The Code of Procedure is a mechanism for settling complaints between members or between members and nonmembers. The Uniform Practice Code establishes standard operating procedures for the settlement of transactions.   (Page 204)

2.   D.   Members or employees of members found to violate the Rules of Fair Practice can be subjected to any penalty in the NASD's arsenal.   (Page 204)

3.   B.   Members and associated persons must submit disputes to arbitration. Customers are subject to arbitration only if they agree to submit to arbitration. Findings under the Code of Arbitration are considered binding on all parties involved.   (Page 207)

4.   D.   The Code of Arbitration is mandatory in member-against-member disputes. In a dispute between a member and a public customer, the member cannot force the public customer to arbitrate, but arbitration may be used at the customer's request.   (Page 204)

5.   B.   The Code of Arbitration covers inter-dealer disputes.   (Page 204)

6.   B.   The Board of Governors may review any DBCC findings within 45 days if it sees fit. In every instance, charges by complainants and replies by respondents must be in writing.

Respondents have 20 calendar days in which to answer a complaint.   (Page 206)

7.   C.   Under the Code of Arbitration, no dispute or claim is eligible for submission to arbitration more than six years after the date of the dispute's occurrence. The statute for arbitration does not extend applicable state statutes of limitations (typically two years).   (Page 207)

8.   B.   The maximum fine in a summary complaint is $2,500, according to the NASD Code of Procedure.   (Page 206)

9.   B.   Disputes regarding the provisions of the Uniform Practice Code (UPC) are handled through the NASD Code of Arbitration. The UPC specifies the mechanics of member-to-member dealings.   (Page 207)

10.   A.   Under the NASD Code of Procedure, both the DBCC and the Board of Governors are empowered to penalize, suspend or expel a member firm or an associated person.   (Page 204)

11.   B.   Arbitration is the preferred method for settling disputes between member firms because it is less costly than litigation.   (Page 207)

12.   A.   In disputes involving more than $30,000, the code dictates that no fewer than three arbitrators but no more than five arbitrators hear the case.   (Page 208)

13.   D.   The respondent in a customer complaint procedure must respond to the notice within 20 calendar days, at which time he may set forth his defense and file a counter or an additional claim.   (Page 205)

49

Lesson Four — Securities Industry Regulations

1. A registered representative may be disciplined for an infraction of the Rules of Fair Practice

   I. at the request of a customer
   II. at the request of the Board of Governors
   III. by the District Business Conduct Committee

   A. I and III only
   B. II only
   C. II and III only
   D. I, II and III

2. The Board of Governors of the NASD has the authority to

   I. suspend a person, prohibiting him from associating with any exchange
   II. censure a partner of a member firm
   III. suspend or expel a member firm from the NASD
   IV. either suspend or bar a person from further association with a member firm

   A. I and III only
   B. II, III and IV only
   C. II and IV only
   D. I, II, III and IV

3. If not appealed to the Board of Governors, findings by a District Business Conduct Committee become effective

   A. immediately
   B. only after review by the SEC
   C. no sooner than 10 days from the date of the decision
   D. no sooner than 45 days from the date of the decision

4. Who can lodge a complaint against a registered rep?

   A. NASD Board of Governors
   B. Client
   C. Member broker-dealer
   D. Anyone

5. Binding arbitration is required in all the following disputes EXCEPT

   A. broker-dealer against broker-dealer
   B. associated person against broker-dealer
   C. broker-dealer against customer
   D. broker-dealer against associated person

6. Which of the following means of settling disputes is attractive to broker-dealers because of its relatively low cost?

    A. Litigation
    B. Coterminous defeasance
    C. Repatriation
    D. Arbitration

7. A customer might choose to go through arbitration with a dispute rather than take it to court because

    A. the arbitrators tend to favor the customer
    B. a customer has no choice and must arbitrate
    C. arbitration is generally less expensive than court procedures
    D. a public customer is not permitted to use arbitration

8. Unless the law directs otherwise, all awards rendered under or proceeding before the arbitration panel shall be

    A. subject to review by the MSRB
    B. subject to review by the SEC
    C. subject to appeal to the federal courts
    D. deemed final and not subject to review or appeal

9. When initiating an arbitration proceeding, the document filed by the initial party that states the relevant facts of the cases and the remedies sought is called the

    A. submission agreement
    B. statement of claim
    C. official statement
    D. director's brief

10. A customer involved in a dispute with a broker-dealer signs the required submission agreement. The customer

    A. must abide by any decision in the customer's favor
    B. must abide by any decision in the firm's favor
    C. must abide by any decision
    D. is not required to abide by any decision

11. For how many years must advertisements, sales literature and market letters be maintained in an easily accessible place?

    A. One
    B. Two
    C. Three
    D. Five

12. When a member firm refers to its previous recommendations, it must also

    I. indicate that the market was generally rising if such is the case
    II. show all of its recommendations of the same type of securities made within the previous twelve months
    III. indicate the date and price of the security at the time of recommendation
    IV. give the amount of profit or loss that would have been realized had an individual acted on all of the recommendations

    A. I, II and III only
    B. II and III only
    C. I, II, III and IV
    D. None of the above

13. Which of the following must be included in a testimonial made on behalf of a member firm and distributed to potential clients?

    I. Qualifications of the person giving the testimonial if a specialized or expert opinion is implied
    II. Length of time the testimonial covers
    III. That the returns and investment performance cited in the testimonial may not be easily duplicated
    IV. Whether compensation was paid to the person giving the testimonial

    A. I, III and IV only
    B. I and IV only
    C. II and III only
    D. I, II, III and IV

14. Which of the following is classified as "sales literature," not as "advertising"?

    A. Reprint of newspaper advertisement
    B. Billboard
    C. Telephone directory listing
    D. Prerecorded telemarketing message

15. Which of the following is classified as "advertising," not as "sales literature"?

    A. Form letter
    B. Reprint of newspaper advertisement
    C. Research report
    D. Tape of a radio commercial

16. Written recommendations prepared by a registered representative need the prior approval of

    A. the appropriate SRO
    B. a principal of the firm
    C. the SEC
    D. the FCC

17. Joe receives a cold call from a registered representative, and he tells the rep he is not interested in this investment or in making any future investments. Which of the following actions is required by the Telephone Consumer Protection Act of 1991?

    A. The rep may send a letter notifying Joe of her intentions before calling again.
    B. A principal of the firm may call Joe the next time.
    C. The rep may never make cold calls again.
    D. No calls may be made to Joe by anyone at the firm.

18. A new customer comes to you with questions about a growth mutual fund. As a registered rep, you may NOT tell the customer

    A. "Because this is a growth fund, your shares will increase in value."
    B. "Your shares may be redeemed at any time, but you should consider this a long-term investment."
    C. "This fund has performed in the top 25 percent of funds with similar objectives over the past ten years, according to the information compiled by ZBest Mutual Fund Rating Service."
    D. "You may choose to have all distributions automatically reinvested in the fund."

19. Which of the following is exempt from the Telephone Consumer Protection Act?

    A. Nonprofit charitable organization calling to sell raffle tickets
    B. Small business calling in the immediate neighborhood
    C. Telemarketing service calling between 8:00 am and 9:00 pm
    D. Radio station calling to survey listeners for an advertiser

20. Which of the following telephone solicitations are exempt from the Telephone Consumer Protection Act?

   I. Calls made by tax-exempt nonprofit organizations
   II. Calls made on behalf of tax-exempt nonprofit organizations
   III. Calls made for debt collection
   IV. Calls made to established business customers

   A. I, III and IV only
   B. I and IV only
   C. II and III only
   D. I, II, III and IV

21. According to the NASD bylaws, which of the following must be recorded for a person who seeks a job that involves handling funds or securities?

   I. Arrest or indictment for any crime involving the purchase, sale or delivery of securities
   II. Denial of membership in any national securities exchange
   III. Disclosure of the person's business connections over the past ten years
   IV. Educational institutions attended within the past ten years

   A. I and II only
   B. I, III and IV only
   C. II and III only
   D. I, II, III and IV

22. Which of the following must be included in an advertisement that identifies a non-branch office of an NASD member?

   A. Statement that the advertisement was filed with the NASD prior to use
   B. NASD approval of the nonbranch's registration
   C. Address and telephone number of the nonbranch's office of supervisory jurisdiction
   D. Name of the registered principal with supervisory responsibility for the non-branch office

23. A husband and wife have both a joint cash account and a joint margin account. In addition, each has an individual retirement account. SIPC would cover

   A. the joint accounts separately and the retirement accounts as one
   B. the retirement accounts separately and the joint accounts as one
   C. all accounts combined as one
   D. all accounts individually and separately

24. Which of the following customer accounts is(are) NOT SIPC-insured?

   I. Customer margin account
   II. JTWROS account with spouse
   III. JTIC commodities account with son
   IV. JTIC account with business partner

   A. I
   B. II and III
   C. II, III and IV
   D. III

25. SIPC provides coverage for which of the following securities held in a customer account?

   I. Common stock
   II. Preferred stock
   III. Rights and warrants
   IV. Corporate bonds

   A. I and II only
   B. II, III and IV only
   C. III and IV only
   D. I, II, III and IV

Answers & Rationale

1. **C.** Members or associated persons may be disciplined only after it is determined that they have violated the rules. This finding could come from the District Business Conduct Committee or the NASD's Board of Governors. (Page 204)

2. **B.** The Board of Governors of the NASD may censure, suspend or expel a member or a person associated with a member. It has no jurisdiction over the exchanges and cannot prohibit any person from associating with them. (Page 205)

3. **D.** If not appealed, District Business Conduct Committee decisions become final 45 days after the decision date. (Page 206)

4. **D.** Anyone can lodge a complaint against a registered rep for infractions of the Rules of Fair Practice. (Page 205)

5. **C.** In disputes involving only associated persons and broker-dealers, all must submit to binding arbitration. In the case of either a broker-dealer against a customer, or a customer against a broker-dealer, the customer is not compelled to submit to arbitration. The customer may *elect* to arbitrate, and in signing documentation to that effect he is bound by the decision of the arbitrators. (Page 207)

6. **D.** Arbitration is a system for resolving disputes between parties by submitting the disagreement to an impartial panel, consisting of one, three or five people. Arbitration expedites binding decisions involving disputes and avoids costly litigation. (Page 207)

7. **C.** Choices A, B and D are false statements. (Page 207)

8. **D.** All decisions made by the arbitration committee are deemed final and binding. (Page 207)

9. **B.** The filing of the claim in a dispute is called the *statement of claim*. (Page 207)

10. **C.** The submission agreement is filed along with the statement of claim when a dispute is submitted for arbitration. Under the NASD's Code of Arbitration Procedure, a customer cannot be forced to submit to arbitration; however, if the customer gives written consent, he must abide by the final decision of the panel. (Page 207)

11. **B.** All advertisements must be maintained on file for three years after use, the first two years in an easily accessible place. (Page 190)

12. **A.** When referring to past recommendations, a member must show the whole universe of recommendations in the past year, not only the winners. A member must indicate whether the overall market was generally rising and the date and price of the security at the time of recommendation. (Page 192)

13. **A.** When a member firm uses a testimonial, the testimonial must be accompanied by the following disclosures: (1) a statement that this person's experience does not necessarily represent that of other customers; (2) any compensation paid, if material; and (3) the qualifications of the testimonial giver if an expert opinion is implied. (Page 194)

14. **A.** A reprint of an advertisement that is distributed to customers is classified as sales literature. All of the other answers make use of the public media and are, therefore, classified as advertising. (Page 189)

15. **D.** Of the answers listed, the radio commercial makes use of the public media and thus is considered advertising. The other answers describe communications that may be made available to the public or to customers and, therefore, they are classified as sales literature. (Page 188)

16. **B.** A written recommendation sent to a customer is classified as sales literature. Therefore, a principal must review and approve the communication before use. (Page 190)

17. **D.** Joe's name must be placed on the firm's "do-not-call list," and no one at the firm may call him. (Page 197)

18. **A.** Share price and investment return will vary, and no mutual fund company can guarantee that an investment will produce positive returns. Reps must comply with rules intended to protect the public; they must not imply that funds are suitable for short-term trading or discuss performance information without revealing the source of the material. Discussing services offered by the fund, such as dividend reinvestment, is permissible. (Page 193)

19. **A.** Exemptions from the Telephone Consumer Protection Act (TCPA) include calls made by nonprofit charitable organizations, calls made to current established business customers, calls without a commercial purpose and calls made with express permission or invitation by the customer. (Page 198)

20. **D.** All of the choices listed describe calls exempted from the TCPA. (Page 198)

21. **D.** Under the NASD bylaws, a broker must have a record of all of the items listed. (Page 182)

22. **C.** A nonbranch office of a broker-dealer must identify the name, address and telephone number of its OSJ on letterheads, business cards, telephone directory listings and advertisements. (Page 189)

23. **B.** SIPC provides up to $500,000 of protection to each separate customer account. Multiple accounts held by the same person would be considered as only one customer for SIPC purposes (remember that the definition of "person" can include individuals, groups, companies, and so on). However, there are different elements of beneficial ownership. If a woman has an account in her name, a man has an account in his name and they are joint owners of a third account, SIPC will treat them as three separate customer accounts. (Page 179)

24. **D.** SIPC coverage applies to accounts holding *securities* only. Commodities accounts, therefore, are not covered. (Page 179)

25. **D.** SIPC provides coverage for up to $500,000 worth of securities held in a customer account. All types of securities are covered up to the maximum. (Page 179)

Final Exam One

1. Which of the following is a characteristic of Treasury bills?

   A. Issued at par
   B. Callable
   C. Issued in bearer form
   D. Registered

2. If a bond is purchased at a premium, the yield to maturity is

   A. higher than the nominal yield
   B. lower than the nominal yield
   C. the same as the nominal yield
   D. the same as the current yield

3. Chip Bullock, age 52, and his wife Clara Bullock, age 56, have a large investment portfolio concentrated in stocks and stock mutual funds, including an international stock fund. They maintain their cash reserves in a money-market account at their local bank. Chip is employed as a consultant and earns a $400,000 salary. The Bullocks are seeking a safe investment because they will need to liquidate a portion of their portfolio when Chip reaches retirement in about five years. They also recognize the need for additional diversification in their portfolio. Which of the following mutual funds is the MOST suitable for the Bullocks?

   A. NavCo Tax-free Municipal Bond Fund
   B. ATF Biotechnology Fund
   C. ATF Overseas Opportunities Fund
   D. ArGood Stock Index Fund

4. When a broker-dealer holds money or securities in its own account, it is doing which of the following?

   A. Underwriting
   B. Hypothecating the securities
   C. Taking a position
   D. Engaging in none of the above

5. A fund seeks maximum current income, safety of principal and capital growth. The fund's portfolio is invested in common stocks, preferred stocks, convertible securities and high-yielding bonds. The diversification of the fund's portfolio can help generate strong total returns while holding volatility to a minimum. This information describes which of the following mutual funds?

   A. ArGood Stock Index Fund
   B. ArGood Investment-grade Bond Fund
   C. NavCo Growth & Income Fund
   D. ZBEST Government Income Fund

6. Which of the following constitutes a discretionary account?

   A. Registered representative's trading account
   B. Broker-dealer's trading account
   C. Account in which the investor gives the broker written authority to buy or sell securities
   D. Mutual fund account allowing periodic withdrawals

7. Rhoda Bear, age 32, and Randy Bear, age 30, have been married for four years. Both Bears work, and they have no children, so their disposable income is relatively high. The Bears live in the suburbs, and they are planning to buy a condominium downtown so that they can enjoy some of their favorite activities on the weekends. They need a safe place to invest the amount they have saved for their down payment for about six months while they shop for the perfect unit. Which of the following mutual funds is the MOST suitable for the Bears?

   A. ATF Capital Appreciation Fund
   B. NavCo Growth & Income Fund
   C. NavCo Cash Reserves Money-Market Fund
   D. ArGood Investment-grade Bond Fund

8. An investor who purchases a Treasury STRIPS is assured of

   I. a locked-in rate of return
   II. a lump-sum payment of principal and interest at maturity
   III. lower taxes because the returns would be taxed at the lower capital gains rate
   IV. little or no reinvestment risk

   A. I
   B. I, II and III
   C. I, II and IV
   D. II and IV

9. From which of the following can you purchase shares of a closed-end investment company after its initial offering?

   A. Investment company directly
   B. Other shareholders through a broker-dealer
   C. Either A or B
   D. Neither A nor B

10. Deductions and charges against a variable life insurance separate account may include

   I. expenses and mortality risk fees
   II. sales load
   III. state premium taxes
   IV. cost of insurance

   A. I and III
   B. I and IV
   C. II and III
   D. II and IV

11. Adam Grizzly is 26 years old and earns $45,000 a year as an advertising executive. He has already accumulated $5,000 in his savings account and is seeking a secure place to invest the amount and begin a periodic investment plan. He knows his long-term time frame means he should be willing to take some risk, but he is uncomfortable with the thought of losing money. Adam would prefer moderate overall returns rather than high returns accompanied by high volatility. Which of the following mutual funds is the MOST suitable for Adam?

A. ATF Capital Appreciation Fund
B. ATF Biotechnology Fund
C. ArGood Balanced Fund
D. ATF Overseas Opportunities Fund

12. An investment company share normally goes ex-dividend

A. on the record date
B. the day after the record date
C. five days after the record date
D. seven days after the record date

13. An investor interested in monthly interest income should invest in

A. GNMAs
B. Treasury bonds
C. a utility company's stock
D. corporate bonds

14. Which of the following would be classified as an investment company?

I. Closed-end company
II. Open-end company
III. Qualified plan company
IV. Nonqualified plan company
V. Fixed-annuity company

A. I and II
B. I, II and V
C. II
D. III, IV and V

15. A teacher has contributed $26,000 to a qualified annuity plan over the past 12 years. The value of the annuity today is $36,000. If the teacher withdraws $15,000 now, what are the tax consequences if the teacher is in the 30 percent tax bracket?

A. $1,500
B. $3,000
C. $4,500
D. No taxes are due on this withdrawal.

16. A convertible bond's market price depends on which of the following?

A. Value of the underlying stock into which the bond can be converted
B. Current interest rates
C. Bond's rating
D. All of the above

17. Where can open-end investment company shares be purchased and sold?

A. In the secondary marketplace
B. From the open-end company
C. In the primary market
D. All of the above

18. An investor has bonds maturing in two weeks. He plans to purchase new bonds with a 10 percent coupon rate. If interest rates decline in the period before the investor can purchase the new bonds, he can expect the income he will receive from the new bonds to

A. increase
B. decline
C. stay the same
D. balloon

19. Under the provisions of an UGMA account, what happens to the account when the minor reaches the age of majority?

A. It should be turned over to the donee.
B. It should be turned over to the donor.
C. It remains an UGMA account.
D. It is liquidated.

20. A corporation needs shareholder approval for which of the following?

    A. Cash dividend
    B. 4-for-1 split
    C. 10 percent stock dividend
    D. Repurchase of 100,000 of its own shares

21. Federal funds are used primarily by

    A. large commercial banks
    B. mutual insurance companies
    C. independent broker-dealers
    D. savings and loans

22. One of the most important functions of a banker's acceptance is its use as a means of

    A. facilitating trades in foreign goods
    B. facilitating trades of foreign securities in the United States
    C. assigning previously declared distributions by foreign corporations
    D. guaranteeing payment of an international bank's promissory note

23. If a corporation wanted to offer stock at a given price for the next five years, it would issue

    A. rights
    B. warrants
    C. callable preferred stock
    D. put options

24. Which of the following withdrawal plans would an investor select if she wanted to receive a fixed payment monthly from the investment company?

    A. Fixed-time
    B. Fixed-share
    C. Fixed-percentage
    D. Fixed-dollar

25. Which of the following come(s) under NASD guidelines concerning sales literature or advertising?

    I. Giving a prepared presentation to the local Kiwanis Club
    II. Distributing a letter to all clients
    III. Distributing copies of a magazine article

    A. I only
    B. II only
    C. II and III only
    D. I, II and III

26. The NASD Board of Governors has the authority to do which of the following?

    I. Suspend a person, prohibiting him from associating with any exchange
    II. Censure a partner of a member firm
    III. Suspend or expel a member firm from membership in the NASD
    IV. Either suspend or bar a person from further association with a member firm

    A. I and III only
    B. II, III and IV only
    C. II and IV only
    D. I, II, III and IV

27. All of the following would be considered typical of money-market funds EXCEPT that

    A. the underlying portfolios are normally made up of short-term debt instruments
    B. most or all are offered as no-load investments
    C. such funds have high betas and are safest in periods of low market volatility
    D. their net asset values normally remain unchanged

28. A customer indicates that she wishes to invest $50,000 in mutual funds. The investments are to be split into three funds, each with its own management company and all of which are growth-oriented health care funds. The registered representative should advise the customer that

   A. this is an excellent idea because it spreads the risk of investing significantly
   B. she will pay greater commissions on the investment when the money is split between three funds than if she put the money into only one fund
   C. she will be able to exchange shares from one fund to another as conditions change without incurring a new sales charge
   D. she should buy individual stocks because mutual funds are for smaller investors only

29. The result of a client investing the same amount of money into a mutual fund at regular intervals over a long period of time is a lower

   A. price per share than cost per share
   B. cost per share than price per share
   C. dollar amount invested
   D. return on the cost basis

30. The NASD Rules of Fair Practice govern the actions of its members. All of the following are considered violations of the rules EXCEPT

   A. churning accounts
   B. recommending low-price speculative stocks to all investors
   C. using discretionary authority
   D. guaranteeing customers against loss

31. On February 14 an investor purchases 1,000 shares of ACE Fund, which has an objective of providing the highest possible level of income on a monthly basis. On February 15, the investor informs his agent that he has changed his mind and wishes to exchange his bond fund shares for shares of a common stock growth fund with an objective of capital appreciation within the same family of funds. The investor's bond fund shares increased in value before the exchange. How will this increase in value be taxed?

   A. As income because the bond fund's objective was to provide current income on a monthly basis
   B. As a short-term gain because the bond fund was held for less than 12 months
   C. As a long-term gain because the exchange of the bond fund shares was made into a common stock fund with an objective of long-term capital appreciation
   D. Because the shares were exchanged within a family of funds, the increase in the bond fund shares' value is not taxed, but it increases the cost base in the common stock fund investment.

32. A complaint filed with the NASD charges that a member or an associated person violated one or more of the Association's rules. Which of the following codes governs the resolution of such matters?

   A. Code of Arbitration
   B. Code of Procedure
   C. Professional Practice Code
   D. Business Conduct Code

33. Which of the following secure(s) an industrial development revenue bond?

   A. State tax
   B. Municipal tax
   C. Trustee
   D. Net lease payments from the corporation

34. Moody's bond ratings are based primarily on an issuer's

    A. marketability
    B. financial strength
    C. capitalization
    D. trading volume

35. A registered representative of an NASD member firm wishes to open an account with another member firm. The executing member shall take all the following actions EXCEPT

    A. notify the employer member in writing before the transaction's execution of its intention to open or maintain the account for the representative
    B. immediately transmit to the employer member duplicate copies of confirmations or other statements with respect to the representative's account
    C. transmit duplicate copies of confirmations or other statements with respect to the representative's account upon the employer member's request
    D. notify the registered representative of the executing member's intent to notify the employer member

36. In its attempt to increase the money supply, the Federal Open Market Committee purchases T bills. This action should cause the yield on T bills to

    A. increase
    B. decrease
    C. remain the same
    D. fluctuate

37. Which of the following do NOT expose the investor to reinvestment risk?

    A. Treasury stock
    B. Treasury bonds
    C. Treasury STRIPS
    D. Treasury notes

38. Distributions from a profit-sharing plan made to an employee after retirement are from the

    A. interest accumulating on the plan's assets
    B. profits on the plan's assets only
    C. amount allocated to the individual's account during the employee's participation in the plan
    D. amount allocated to the individual's account plus accumulated earnings during the employee's participation in the plan only

39. An individual calculating taxable income she received from a municipal bond fund investment for this year would consider which of the following?

    A. Part of the income distribution she received as a dividend is taxable at ordinary income tax rates.
    B. All of the income distribution she received as a dividend is taxable at ordinary income tax rates.
    C. Any capital gains distributions she received from the fund are taxable at ordinary income tax rates.
    D. All distributions, both income and gains, she received from the fund are exempt from federal income tax.

40. If TIP Company's dividend decreases by 5 percent and its stock's market value decreases by 7 percent, the stock's current yield will

    A. increase
    B. decrease
    C. remain at 5 percent
    D. remain at 7 percent

41. If a variable annuity has an assumed investment rate of 5 percent and the annualized return of the separate account is 4 percent, what are the consequences?

    I. The accumulation unit's value will rise.
    II. The annuity unit's value will rise.
    III. The accumulation unit's value will fall.
    IV. The annuity unit's value will fall.

    A. I and II
    B. I and IV
    C. II and III
    D. III and IV

42. ACE, an open-end investment company, has the following financial information:

Dividend income	$2,000
Interest income	$900
Long-term gains	$1,000
Expenses	$900

    To qualify as a regulated investment company, ACE must distribute what amount to its investors?

    A. $1,800
    B. $2,700
    C. $3,510
    D. $3,600

43. June Polar is 65 years old. Her payroll deduction contributions into a nonqualified tax-deferred annuity total $10,000, and the account's current value is $16,000. For tax purposes, what is June's cost basis?

    A. $0
    B. $6,000
    C. $10,000
    D. $16,000

44. If Mrs. Polar's payroll deductions into a qualified tax-deferred annuity total $10,000 and her current value in the account is $16,000, her cost basis for tax purposes would be

    A. $0
    B. $6,000
    C. $10,000
    D. $16,000

45. An investor is looking into the purchase of Series EE bonds through payroll deduction at his place of employment. If the investor decides to purchase the Series EE bonds, he will receive the interest earned

    A. monthly
    B. semiannually
    C. annually
    D. at redemption

46. Which of the following describe premiums for a scheduled-payment variable life policy?

    I. Fixed as to the premium amount
    II. Variable as to the premium amount, depending on the policy's face amount
    III. Fixed as to time of payment
    IV. Variable as to time of payment

    A. I and III
    B. I and IV
    C. II and III
    D. II and IV

47. An investor is in the annuity stage of a variable annuity purchased 15 years ago. During the present month, the annuitant receives a check for an amount that is less than the previous month's payment. Which of the following events caused the annuitant to receive the smaller check?

   A. The account's performance was less than the previous month's performance.
   B. The account's performance was greater than the previous month's performance.
   C. The account's performance was less than the assumed interest rate.
   D. The account's performance was greater than the assumed interest rate.

48. For a customer, a registered representative may arrange the purchase of an interest in a privately offered stock only if the representative

   I. informs her broker-dealer after the trade
   II. informs her broker-dealer before the trade
   III. provides all documents and information as required by her broker-dealer
   IV. Because the sale is private, the representative does not have to do anything out of the ordinary.

   A. I and II
   B. II
   C. II and III
   D. IV

49. Which of the following statements is true of the expense ratio of an open-end investment company?

   A. It is computed exclusive of the management fee.
   B. It is computed inclusive of the management fee.
   C. It is computed taking into account the management fee only.
   D. It shows the extent of leverage in the fund.

50. A mutual fund paid $.30 in dividends and $.75 in capital gains during the year. The offering price at the end of the year is $6.50. The fund's current yield for the year is

   A. 4.6 percent
   B. 6.9 percent
   C. 11.5 percent
   D. 16.2 percent

51. Fees such as mortality and risk expenses are deducted from the

   I. premium payment for flexible premium policies
   II. premium payment for fixed premium policies
   III. benefit base for scheduled premium policies
   IV. benefit base for fixed premium policies

   A. I and II
   B. I and IV
   C. II and III
   D. III and IV

52. The separate account funding a variable annuity that purchases shares in a mutual fund offered by the life insurance company is considered

   A. a unit investment trust
   B. a face-amount certificate company
   C. a management investment company
   D. none of the above

53. After opening an account in a mutual fund, an investor generally can make additional periodic investments in minimum amounts of

   A. $50
   B. $100
   C. $500
   D. The amount varies from fund to fund.

54. Which of the following characteristics describe stock rights?

    I. Short-term instruments that become worthless after the expiration date
    II. Most commonly offered in connection with debentures to sweeten the offering
    III. Issued by a corporation
    IV. Traded in the securities market

    A. I and II
    B. I and III
    C. I, III and IV
    D. II, III and IV

55. Ada and Angus Bullwether are tenants in common in a joint account. Which of the following statements is(are) true of this arrangement?

    I. If one of them dies, the survivor will not automatically assume full ownership.
    II. They need not have equal interest in the account.
    III. They may have a disproportionate interest in the property in the account.

    A. I only
    B. I and II only
    C. II and III only
    D. I, II and III

56. Which of the following statements is true of a prospectus for an individual variable annuity contract?

    I. It must provide full and fair disclosure.
    II. It is required by the Securities Act of 1933.
    III. It must be filed with the SEC.
    IV. It must precede or accompany every sales presentation.

    A. I only
    B. I, III and IV only
    C. II and III only
    D. I, II, III and IV

57. In a mutual fund, the amount of increases or decreases in the NAV over the past years can be reviewed in the

    A. official statement
    B. customer account form
    C. prospectus
    D. tombstone

58. The NASD's Rules of Fair Practice prohibit members from

    I. lending a client's securities without prior authorization from the client
    II. inducing a client to purchase shares of a mutual fund by implying the client will profit from a pending dividend
    III. receiving discounts in securities transactions from another member

    A. I and II only
    B. II and III only
    C. III only
    D. I, II and III

59. A broker-dealer decides to give a $300 bonus to the registered representative from any other member firm who sells the most shares in a joint sales contest. This arrangement is

    I. unacceptable
    II. acceptable if the SEC approves
    III. acceptable if the underwriter is an NASD member
    IV. acceptable as long as it is not considered compensation

    A. I
    B. I and IV
    C. II
    D. II and III

60. Which of the following statements about sales charges is(are) true?

    I. Under NASD rules, mutual fund sales charges may not exceed 8.5 percent of the offering price.
    II. Under NASD rules, mutual fund sales charges may not exceed 8.5 percent of the shares' net asset value.
    III. An investment company must offer rights of accumulation, breakpoints and reinvestment of dividends at NAV to charge an 8.5 percent sales charge.
    IV. Under the Investment Company Act of 1940, the maximum sales charge for purchases of mutual fund shares under a contractual plan is 9 percent.

    A. I
    B. I and III
    C. I, III and IV
    D. II, III and IV

61. An owner of common stock has which of the following rights?

    I. To determine when dividends will be issued
    II. To vote at stockholders' meetings or by proxy
    III. To receive a predetermined fixed portion of the corporation's profit in cash when declared
    IV. To buy restricted securities before they are offered to the public

    A. I, III and IV
    B. II
    C. II, III and IV
    D. II and IV

62. Bea Kuhl is participating in a periodic payment plan. Fifty percent of her first year's payments are taken as a sales charge. What is the maximum the sales charge can average over the life of the plan?

    A. 8.5 percent
    B. 9 percent
    C. 16 percent
    D. 20 percent

63. In a mutual fund, a shareholder who elected not to receive share certificates can liquidate all or a portion of his holdings and receive payment from the fund if the fund receives which of the following from the shareholder?

    I. Written request
    II. Signed stock power
    III. Signature guarantee

    A. I
    B. I and II
    C. I and III
    D. II and III

64. Joe receives a cold call from a registered representative, and he tells the rep he is not interested in this investment or in making any future investments. Which of the following actions is required by the Telephone Consumer Protection Act of 1991?

    A. The rep may send a letter notifying Joe of her intentions before calling again.
    B. A principal of the firm may call Joe the next time.
    C. The rep may never make cold calls again.
    D. No one at the firm may call Joe again.

65. Your firm's market analyst believes the current bullish market in equities will continue. Which of the following mutual funds would be MOST suitable for a growth-oriented investor?

    A. Bond
    B. Blue-chip stock
    C. GNMA
    D. Preferred stock

66. Contract holders must be given the right to vote on matters concerning separate account personnel at the

    A. beginning of separate account operations
    B. first meeting of contract holders within one year of beginning operations
    C. meeting of contract holders after one year of selling the first variable life policy
    D. According to federal law, contract holders cannot vote on separate account personnel.

67. A separate account funding a variable life contract is considered to be a(n)

    A. investment company issuing periodic payment plan certificates
    B. insurance company issuing periodic payment plan certificates
    C. investment company issuing variable annuity contracts
    D. fixed annuity company issuing variable payment contracts

68. Separate accounts funding a variable life contract and certain personnel working for the accounts must be registered under which of the following securities acts?

    I. Securities Act of 1933
    II. Securities Exchange Act of 1934
    III. Investment Company Act of 1940
    IV. Investment Advisers Act of 1940

    A. I, II and III only
    B. II only
    C. III and IV only
    D. I, II, III and IV

69. Adam Grizzly invests $3,000 in open-end investment company shares. After 60 days, he signs a letter of intent for a $10,000 breakpoint and backdates the letter two months. Six months later, he deposits $10,000 into the fund. He receives a reduced sales charge on

    A. the $3,000 investment only
    B. $7,000 of the investment only
    C. the $10,000 investment only
    D. the entire $13,000 investment

70. An owner of preferred stock has which of the following rights?

    I. To determine when dividends will be issued
    II. To vote at stockholders' meetings or by proxy
    III. To a predetermined fixed portion of the corporation's profit in cash when declared
    IV. To determine who sits on the board of directors

    A. I, III and IV
    B. II, III and IV
    C. II and IV
    D. III

71. Some open-end investment companies offer their investors a conversion privilege, which permits an investor to

    A. exchange general securities for shares in a mutual fund's portfolio
    B. delay payment of taxes on investment company shares that have appreciated in value
    C. purchase additional fund shares from dividends paid by the fund
    D. exchange shares of one mutual fund for those of another fund under the same management, at net asset value

72. Which of the following would be eligible for membership in the NASD?

    A. Bank organized under state and federal laws
    B. Closed-end investment company
    C. Broker or dealer whose regular course of business consists of transactions in securities or the investment banking business
    D. All of the above

73. Joe Kuhl uses the FIFO method to determine his capital gains. What does this mean?

    A. The IRS will assume a liquidation of the first shares Joe acquired.
    B. Joe will indicate the specific shares that he redeemed without regard to when he purchased them.
    C. The last shares purchased are the first shares to be redeemed.
    D. None of the above applies in this case.

74. Tex Longhorn is about to buy a variable annuity contract. He wants to select an annuity that will give him the largest possible monthly payment. Which of the following payout options would do so?

    A. Life annuity with period certain
    B. Unit refund life option
    C. Life annuity with 10-year period certain
    D. Life only annuity

75. Porter Stout has $350,000 in securities and $201,000 in cash with his brokerage firm. If the brokerage firm were forced to liquidate, how much of the account would SIPC cover?

    A. $250,000 of the securities and all of the cash
    B. All of the securities and $150,000 of the cash
    C. All of the securities and $100,000 of the cash
    D. All of the cash and $299,000 of the securities

76. If a customer submits a sell order to his broker-dealer after the close of the New York Stock Exchange, the customer receives a price based on the net asset value computed

    A. the previous business day
    B. the same day regardless of when the order is received
    C. the next time the fund computes it
    D. within the next two business days

77. Hugh Heifer originally invested $20,000 into the ACE Fund and has reinvested dividends and gains of $8,000. His shares in ACE are now worth $40,000. He converts his investment in ACE to the ATF Fund, which is under the same management as ACE. In this case, which of the following statements is true?

    A. He retains his cost basis of $28,000 in the ATF Fund.
    B. He must declare $12,000 as a taxable gain upon conversion into the ATF Fund.
    C. He retains a $20,000 cost basis in the ATF Fund because of the conversion privilege.
    D. He is not liable for taxes in the current year because he did not have constructive receipt of the money at conversion.

78. Which of the following ALFA Enterprises securities is MOST affected by a change in ALFA's earnings?

    A. 10 percent debentures maturing in 10 years
    B. 6 percent preferred stock
    C. Common stock
    D. Treasury stock

79. Chip Bullock is the sole owner of a business. He earns $160,000 a year and makes the maximum contribution to a defined benefit Keogh plan. How much money may he contribute to his IRA?

    A. $0
    B. $2,000
    C. $15,000
    D. $30,000

80. The Securities Exchange Act of 1934 does which of the following?

    I. Requires registration of securities
    II. Requires registration of broker-dealers with the SEC
    III. Prohibits inequitable and unfair trade practices
    IV. Provides for regulation of the over-the-counter market

    A. I only
    B. II and III only
    C. II, III and IV only
    D. I, II, III and IV

81. A no-load fund sells its shares to the public

    A. through a network of underwriters and dealers
    B. through a dealer and its sales representatives
    C. by underwriter only
    D. by a direct sale from the fund to the investor

82. Gordy Guernsey owns a variable annuity contract, and the AIR stated in the contract is 5 percent. In January, the realized rate of return in the separate account was 7 percent, and Gordy received a check based on this return for $200. In February, the rate of return was 10 percent, and Gordy received a check for $210. To maintain the same payment Gordy received in February, what rate of return would the separate account have to earn in March?

    A. 3 percent
    B. 5 percent
    C. 7 percent
    D. 10 percent

83. Which of the following statements about sales literature for a mutual fund is(are) true?

    I. The material used to solicit the sale of mutual fund shares may require approval by a principal of the firm.
    II. The NASD must approve all mutual fund sales literature within three days of its first use.
    III. If the mutual fund sponsor has had the literature reviewed by the NASD in advance, the firm requires no further approvals.

    A. I and III only
    B. II only
    C. III only
    D. I, II and III

84. When would an investor be liable for tax on reinvested distributions from an open-end investment company?

    A. When she sells the shares purchased from the distribution
    B. When she has held the shares purchased with the distribution for 12 months
    C. At the time the distribution is made
    D. None of the above

85. According to the NASD Rules of Fair Practice, a member firm may give certain selling concessions to

    A. the general public
    B. other NASD member firms
    C. nonmember broker-dealers
    D. all of the above

86. An investor who owns shares of a mutual fund actually owns

    A. an undivided interest in the fund's debt capitalization
    B. specific shares of stock in the fund's portfolio
    C. an undivided interest in the fund's portfolio
    D. certain unspecified securities among those owned by the fund

87. A 6¼ percent municipal bond has a yield to maturity of 6¾ percent. From this information, it can be determined that the municipal bond is trading

    A. flat
    B. at par
    C. at a discount
    D. at a premium

88. The Securities Act of 1933 requires that which of the following be offered only by prospectus?

    I. Treasury bonds
    II. Mutual fund shares
    III. Variable annuities
    IV. Unit investment trusts

    A. I and II
    B. II and III
    C. II, III and IV
    D. III and IV

89. A customer decides to buy shares of an open-end investment company. When is the price of the shares determined?

    A. At the next calculation of net asset value the day the fund custodian receives proper notification from the customer
    B. At the next calculation of net asset value the day the broker-dealer wires the fund's underwriter on behalf of the customer
    C. Both A and B
    D. Neither A nor B

90. ACE Fund has prepared a piece of sales literature to be distributed to individuals who respond to ACE's tombstone ad. If the fund sends the literature to a prospect, which of the following statements is true of the material?

    A. It must contain directions for obtaining a prospectus.
    B. It must include the good points contained in the prospectus.
    C. It must contain the SEC disclaimer.
    D. It must be accompanied by a prospectus.

91. Which of the following characteristics describes a hot issue?

    A. Offered below the market price
    B. Offered above the market price
    C. Begins to trade above the initial offering price
    D. Begins to trade below the initial offering price

92. Your customer tells you he wants a source of retirement income that is stable, but that also could offer some protection against purchasing power risk in times of inflation. You should recommend

    A. a variable annuity
    B. a fixed annuity
    C. a combination annuity
    D. common stocks and municipal bonds

93. Which of the following characteristics describes a prospectus?

   A. Complies with the full and fair disclosure requirements of the Securities Act of 1933
   B. Used to solicit indications of interest in a new issue
   C. Filed with the SEC and not available to the general public
   D. Filed with the SEC semiannually

94. Which of the following must be paid before a corporation can offer a cash common stock dividend?

   I. Straight preferred stock dividends
   II. Bond interest
   III. Cumulative preferred stock dividend arrearages
   IV. Callable preferred stock dividends

   A. I only
   B. II only
   C. I, III and IV only
   D. I, II, III and IV

95. Which type of nonmarketable security pays semiannual interest?

   A. Series EE bonds
   B. Treasury bonds
   C. Series HH bonds
   D. Agency issues

96. Which of the following statements about a straight life variable annuity is(are) true?

   I. The number of annuity units a client redeems never changes.
   II. The number of accumulation units a client owns never changes.
   III. If the client dies during the annuity period, the remaining funds are distributed to the beneficiary.
   IV. The monthly payout is fixed to the Consumer Price Index.

   A. I
   B. I and II
   C. I, II and III
   D. II, III and IV

97. The Investment Company Act of 1940 requires that mutual funds pay dividends from their

   A. capital gains
   B. net income
   C. gross income
   D. portfolio earnings

98. Tex Longhorn is 61 years old. He would like to take a lump-sum distribution from his Keogh plan. What would be the tax treatment of this distribution?

   A. Eligible for five-year income averaging
   B. Taxed at long-term capital gains rates
   C. 10 percent penalty
   D. 50 percent penalty

99. An NASD broker-dealer trading in shares of an open-end investment company cannot buy shares of the fund

   A. to cover existing orders
   B. for the firm's own investment purposes
   C. at a discount
   D. for the purpose of resale at a later date

100. Which of the following has the authority to approve an investment adviser's contract with the investment company?

   A. NASD District Business Conduct Committee
   B. Board of directors of the fund
   C. Board of Governors of the NASD
   D. SEC

Answers & Rationale

1. **D.** A registered security is one whose owner is designated on records maintained for this purpose. Even though T bills are book-entry securities and no certificates are issued, ownership records are maintained and, therefore, they are considered registered. (Page 36)

2. **B.** A bond purchased at a premium is purchased for an amount greater than the face amount of the bond at maturity. The premium paid reduces the yield of the bond if held until maturity. (Page 28)

3. **A.** The Bullocks are almost entirely invested in the stock market. As they approach retirement, they should shift some of their portfolio to bonds. Because they are in a high tax bracket, a municipal bond fund best meets their objectives of diversification and safety. (Page 95)

4. **C.** When a dealer holds securities for its own account, it is considered to be taking a position. (Page 55)

5. **C.** Growth and income funds invest in common stocks, preferred stocks, convertible securities and high-yielding bonds. (Page 94)

6. **C.** In a discretionary account, a representative has been given authority to select the amount and type of investment for a client. The authorization must be written. (Page 118)

7. **C.** Rhoda and Randy Bear are preparing to make a major purchase within the next few months. They require a highly liquid investment to keep their money safe for a short amount of time. The money-market fund best matches this objective. (Page 96)

8. **C.** Even though an investment in a Treasury STRIPS does not yield a regular cash flow, paying all of its interest at maturity, the difference between the purchase price and the mature value is still taxed as ordinary income and must be accrued on a yearly basis. (Page 38)

9. **B.** Closed-end investment company shares are traded in the secondary marketplace (OTC or exchange). Therefore, shares are purchased from other shareholders through broker-dealers. Closed-end funds, unlike open-end funds, cannot issue shares directly to shareholders. (Page 82)

10. **B.** Cost of insurance and mortality and expense risk fees are deducted from the separate account. Sales loads and premium taxes are deducted from the premium. (Page 147)

11. **C.** Adam Grizzly is a young investor at the beginning of his earnings cycle. For other investors in his situation, an aggressive growth fund might help achieve maximum capital appreciation over a long-term time frame. However, Adam is risk averse and has not had any experience with investing in the securities markets. A balanced fund is a good place to begin investing for high total return and low volatility. (Page 94)

12. **B.** An investor purchasing shares on the record date becomes a shareholder of record and is entitled to the dividend declared. Orders received after the pricing of shares or the record date would be processed the next day and would purchase shares ex-dividend. (Page 108)

13. **A.** The mortgages underlying GNMA modified pass-through certificates pay interest on a monthly basis. The GNMA then passes this monthly income through to investors in GNMA pass-through certificates. (Page 39)

14. **A.** Open- and closed-end funds are classified as investment companies. Plan companies offer plans in which an investment company may be selected as an investment vehicle, but they are not investment companies themselves. Only insurance companies offer fixed annuities. (Page 82)

15. **C.** Contributions to a qualified annuity are taxable when withdrawn at ordinary income tax

rates. Because, in this case, the teacher withdraws $15,000, that amount is subject to tax. Thirty percent of $15,000 equals a tax liability of $4,500.
(Page 162)

16. **D.** All of the factors listed affect a convertible bond's price. The rating of a bond reflects the issuing company's health and, therefore, indirectly affects the value of the investment.
(Page 33)

17. **B.** Open-end company shares are bought and sold from the investment company.
(Page 82)

18. **C.** Fluctuations in interest rates may affect a bond's price, but will not affect the income payable from the bond. The percentage interest payable for use of money is stated on the face of a bond and is part of the bond indenture, a legal obligation on the part of the issuing company.
(Page 20)

19. **A.** When the minor reaches the age of maturity, proceeds must be handed over to the child (donee) under the terms of the Uniform Gifts to Minors Act.
(Page 120)

20. **B.** Shareholders have a right to vote on such items as mergers, reorganizations, recapitalizations and stock splits.
(Page 5)

21. **A.** The federal funds rate is the rate of interest at which member banks of the Federal Reserve System borrow excess funds from other members, usually on an overnight basis.
(Page 64)

22. **A.** A banker's acceptance is a time draft typically used to facilitate an overseas trading venture. It is guaranteed by a bank on behalf of a corporation in payment for goods or services.
(Page 46)

23. **B.** A warrant is a purchase option for stock for a long period of time. The warrant allows the holder to purchase common stock for a set price. Rights and options have short lives.
(Page 17)

24. **D.** A fixed-dollar plan is the only type of plan that fixes a definite dollar payment.
(Page 125)

25. **D.** Sales literature is any public solicitation concerning securities.
(Page 189)

26. **B.** The NASD Board of Governors may censure, suspend or expel a member or a person associated with a member. It has no jurisdiction over the exchanges and cannot prohibit any person from associating with them.
(Page 205)

27. **C.** Money-market funds have no price volatility; the rate of interest on money-market funds fluctuates in conjunction with that on the instruments underlying the original money-market certificates.
(Page 96)

28. **B.** Because the funds are under separate management, the load charged on each separate investment will most likely be at the maximum. If the customer invests the entire sum within one fund or a family of funds, a reduced sales charge may be available.
(Page 103)

29. **B.** By investing a predetermined amount of money periodically for a long period of time, the investor uses the concept of *dollar cost averaging*. The result is to reduce the cost per share compared to the average market price.
(Page 122)

30. **C.** Use of discretionary authority does not violate the Rules of Fair Practice, but abuse of that authority by excessive trading and the misuse of a customer's funds or securities is. Choices A, B and D are clear violations. Recommendations should be based on the customer's financial status and objectives. Low-priced stocks may result in a higher percentage of commission. Brokers that make a practice of selling low-priced stocks are often called *penny brokers*.
(Page 201)

31. **B.** Because the investor held the bond fund shares for less than 12 months, the gain is short term. An exchange privilege does not exempt the transfer of funds from taxation. The exchange is a taxable event.
(Page 109)

32. **B.** Any complaint charging that a member firm or an associated person violated one or more of the NASD's rules is handled under the Code of Procedure. Complaints, which charge that specific rules were violated, should not be confused with disputes, which tend to deal more with business ethics, failures to perform and misunderstandings. Disputes are submitted for resolution under the NASD's Code of Arbitration.   (Page 204)

33. **D.** Municipalities issue IDRs to construct a facility that will be used by, or is being constructed for the benefit of, a corporation. When this is done, the corporation must sign a long-term lease. Although classified as municipal securities, IDRs are backed by the revenues of the corporation participating in the project.   (Page 45)

34. **B.** Bond ratings are credit ratings for an issuer. They measure the issuer's ability to repay principal and interest.   (Page 23)

35. **B.** When an employee opens an account with another member, the executing member notifies the employee that it will inform the employing member that the account is to be opened, and copies of confirmations and other reports will be available upon request. (Page 116)

36. **B.** The purpose of the FOMC purchase is to increase the attractiveness of the market price of T bills. Because the price will be driven up by an increased market demand and a decreased supply, yields should decrease.   (Page 65)

37. **C.** STRIPS are special bonds issued by the Treasury department and split into individual principal and interest payments, which are then resold in the form of zero-coupon bonds. Because zeros pay no interest, an investor realizes gains in the form of increased basis as a bond matures and receives no income payments to reinvest.
(Page 38)

38. **D.** Distributions from a profit-sharing plan are made from the individual's account, reflecting the accrued amount of contributions and earnings on the contributions. Contributions to the plan normally are based on a predetermined percentage of profits.   (Page 164)

39. **C.** Interest in the form of dividends paid from a municipal bond fund would be exempt from federal income tax. Gains from the sale of portfolio securities would be subject to ordinary income tax.   (Page 95)

40. **A.** Because the dividend rate decreased at a rate less than the stock's market value, the current yield will be greater.   (Page 11)

41. **B.** The accumulation unit will increase in value because the portfolio earned 4 percent; however, the annuity unit's value will decrease because the portfolio's actual return of 4 percent was less than the assumed interest rate of 5 percent necessary to maintain payments.
(Page 141)

42. **A.** To qualify as a regulated investment company, at least 90 percent of net investment income (without regard to gains) must be distributed. Net investment income equals dividend income ($2,000 in this case) plus interest income ($900) minus expenses ($900), to equal $2,000. Ninety percent of $2,000 is $1,800.   (Page 107)

43. **C.** Contributions to a nonqualified annuity are made after taxes. The annuity's growth is deferred, representing ordinary income when withdrawn. Cost basis is $10,000.   (Page 143)

44. **A.** Contributions to a tax-qualified annuity are made before taxes. The growth is deferred. Mrs. Polar has no cost basis in this question. The entire $16,000 will be taxed as ordinary income.
(Page 162)

45. **D.** Interest on Series EE bonds is received at redemption of the bonds.   (Page 38)

46. **A.** Scheduled payment VLI contracts have fixed premiums and payment periods. (Page 145)

47. **C.** In the annuity stage of a variable annuity, the amount received depends on the account performance compared to the assumed interest

rate. If actual performance is less than the AIR, the payout's value declines. (Page 141)

48. **C.** In a private securities transaction, the representative must obtain permission for the sale from his broker-dealer before the transaction. The transaction must be through the broker-dealer's books, and any information the broker-dealer requests must be supplied. The broker-dealer is still responsible for the representative's actions in this private transaction. (Page 200)

49. **B.** The expense ratio includes the expenses of operating the fund compared to fund assets. Expenses included in the ratio are management fees, administrative fees, brokerage fees and taxes. (Page 97)

50. **A.** A mutual fund's current yield is current income ($.30 dividend in this case) divided by the net asset value ($6.50). Gains are not included in calculation of current yield; they are accounted for separately. (Page 108)

51. **D.** Expenses are deducted from the benefit base (cash value) for both scheduled and flexible premium VLI contracts. (Page 147)

52. **A.** A separate account purchasing shares of mutual funds to fund variable contracts does not actively manage the securities held; instead, the account holds the shares in trust for the contract holders. This account is classified as a unit investment trust under the act of 1940. (Page 136)

53. **D.** Minimum amounts differ from fund to fund, and a registered rep must refer to the prospectus for each fund. (Page 92)

54. **C.** A corporation issues rights allowing subscribers to purchase stock within a short period of time at a reduced price from the stock's current market price. The right does not have to be exercised, but may be traded in the secondary market. Warrants are commonly used as sweeteners in debenture offerings. (Page 16)

55. **D.** Under tenants in common, owners may have fractional interests in the undivided owner-

ship of an asset. The interest passes to the decedent's estate at death, unlike JTWROS, wherein the survivor succeeds to the interest. (Page 117)

56. **D.** A variable annuity is a security and, therefore, must be registered with the SEC. As part of the registration requirements, a prospectus must be filed and distributed to a prospective investor before or during any solicitation for sale. (Page 137)

57. **C.** Changes in NAV are found in the prospectus for at least 10 years if the fund has existed that long. (Page 90)

58. **A.** The Rules of Fair Practice prohibit unauthorized borrowing (theft) and selling of dividends. Discounts to other NASD members are allowed if a dealer agreement has been signed. (Page 202)

59. **A.** Gifts exceeding $100 per person per year are not allowed. (Page 201)

60. **C.** The NASD limits sales charges to 8.5 percent of the POP as a maximum. If the fund does not allow for breakpoints, reinvestment of dividends at net or rights of accumulation, the maximum is less than 8.5 percent. Under the Investment Company Act of 1940, the maximum sales charge on mutual funds is deferred to the NASD rules, while a contractual plan specifically may charge 9 percent over the life of the plan. (Page 100)

61. **B.** The stockholder has the right to vote and the right to dividends if and when declared (although not to a fixed dividend). A restricted security has prescribed limits on resale generally requiring registration. (Page 5)

62. **B.** The maximum sales charge on a contractual plan, whether front-end load or spread load, is 9 percent over the life of the plan. (Page 123)

63. **C.** An order for redemption without a certificate being issued requires a written request and a signature guarantee. A signed stock power

would be required if the shareholder had possession of the mutual fund certificates.   (Page 106)

64. **D.** Under the provisions of the Telephone Consumer Protection Act of 1991, Joe's name must be placed on the firm's do-not-call list, and no one at the firm may call him again. (Page 197)

65. **B.** Blue-chip stocks are equity securities that should increase in value when the overall stock market rises. The other choices are fixed-income securities.   (Page 94)

66. **B.** Contract holders must be given the right to vote on company personnel (directors, adviser, custodian, etc.) at the first meeting held within one year of the start of operations.   (Page 149)

67. **A.** The Investment Company Act of 1940 defines an insurance company offering VLI contracts as an investment company offering periodic payment plan certificates. The separate account may be organized as either an open-end investment company or a unit investment trust.
(Page 145)

68. **D.** Companies offering VLI contracts must register under the Investment Company Act of 1940; the VLI contracts must be registered under the Securities Act of 1933; representatives selling the contracts must register under the Securities Exchange Act of 1934; and the adviser managing the separate account must register under the Investment Advisers Act of 1940.   (Page 143)

69. **D.** The entire investment qualifies for the reduced load. A letter of intent covers purchases within a 13-month period and may be backdated 90 days. Adam Grizzly actually had 11 months in which to make the additional investment.
(Page 104)

70. **D.** The preferred stockholder generally has no right to vote, but carries a prior right to dividends if and when declared. A restricted security has prescribed limits on resale generally requiring registration.   (Page 8)

71. **D.** The exchange, or conversion, privilege allows an investor to exchange shares of one fund for those of another fund under the same management without paying an additional sales charge (although the exchange is still a taxable event).
(Page 105)

72. **C.** Broker-dealers in the securities business may become members; banks cannot. A closed-end fund is an investment company, not a broker-dealer.   (Page 182)

73. **A.** FIFO means "first in, first out." Choice C describes LIFO (last in, first out); choice B describes share identification.   (Page 110)

74. **D.** Generally, a life only contract pays the most per month because payments cease at the death of the annuitant.   (Page 140)

75. **C.** SIPC covers cash and securities up to $500,000, but only $100,000 in cash.   (Page 179)

76. **C.** Orders to redeem shares are executed at the next computed price.   (Page 99)

77. **B.** The exchange privilege offers exchange without an additional sales charge, but the exchange is still taxable. Hugh is taxed on the gain of $12,000 ($40,000 – $28,000).   (Page 105)

78. **C.** Changes in earnings strongly affect common stock prices.   (Page 8)

79. **B.** The maximum contribution is the lesser of 100 percent earned income or $2,000.
(Page 152)

80. **C.** The Securities Act of 1933 (paper act) requires registration of securities. To prevent manipulative and deceptive practices, the act of 1934 (people act) requires registration of people and exchanges transacting securities business. The NASD is the SRO of the OTC market, but the SEC has final authority.   (Page 176)

81. **D.** Because there is no load, there is no underwriter. The fund sells directly to the public.
(Page 99)

82. **B.**   If the actual rate of return equals the assumed interest rate, the check will stay the same. Recall that the payout is based on an accumulated value to be distributed over the life of the annuitant (like compounding). Therefore, for Gordy to receive the $210 in March, the account must earn 5 percent.   (Page 141)

83. **A.**   A firm's principal must approve sales literature before use. If the NASD has reviewed the literature, it need not be submitted by every broker-dealer intending to use it.   (Page 191)

84. **C.**   Reinvested income and gains distributions are taxable in the year they are received.   (Page 109)

85. **B.**   Members may give other members concessions, but must deal with the public and non-members at the public offering price.   (Page 99)

86. **C.**   Each shareholder owns an undivided (mutual) interest in the mutual fund's portfolio.   (Page 92)

87. **C.**   The YTM is greater than the nominal yield, meaning the price must be less than par. The bond is selling at a discount.   (Page 28)

88. **C.**   Treasury securities are exempt from registration requirements, as are municipal issues, and do not require a prospectus.   (Page 171)

89. **C.**   The price for mutual fund shares is the next price calculated by the fund after receiving the request.   (Page 99)

90. **D.**   Any solicitation requires a prospectus to be delivered before or during the solicitation. (Sales literature is solicitation.)   (Page 190)

91. **C.**   A hot issue is a new issue of common stock that begins to trade in the secondary market at an immediate premium to the initial offering price.   (Page 175)

92. **C.**   Because the investor wants the objectives provided by both a fixed and a variable annuity, a combination annuity would be suitable.   (Page 138)

93. **A.**   A prospectus is a disclosure document that reveals material information about the issuer to the SEC and the public.   (Page 171)

94. **D.**   A corporation must pay interest to its bondholders and dividends to its preferred stockholders before it may pay a dividend to common stockholders.   (Page 8)

95. **C.**   Series EE bonds are sold at a discount and mature to face value; T bonds and agency issues are marketable debt. HH bonds are nonmarketable and pay interest semiannually.   (Page 38)

96. **A.**   Annuity units are fixed; their current value, when cashed in, determines the payout amount. A life only annuity ceases payments at the death of the annuitant. The company keeps any undistributed payments. Accumulation units fluctuate in value and number during the accumulation period.   (Page 140)

97. **B.**   Dividends are paid from net income (interest plus dividends plus short-term gains, when identified minus expenses).   (Page 107)

98. **A.**   The distribution would be taxed as ordinary income, but would also qualify for five-year income averaging (TRA 1986). A 10 percent penalty would apply if Tex were younger than age 59½; the 50 percent penalty would apply if he did not take the distribution according to his life expectancy by April 1st of the year following the year he turned 70½.   (Page 158)

99. **D.**   A broker-dealer may purchase shares only to fulfill existing orders or for its own investment account, not for inventory.   (Page 90)

100. **B.**   The investment adviser's contract is approved by the fund's board of directors and often a majority vote of the outstanding fund shares. An investment adviser must be *registered* with the SEC, not *approved* by the Commission.   (Page 88)

51

Final Exam Two

1. Max Leveridge is a retired widower, age 72, seeking a moderate level of current income to supplement his Social Security benefits and his company pension plan. Max is a Depression-era grandfather of six, with a very conservative attitude toward investments. An equally important investment goal for him is capital preservation. Which of the following mutual funds is the MOST suitable for Max?

   A. ZBEST Government Income Fund
   B. ArGood Balanced Fund
   C. ACE Equity Income Fund
   D. ArGood Investment-grade Bond Fund

2. An individual purchasing a flexible premium variable life contract should know that the

   I. premiums are discretionary as to timing and amount
   II. death benefit may equal the contract's face amount
   III. death benefit may equal the contract's face amount plus cash value
   IV. performance of the separate account directly affects the policy's cash value and duration

   A. I, II and III only
   B. I, III and IV only
   C. IV only
   D. I, II, III and IV

3. What is(are) a respondent's responsibilities when the party learns that it is involved in an arbitration dispute?

 I. The respondent must file the appropriate forms with the Director of Arbitration within 20 calendar days of the receipt of service.

 II. In its answer, the respondent must put forth all defenses to the statement of claim.

 III. The respondent may set forth a counterclaim, if any, against the initiating party or a third party.

 A. I only
 B. I and II only
 C. III only
 D. I, II and III

4. Which of the following characteristics describe T bills?

 I. Issued at face value
 II. Issued at a discount
 III. Pay semiannual interest
 IV. Pay all interest upon maturity

 A. I and III
 B. I and IV
 C. II and III
 D. II and IV

5. A stock's market value is determined by which of the following?

 A. Board of directors
 B. What individuals will pay for it
 C. Vote of the stockholders
 D. Company's financial condition

6. Which of the following Treasury securities allows an investor to lock in a yield for an extended period of time by minimizing reinvestment risk?

 A. Treasury bill
 B. Treasury STRIP
 C. Treasury bond
 D. Treasury note

7. Which of the following debt instruments pays NO interest?

 A. STRIP
 B. T note
 C. T bond
 D. T stock

8. A mutual fund previously invested in bonds with medium-length maturities. As the bonds matured, the fund reinvested the proceeds and purchased long-term bonds with maturities of up to 20 years. What would have happened to the fund if the reinvestment had occurred during a period when interest rates were rising?

 I. Decrease in yield
 II. Decrease in income
 III. Increase in yield
 IV. Increase in income

 A. I and II
 B. I and IV
 C. II and III
 D. III and IV

9. A company that has paid its common stockholders a dividend would be required to also have made distributions to which of the other securities issued by the company?

 I. Bonds
 II. Convertible bonds
 III. Preferred stock
 IV. Convertible preferred stock

 A. I and II only
 B. I and III only
 C. II and III only
 D. I, II, III and IV

10. Which of the following corporate bonds is usually backed by other investment securities?

 A. Mortgage bond
 B. Equipment trust certificate
 C. Collateral trust bond
 D. Debenture

11. Which of the following would be the best time for an investor to purchase long-term fixed-interest-rate bonds?

    A. When short-term interest rates are high and are beginning to decline
    B. When short-term interest rates are low and are beginning to rise
    C. When long-term interest rates are low and are beginning to rise
    D. When long-term interest rates are high and are beginning to decline

12. If not appealed to the Board of Governors, a District Business Conduct Committee's findings become effective

    A. immediately
    B. only after review by the SEC
    C. no sooner than 10 days from the date of the decision
    D. no sooner than 45 days from the date of the decision

13. Interest rates have been rising for the past few days. What has happened to the price of bonds traded in the bond market during this time?

    A. Increased
    B. Decreased
    C. Stayed the same
    D. Bond prices are not affected by interest rates.

14. Which of the following funds would provide high appreciation potential together with high risk?

    A. Balanced
    B. Bond
    C. Income
    D. Sector

15. In a period of deflation, corporate bond prices do which of the following?

    A. Increase
    B. Decrease
    C. Stay the same
    D. Fluctuate

16. The formula used to determine the tax-equivalent yield between a taxable and a nontaxable bond and to compare corporate return with municipal return is

    A. nominal yield divided by 100 percent minus the investor's tax bracket
    B. nominal yield plus 100 percent minus the investor's tax bracket
    C. nominal yield multiplied by 100 percent minus the investor's tax bracket
    D. nominal yield minus 100 percent minus the investor's tax bracket

17. The interest from which of the following bonds is exempt from federal income tax?

    I. State of California
    II. City of Anchorage
    III. Treasury
    IV. GNMA

    A. I and II only
    B. I, II and IV only
    C. III and IV only
    D. I, II, III and IV

18. Your customers would like to have $40,000 set aside when their child starts college, but do not want to invest in anything that could endanger their principal. In this situation, you should recommend

    A. zero-coupon bonds or Treasury STRIPS
    B. corporate bonds with high rates of interest payment
    C. municipal bonds for their long-term tax benefits
    D. Treasury bills

19. Which of the following are money-market instruments?

    I. Bankers' acceptances
    II. Treasury bills
    III. Commercial paper
    IV. Treasury bonds maturing in six months

    A. I and II only
    B. I, II and III only
    C. III and IV only
    D. I, II, III and IV

20. A fund seeks to duplicate the price and yield performance of Standard & Poor's composite index of 500 stocks. The fund invests in each of the index's 500 stocks in approximately the same proportion as the composition of the index. The portfolio is not actively traded and, therefore, features a low turnover ratio. This information describes which of the following mutual funds?

   A. ATF Biotechnology Fund
   B. ZBEST Asset Allocation Fund
   C. NavCo Cash Reserves Money-Market Fund
   D. ArGood Stock Index Fund

21. The annuity unit of a variable annuity changes in value in a manner that corresponds most closely to changes in which of the following?

   I. Dow Jones Index
   II. Cost of living index
   III. Value of securities the insurance company holds
   IV. Value of securities kept in a separate account

   A. I and III only
   B. I, III and IV only
   C. IV only
   D. I, II, III and IV

22. Which of the following may be purchased for the portfolio of a long-term municipal bond fund?

   I. Common stock
   II. Corporate bonds
   III. Preferred stock
   IV. Long-term municipal bonds

   A. I and II
   B. I and IV
   C. II and III
   D. IV

23. Banks pay the federal funds rate for

   A. short-term bank loans from the government
   B. loans offered by major New York City banks
   C. loans from other banks
   D. loans from broker-dealers

24. The over-the-counter market could be characterized as what type of market?

   A. Auction
   B. Double-auction
   C. Negotiated
   D. None of the above

25. The ex-dividend date is which of the following?

   I. Date on and after which the buyer is entitled to the dividend
   II. Date on and after which the seller is entitled to the dividend
   III. Second business day before the record date
   IV. Second business day after the record date

   A. I and III
   B. I and IV
   C. II and III
   D. II and IV

26. Geographic diversification of municipal securities investments protects against all of the following EXCEPT

   A. adverse legislation in a certain area
   B. economic decline in a certain area
   C. a change in interest rates
   D. default by a particular issuer

27. August Polar has $800 to invest in the Amusement Technology Fund. If the shares are currently priced at $21.22 each, August can purchase how many shares?

   A. None because the minimum trading unit is 100 shares
   B. 37, with $14.85 in change
   C. 37.7
   D. 38

28. When examining a diversified common stock fund's portfolio, you would MOST likely find

   A. all growth stocks within one particular industry
   B. stocks of many companies within many industries
   C. mostly convertible bonds and other debt instruments
   D. There is no telling what you would find.

29. 12b-1 fees can be used to pay all of the following EXCEPT

   A. advertising costs
   B. commissions on portfolio securities transactions
   C. mailing expenses
   D. prospectus printing costs

30. Which of the following statements are true concerning a flexible premium contract?

   I. The contract holder determines premium amounts.
   II. The contract holder determines the death benefit.
   III. Cash value is affected by separate account performance.
   IV. The contract may lapse due to insufficient cash value.

   A. I and II only
   B. I, II and III only
   C. III and IV only
   D. I, II, III and IV

31. Wall Street closely monitors Federal Open Market Committee activities because of the effect of the FOMC's decisions on all of the following EXCEPT

   A. money supply
   B. interest rates
   C. exchange rates
   D. money velocity

32. Which of the following statements describes a balanced fund?

   A. It has some portion of its portfolio invested in both debt and equity instruments at all times.
   B. It has equal amounts of common stock and corporate bonds at all times.
   C. It normally has equal amounts of common and preferred stock at all times.
   D. None of the above statements is true.

33. All of the following are advantages of mutual fund investment EXCEPT

   A. the investor's personal control over her investment in the fund portfolio
   B. exchange privileges within a family of funds managed by the same management company
   C. the ability to invest almost any amount at any time
   D. the ability to qualify for reduced sales loads based on accumulation of investment within the fund

34. According to the Investment Company Act of 1940, which of the following statements are true?

   I. A company must have $1 million in assets before it may begin operations.
   II. At least 40 percent of a board of directors must be noninterested persons.
   III. A fund must have at least 100 shareholders.
   IV. A fund may not borrow more than 33⅓ percent of its asset value.

   A. I and III only
   B. II, III and IV only
   C. II and IV only
   D. I, II, III and IV

35. An investor in the 28 percent tax bracket has a $5,000 loss after netting all capital gains and losses realized. How much may the investor deduct from income this year?

   A. $0
   B. $2,500
   C. $3,000
   D. $5,000

36. Which of the following statements is true of an open-end investment company's NAV?

   I. It is calculated seven days a week.
   II. It is calculated as stipulated in the prospectus.
   III. It takes into account cash the fund holds, but has not invested.
   IV. When divided by the number of shares outstanding, it equals the net asset value per share.

   A. I and IV
   B. II, III and IV
   C. III
   D. IV

37. A mutual fund's net asset value per share fluctuates relative to the

   A. value of the fund's portfolio
   B. law of supply and demand
   C. number of shareholders
   D. S&P 500 market index

38. Which of the following statements is true of net asset value per share?

   I. It increases if the fund's assets appreciate in value.
   II. It decreases if the fund distributes a dividend to shareholders.
   III. It decreases when shares are redeemed.
   IV. It increases if shareholders reinvest dividend and capital gains distributions.

   A. I and II
   B. I and III
   C. II and III
   D. II and IV

39. Grandpa Leveridge is in the 28 percent tax bracket. He opens an UGMA for his granddaughter Minnie. Minnie's mother Lotta is in the 30 percent tax bracket. When Minnie reaches the age of majority, the account will be taxed at which of the following rates?

   A. 28 percent
   B. 30 percent
   C. Minnie's parents' joint rate
   D. Minnie's rate

40. Which of the following characteristics describes secondary distribution?

   A. Accomplished without an investment banker
   B. Used to achieve a better price than the current market
   C. Method of redistributing a large block of stock without significantly affecting the market price
   D. New issue of stock or bonds being offered by a "second tier" company

41. A mutual fund's net asset value is $9.30. If its sales charge is 7 percent, its offering price is

   A. $9.95
   B. $9.97
   C. $10.00
   D. $10.70

42. If a mutual fund levies an 8½ percent sales charge, the fund must offer all of the following EXCEPT

   A. exchange privileges
   B. breakpoints
   C. rights of accumulation
   D. dividend reinvestment at NAV

43. If an investment company offers rights of accumulation and an investor wishes to get a reduced sales charge, the client must deposit sufficient funds within

   A. 45 days
   B. 13 months
   C. There is no time limit.
   D. Each fund has its own requirements.

44. Amusement Technology Fund permits rights of accumulation. Max Leveridge has invested $9,000 and has signed a letter of intent for a $15,000 investment. His reinvested dividends during the 13 months total $720. How much money must Max contribute to fulfill the letter of intent?

   A. $5,280
   B. $6,000
   C. $9,000
   D. $15,000

45. You have decided to buy 100 shares of ACE Fund, which prices its shares at 5:00 p.m. every business day. You turn in your order at 3:00 p.m., when the shares are priced at $10 NAV, $10.86 POP. The sales load is 7.9 percent. What will your 100 shares cost?

   A. $1,000
   B. $1,079
   C. $1,086
   D. 100 times the offering price, which will be calculated at 5:00 p.m.

46. Which of the following affect(s) the cash value of a variable life insurance contract?

   I. Policy loans
   II. Halt in premium payments
   III. Decline in the separate account value
   IV. Mortality risk fee

   A. I only
   B. I and II only
   C. III only
   D. I, II, III and IV

47. Hugh Heifer wants to redeem 1,000 shares of ACE Fund. Hugh submits his request for redemption, which ACE receives at noon. ACE prices its shares at the close of the NYSE each day, at which time the shares are priced at $12.50 NAV, $13.50 ask. ACE also charges a 1 percent redemption fee. Hugh receives what amount for his shares?

   A. $12,375
   B. $12,500
   C. $13,365
   D. $13,500

48. The ex-dividend date for mutual fund shares is

   A. seven days before the record date
   B. two business days before the record date
   C. the same day as the record date
   D. the day following the record date

49. Klaus Bruin buys shares of ZBest Invest Mutual Fund shortly before the ex-dividend date. Before he buys the shares, Klaus should understand that

   A. the price of the shares will decline on the ex-dividend date by the amount of the distribution
   B. if he reinvests the dividend, he will not be liable for taxes on the dividend received
   C. there is a great advantage to his purchasing the shares immediately so that he can receive the dividend
   D. all of the above may be true

50. Which of the following makes up the net investment income of an open-end investment company?

    A. Net gains on sales of securities
    B. Dividends, interest and unrealized gains
    C. Income from dividends and interest paid by securities the fund holds minus the operating expenses
    D. Ninety percent of the fund's net asset value

51. Which of the following statements are true of mutual fund dividend distributions?

    I. The fund pays dividends from net income.
    II. A single taxpayer may exclude $100 worth of dividend income from taxes annually.
    III. An investor is liable for taxes on distributions whether a dividend is a cash distribution or is reinvested in the fund.
    IV. An investor is liable for taxes only if he receives a distribution in cash.

    A. I and II
    B. I, II and III
    C. I and III
    D. II and IV

52. Greta Guernsey redeemed 200 of her 500 mutual fund shares. She has not designated which shares were redeemed. Which of the following methods does the IRS use to determine which shares she redeemed?

    A. Identified shares
    B. Wash sale rules
    C. LIFO
    D. FIFO

53. ACE, an open-end investment company, operates under the conduit, or pipeline, tax theory. Last year, it distributed 91 percent of all net investment income as a dividend to shareholders. Therefore, which of the following statements is true?

    A. ACE paid taxes on 9 percent of its net investment income last year.
    B. ACE paid taxes on 9 percent of its net investment income and capital gains last year.
    C. ACE paid taxes on 91 percent of its net investment income last year.
    D. ACE paid no taxes last year because it qualified as a regulated investment company under IRC Subchapter M.

54. Your client has a $21,000 net capital loss this year. He plans to apply the maximum deduction toward his ordinary income for the year. After this year, he may do which of the following?

    A. Carry $3,000 of the loss forward
    B. Carry the loss forward indefinitely and deduct a maximum of $3,000 per year
    C. Carry the loss forward indefinitely and offset capital gains only
    D. Not carry the loss forward

55. On January 10, 1987, Adam Grizzly purchases 1,000 shares of the ArGood open-end investment company. On January 22, 1987, ArGood sells 25,000 shares of TCB at a profit. ArGood originally purchased the TCB on June 24, 1984. On February 15, 1987, ArGood distributes the gain from the sale of TCB to shareholders. How is Adam taxed on this distribution?

    A. The income is taxed as a long-term gain, the same rate as ordinary income.
    B. The income is taxed as a long-term gain qualifying for the 60 percent exclusion.
    C. If Adam has been using automatic reinvestment, he is not taxed at all.
    D. Adam is not taxed because he did not sell the TCB; ArGood is liable for all taxes.

56. A mutual fund prospectus displays all of the following EXCEPT

    A. a breakpoint schedule
    B. the investment adviser's name
    C. the SEC disclaimer
    D. performance predictions

57. Which of the following statements is true of your open-end investment company client's decision not to take automatic reinvestment of dividend and capital gains distributions?

    A. It does not change the tax status of these distributions.
    B. It lowers the client's proportionate ownership in the fund each time a distribution is made.
    C. It is the way individuals requiring income payments often invest.
    D. It results in all of the above.

58. Gwinneth Stout has a large investment in the ATF open-end investment company. She has selected a fixed-time withdrawal plan. The computation for the withdrawal plan is based on the

    A. NAV each period
    B. NAV at the first payment
    C. POP each period
    D. POP at the first payment

59. Karen Kodiak is 24 years old, earning $20,000 as a radio sports announcer. She is seeking to invest $1,000 in savings. She does not want a fund that undergoes extreme fluctuations in net asset value. Instead, she is looking for maximum diversification and will accept a moderate amount of risk. Which of the following mutual funds is MOST suitable for Karen?

    A. ZBEST Asset Allocation Fund
    B. NavCo Cash Reserves Money-Market Fund
    C. ATF Biotechnology Fund
    D. ATF Capital Appreciation Fund

60. A customer chooses a voluntary accumulation plan and signs up for automatic checking account deductions of $100 a month. She tells the registered representative that she intends to continue the plan for 10 years. Based on this information, which of the following statements is true?

    A. Her decision to invest is binding, and she must continue to invest for 10 years.
    B. She can terminate the plan at her option.
    C. She will be charged a late fee on investments not made in a timely fashion.
    D. She can terminate the plan if she agrees to pay the balance in lump sum.

61. When voting rights are extended to contract holders of variable life insurance contracts, there is one vote for each

    A. contract owned
    B. dollar of cash value credited to the contract
    C. $100 of cash value funded by the insurance company's general account
    D. $100 of cash value funded by the insurance company's separate account

62. The investment objective of a separate account funding variable life insurance may be changed

    A. with a majority vote of shares
    B. by order of the state insurance commissioner
    C. if either A or B occurs
    D. under no circumstances

63. Which of the following statements is true of a separate account registering as an investment company that offers variable life contracts under the Investment Company Act of 1940?

    I. It must have a minimum net capital of $100,000 before operations may begin.
    II. It must have a minimum net capital of $1 million before operations may begin.
    III. It may operate if the insurer has a minimum net capital of $1 million.

    A. I
    B. I and III
    C. II
    D. II and III

64. Under the Uniform Gifts to Minors Act, the owner of the securities held in the account is the

    A. custodian
    B. minor
    C. parent of the minor
    D. donor of the securities

65. A fund seeks to achieve maximum capital appreciation, with little or no pursuit of current income. The fund invests in stocks of small and medium-sized companies that demonstrate significant long-term growth potential. The fund's management believes that despite year-to-year fluctuations, the strategy of investing in companies that show strong earnings growth can result in superior investment returns. This information describes which of the following mutual funds?

    A. ATF Capital Appreciation Fund
    B. NavCo Growth & Income Fund
    C. ACE Equity Income Fund
    D. NavCo Tax-free Municipal Bond Fund

66. Armand A. Legge has been investing $100 a month in the Amusement Technology Fund over the past five months. His purchases are as follows:

Month	Price/Share	Quantity
1	10	10
2	20	5
3	25	4
4	5	20
5	10	10

What is the difference between the investor's average cost and the average price he paid for the shares?

    A. $3.80
    B. $7.14
    C. $10.20
    D. $14.00

67. The price of closed-end investment company shares is determined by

    A. supply and demand
    B. the New York Stock Exchange
    C. the board of directors
    D. the net asset value plus the sales charge

68. The AIR on a variable annuity is 5 percent. In April, the annuitant receives a payment of $300 when the separate account earns 5 percent. In May, the payment increases to $325 when the separate account earns 9 percent. What must the separate account earn in June to maintain the $325 payment?

    A. Less than 5 percent
    B. 5 percent
    C. Between 5 percent and 9 percent
    D. 9 percent

69. Customers could pay a commission, rather than a sales charge, for shares of a(n)

    A. no-load fund
    B. mutual fund
    C. open-end investment company
    D. closed-end investment company

70. According to the NASD, the maximum sales charge on a variable annuity contract is

    A. 8.5 percent of the total amount invested
    B. 8.5 percent of the net amount invested
    C. 9 percent of the total amount invested
    D. unlimited

71. Which of the following statements regarding variable annuities are true?

    I. The number of accumulation units is fixed.
    II. The number of accumulation units varies.
    III. The number of annuity units is fixed.
    IV. The number of annuity units varies.

    A. I and III
    B. I and IV
    C. II and III
    D. II and IV

72. At age 65, Randy Bear purchased an immediate variable annuity contract. Randy made a lump-sum $100,000 initial payment and selected a life income with 10-year period certain payment option. Randy lived until age 88. The insurance company made payments to Randy

    A. until his initial payment of $100,000 was exhausted
    B. for 10 years
    C. for 23 years
    D. at a fixed rate for 10 years and at a variable rate up until his death

73. August Polar invests $200 monthly into a mutual fund. His daughter June enters college, and August would like to send her $100 monthly. Which of the following should August's registered representative recommend?

    A. Invest $100 monthly into the mutual fund, and send June $100 monthly.
    B. Invest $200 monthly into the mutual fund, and send all dividends to June.
    C. Invest $200 monthly into the mutual fund, and redeem shares when needed.
    D. Begin a systematic withdrawal program of $100 monthly.

74. Which of the following statements is(are) true of a variable annuity's separate account?

    I. It is used for the investment of monies paid by variable annuity contract holders.
    II. It is separate from the insurance company's general investments.
    III. It is operated in a manner similar to an investment company.
    IV. It is as much a security as it is an insurance product.

    A. I only
    B. I and II only
    C. II and III only
    D. I, II, III and IV

75. Similarities between a mutual fund and a variable annuity's separate account include which of the following?

    I. The investment portfolio is professionally managed.
    II. The client may vote for the board of directors or board of managers.
    III. The client assumes the investment risk.
    IV. The payout plans guarantee the client income for life.

    A. I, II and III only
    B. II and IV only
    C. III and IV only
    D. I, II, III and IV

76. Angus Bullwether has $100,000 to invest. He will need the money when he retires in six months. Which of the following is the MOST suitable investment for Angus?

   A. Growth fund
   B. Immediate variable annuity
   C. International stock fund
   D. Money-market fund

77. Your customer is 68 years old, retired and in good health. She is concerned about budgeting her money and needs funds for day-to-day living expenses starting now. As her representative, you might suggest that she purchase

   A. all the whole life insurance that she can afford
   B. a periodic-payment deferred variable annuity
   C. a single-payment deferred variable annuity
   D. an immediate annuity

78. An insurance company offering a variable annuity makes payments to annuitants on the 15th of each month. The contract has an assumed interest rate of 3 percent. In July of this year, the contract earned 4 percent. In August the account earned 6 percent. If the contract earns 3 percent in September, the payments to annuitants will be

   A. greater than the payments in August
   B. less than the payments in August
   C. the same as the payments in August
   D. less than the payments in July

79. Klaus Bruin, age 48, and his wife Sandy Bruin, age 50, have a combined annual income of more than $200,000. Their portfolio consists of common stocks and bonds that offer a wide range of safety and return potential. The Bruins are becoming ever more concerned about the effects of rising inflation in the United States economy. They are seeking to invest a small percentage of their portfolio in a fund that will provide additional diversification. Which of the following mutual funds is the MOST suitable for the Bruins?

   A. NavCo Tax-free Municipal Bond Fund
   B. ArGood Investment-grade Bond Fund
   C. ATF Overseas Opportunities Fund
   D. ZBEST Government Income Fund

80. According to the NASD Rules of Fair Practice, a member firm may give certain selling concessions to

   A. the general public
   B. other NASD member firms
   C. nonmember broker-dealers
   D. all of the above

81. If a customer, age 52, cashes in his annuity contract before payout begins, which of the following statements is(are) true?

   I. He will be taxed at the ordinary income tax rate on earnings exceeding cost base.
   II. He will have to pay a 10 percent penalty on the amount withdrawn that exceeds cost base.
   III. He will have to pay a 5 percent penalty on the amount withdrawn that exceeds cost base.
   IV. He will be taxed at ordinary rates on the amount withdrawn, which represents cost base, and will be taxed at capital gains rates on the amount withdrawn that exceeds cost base.

   A. I
   B. I and II
   C. I and III
   D. III and IV

82. If a customer, age 35, invests $100 a month in a variable annuity for seven years and suddenly dies, which of the following statements is true?

    A. The customer's beneficiaries will not receive any money until the year in which the customer would have turned age 59½.
    B. The insurance company keeps all contributions made to date because the contract was not annuitized.
    C. The customer's beneficiaries will receive only the amount contributed.
    D. If the contract were insured, the customer's beneficiaries would receive the greater of the contributions or current value of the account.

83. When a customer withdraws money from an IRA after age 59½, which of the following statements is true?

    A. The amount withdrawn is subject to a 10 percent penalty.
    B. The amount withdrawn is subject to taxes at the capital gains rate.
    C. The entire amount in the IRA is subject to taxation at the ordinary rate, regardless of the amount withdrawn.
    D. The amount withdrawn is subject to taxation at ordinary income tax rates.

84. Which of the following statements is(are) true about a qualified, noncontributory defined benefit plan?

    I. Contributions are taxable.
    II. Distributions are taxable.
    III. Contributions may vary.

    A. I and II
    B. II
    C. II and III
    D. III

85. Which of the following defines the purpose of dollar cost averaging?

    A. To obtain a lower average price per share than average cost per share
    B. To obtain a lower average cost per share than average price per share
    C. To take advantage of a nonfluctuating market
    D. To buy more shares at higher prices

86. Keogh plans are retirement programs designed for use by nonincorporated businesses. These plans allow the self-employed individual to contribute on a tax-deductible basis the

    A. lesser of 25 percent of postcontribution income or $30,000
    B. lesser of 25 percent of precontribution income or $30,000
    C. greater of 25 percent of postcontribution income or $30,000
    D. greater of 25 percent of precontribution income or $30,000

87. June Polar is a retired teacher participating in a qualified tax-sheltered annuity. Contributions made on her behalf total $15,000. This year, she received a lump-sum payment of $21,000. How would this payment be taxed?

    A. As a capital gains distribution
    B. As ordinary income
    C. $6,000 as capital gains and the remainder as ordinary income
    D. As ordinary income, except for the $15,000, which represents return of her contribution

88. ALFA Securities, an NASD member, wants to buy shares in ATF Mutual Fund from the fund's sponsor at a discount. This arrangement is possible if ATF's sponsor

    A. is not an NASD member
    B. is also an NASD member and a sales agreement between the two firms is in effect
    C. has a sales agreement with ALFA Securities
    D. meets any of the above restrictions

89. Under what conditions does the Investment Company Act of 1940 require a written statement disclosing the source of a dividend payment?

    A. Whenever a dividend is paid
    B. Whenever net income is part of the dividend
    C. Whenever all or part of the dividend payment comes from a source other than current income or accumulated undistributed net income
    D. The Investment Company Act of 1940 does not require disclosure; only the Internal Revenue Code requires disclosure of the dividend amount.

90. When the annual report is used as sales literature, which of the following statements are true?

    I. The principal of the firm must approve its use as such.
    II. The prospectus must accompany the report.
    III. The figures contained in the report must be as of a specific date.
    IV. The report must contain the complete portfolio list.

    A. I, II and III only
    B. I and IV only
    C. II, III and IV only
    D. I, II, III and IV

91. In the sale of open-end investment company shares, which of the following statements is true of the prospectus?

    A. It is not necessary.
    B. It must be delivered to the client either before or during the sales solicitation.
    C. It must be delivered before the sales solicitation.
    D. It must be delivered at or before the delivery of the fund share certificate.

92. Which of the following persons would MOST likely become a member(s) of the NASD?

    I. Person convicted of a crime involving fraudulent conversion in the securities business within the past 10 years
    II. Person who transacts business for his own account and for others in the over-the-counter market
    III. Person acting as a specialist on the New York Stock Exchange only

    A. I and III only
    B. II only
    C. II and III only
    D. I, II and III

93. Mutual fund performance statistics must show results for which of the following periods?

    I. 1 year
    II. 3 years
    III. 5 years
    IV. 10 years

    A. I
    B. I, III and IV
    C. II and III
    D. II, III and IV

94. Which of the following individuals may NOT purchase shares of a hot issue of stock?

    A. General partner of a member firm
    B. Spouse of the person who is the managing underwriter of the issue
    C. Senior officer of a bank
    D. All of the above

95. Which of the following statements is(are) true of a sale of securities in a dollar amount just below the point at which an investor could take advantage of a lower sales charge by making a larger purchase?

    I. It is called a breakpoint sale.
    II. It would not be a conflict of interest.
    III. It is contrary to just and equitable principles of trade.
    IV. It requires the approval of the District Business Conduct Committee.

    A. I
    B. I and III
    C. I and IV
    D. II

96. NASD rules permit members to do which of the following?

    A. Execute an order to sell shares of a customer's securities, knowing that delivery of these shares will be two weeks later
    B. Continue to compensate a registered representative for sales made while the representative was working for the firm according to a previous contract
    C. Arrange for a customer to receive $5,000 worth of credit to purchase mutual fund shares
    D. Give a selling concession to a nonmember firm because of the large number of shares the nonmember is purchasing

97. While recommending the purchase of a security, a registered representative presented material indicating a possible upward move in the price of the recommended security. This recommendation to buy was probably

    I. fraudulent
    II. in violation of the Rules of Fair Practice
    III. not suitable for all investors
    IV. acceptable if the statements about prices and earnings were clearly labeled as forecasts

    A. I
    B. I and II
    C. III
    D. III and IV

98. An employee involved in the management of an NASD member's business, particularly in the supervision of business solicitation or in training, must be registered as a

    A. broker
    B. dealer
    C. partner
    D. principal

99. Which Federal Reserve Board regulation prohibits brokers and dealers from extending credit for the purchase of open-end investment company shares?

    A. Regulation A
    B. Regulation G
    C. Regulation U
    D. Regulation T

100. The NASD's Code of Procedure contains guidelines for

    A. handling violations of the NASD's Rules of Fair Practice
    B. reviewing and approving accounts, trades, correspondence and sales literature
    C. resolving disputes between two NASD members
    D. resolving disputes between NASD members and non–NASD firms

Answers & Rationale

1. **A.** Max Leveridge requires maximum safety and current income. While all fixed-income funds aim to provide current income, the U.S. government bond fund offers the best combination of safety and a higher yield than a money-market fund. (Page 95)

2. **D.** A flexible premium policy allows the insured to determine the amount and timing of premium payments. Depending on the policy, the death benefit may equal the face value of the contract, a percentage of cash value or a combination of the two. If separate account performance is such that cash value drops below an amount necessary to maintain the policy in force, the policy lapses. (Page 149)

3. **D.** Anyone can bring charges of rule violations against a member firm or an associated person, including customers, which is the reason each branch office must maintain library copies of the NASD's Bylaws, Rules of Fair Practice and Code of Procedure. (Page 205)

4. **D.** T bills are issued at a discount and pay all interest upon maturity. (Page 36)

5. **B.** Market value of stock is determined by supply and demand. (Page 8)

6. **B.** This is actually a three-part question pertaining to locking in yield, a long period of time and reinvesting with minimum risk. The long time aspect is easily handled in that bonds are longer term securities than notes or bills. STRIPS (Separate Trading of Registered Interest and Principal of Securities) are T bonds with the coupons removed. The choice between bonds and STRIPS is simplified when reinvestment risk is considered. STRIPS don't pay interest; instead, they are sold at a deep discount and mature at face par value. Consequently, there are no interest payments to be reinvested and no reinvestment

risk. This is also how the investor locks in a yield. (Page 38)

7. **A.** STRIPS (Separate Trading of Registered Interest and Principal of Securities) are T bonds with the coupons removed. STRIPS don't pay interest; instead, they are sold at a deep discount and mature at face par value. (Page 38)

8. **D.** The longer a bond's maturity, the greater the risk to the investor. As a result, long-term bonds pay higher interest rates than medium- or short-term bonds. If a fund replaces medium-term bonds with long-term bonds, you would expect the long-term bonds to pay higher interest rates and, thus, more income. Additionally, as interest rates increase, so do yields. For example, a fund has a medium-term bond paying 8 percent. The income from the bond is $80 annually. The bond matures, and the fund receives $1,000 as a return of principal. The fund purchases a long-term bond paying 9 percent, or $90, annually (income to the fund increases by $10). Additionally, if interest rates are rising, price is declining. Thus, the 9 percent long-term bond will not cost $1,000, but say $950. Therefore, the current yield of the 9 percent bond will be 9.47 percent ($90 × $950)—yield is up. (Page 27)

9. **D.** Because common stock is paid last (most junior), other securities the firm issued will receive distributions (interest payments on debt securities and dividends on senior equity securities). (Page 8)

10. **C.** Collateral trust bonds are backed by other securities, while mortgage bonds are backed by real estate. Equipment trust certificates are backed by equipment. Debentures are secured by the company's promise to pay. (Page 30)

11. **D.** The best time to buy long-term bonds is when long-term interest rates have peaked. In addition to the high return, as interest rates fall the value of existing bonds will rise. (Page 28)

12. **D.** If not appealed, District Business Conduct Committee decisions become final 45 days after the decision date. (Page 205)

13. **B.** When interest rates rise, bond prices fall. (Page 27)

14. **D.** A sector, or specialized, fund offers a higher appreciation potential, coupled with higher risk, than an income-oriented fund. (Page 94)

15. **A.** In a period of deflation, interest rates fall. When interest rates drop, bond prices increase. (Page 27)

16. **A.** Tax-equivalent yield on bonds issued between municipalities and corporations is determined by dividing a municipal bond's nominal yield by the difference between 100 percent and the investor's tax bracket. In reality, because municipal securities are quoted in yields to maturity, the truest measure of equivalency uses a bond's yield to maturity. (Page 43)

17. **A.** Municipal bonds are exempt from federal income tax. Direct federal debt, such as Treasury bonds, is subject to federal income tax, but is exempt from state tax. GNMA bonds are subject to both federal and local taxes. (Page 42)

18. **A.** Zero-coupon bonds represent the lowest risk coupled with the highest return of all the investments listed. They offer no current income. (Page 38)

19. **D.** Money-market securities are made up of short-term, high-yield debt issues. All of the items listed here are considered short term—even the bonds because they will mature in less than one year. (Page 45)

20. **D.** Index funds seek to duplicate the price and yield performance of a selected index. (Page 94)

21. **C.** An annuity unit's value reflects changes in the assets held in the life insurance company's separate account. (Page 141)

22. **D.** A long-term municipal bond fund may invest only in securities matching its investment objective. (Page 88)

23. **C.** The federal funds rate is the rate of interest at which member banks of the Federal Reserve System can borrow excess funds from other members, usually on an overnight basis. The rate is subject to change and often does on a daily basis. (Page 47)

24. **C.** The New York Stock Exchange is an auction market, and the OTC market is a negotiated market. (Page 54)

25. **C.** Stocks sold on the ex-dividend date entitle the seller to the dividend. Stocks sell ex-dividend two business days before the record date. (Page 58)

26. **C.** If the interest rates change, geographic diversification will not help. A change in interest rates affects all of the yields. (Page 72)

27. **C.** August can purchase 37.7 shares. Mutual fund shares may be sold in full or fractional amounts and do not trade in round lots of 100 shares. (Page 92)

28. **B.** A diversified common stock fund contains stocks from many companies and many industries. (Page 82)

29. **B.** 12b-1 fees cover advertising costs, mailing expenses and prospectus printing costs. (Page 101)

30. **D.** All of the statements listed are true. (Page 149)

31. **C.** The FOMC is one of the most influential committees in the Federal Reserve System, and its decisions affect money supplies, interest rates and even the speed at which dollars turn over (money velocity). The foreign exchange rate is set in the interbank market. (Page 65)

32. **A.** Balanced funds carry both equity and debt issues, although they needn't maintain equal amounts of these issues. (Page 94)

33. **A.** Control of the investment is given over to the investment manager. All of the other items mentioned are considered advantages. (Page 92)

34. **B.** A company must have commitments for at least $100,000 in assets before it begins. All of the other items are true.   (Page 87)

35. **C.** The maximum deduction of capital losses in any one year is $3,000. Any remaining losses can be carried forward into the next year.   (Page 110)

36. **B.** NAV must be calculated at least every business day, but not on weekends or holidays. It takes into account all of the fund's assets and is arrived at by totaling the assets and dividing that amount by the number of shares outstanding.   (Page 100)

37. **A.** Share prices fluctuate in relation to the assets held in the fund's portfolio.   (Page 100)

38. **A.** Share prices increase when assets in the portfolio increase in value. Share prices decrease when the fund distributes a dividend because shareholders receive either cash or additional shares. Redeeming or purchasing shares does not affect share prices, only total assets. Reinvesting dividends or capital gains has no effect on share prices either.   (Page 100)

39. **D.** In an UGMA, when Minnie reaches the age of majority the account is taxed at Minnie's rate.   (Page 121)

40. **C.** A secondary distribution is the sale of stock that has been previously issued and owned. A key purpose of a secondary distribution is to redistribute a large block of stock without significantly affecting the market price. Like a primary distribution, an underwriting manager makes distribution arrangements and a syndicate may be formed. In a secondary distribution, the securities are usually offered at a fixed price that is closely related to the current market price so as not to upset the market significantly.   (Page 50)

41. **C.** To determine the selling price of the shares when given the NAV, divide the NAV by 100 percent minus the sales load: NAV ÷ 100% − SL% = Selling price. In this case, $9.30 divided by 100 percent minus 7 percent equals $10.   (Page 102)

42. **A.** Funds charging the full 8½ percent sales load must offer breakpoints, rights of accumulation and dividend reinvestment at NAV. Exchange privileges are the exception. (Page 103)

43. **C.** Rights of accumulation are good for not less than 10 years, while the letter of intent has a 13-month limit.   (Page 105)

44. **B.** Max must put in the full $15,000, so he owes an additional $6,000. Reinvested dividends and changes in the NAV do not affect the amount required.   (Page 104)

45. **D.** Mutual funds use forward pricing. You will pay the offering price calculated at 5:00 p.m.   (Page 99)

46. **D.** All of the choices listed may affect VLI cash value.   (Page 148)

47. **A.** Hugh receives $12.50 per share less a redemption fee of 1 percent; $12.50 times 100 shares is $12,500. A 1 percent redemption fee is $125, so Hugh receives $12,375.   (Page 106)

48. **D.** A mutual fund's board of directors sets the record date. Because the fund uses forward pricing and a transaction occurs the day the order is received, the investor would be a shareholder of record if the transaction is completed by the time the fund prices its shares. The ex-dividend date for corporate stocks in the secondary market is two business days before the record date.   (Page 108)

49. **A.** Share prices decline on the ex-dividend date. Dividend distributions cause a tax liability, so the purchase of shares right before an ex-dividend date is not a good idea.   (Page 108)

50. **C.** Dividends and interest paid on securities held in the portfolio make up investment income. From this, the fund pays its expenses before the investment income becomes *net* investment income. (Page 107)

51. **C.** The fund pays dividends from net income, and the investor is liable for taxes on all distributions. (Page 109)

52. **D.** When a customer does not choose a method, the IRS uses FIFO. (Page 110)

53. **A.** ACE pays taxes on any portion of income it does not distribute as long as it distributes at least 90 percent. ACE paid taxes on 9 percent. (Page 107)

54. **B.** Capital losses can be used to offset capital gains. A client can use $3,000 of capital losses per year to offset ordinary income. After using $3,000 this year, your client will have $18,000 to carry forward in future years until the loss is exhausted. (Page 110)

55. **A.** Adam owned shares of the mutual fund when it distributed the gain, and he is liable for the taxes. This is considered a long-term gain, which is currently taxed as ordinary income. (Page 108)

56. **D.** The mutual fund prospectus must not provide performance predictions. (Page 86)

57. **D.** Reinvestment does not change the tax status, while taking distributions lowers proportionate ownership. An investment of this type allows an investor to take distributions without touching the principal. (Page 109)

58. **A.** At first, withdrawal of funds is based on the NAV. Subsequently, it is determined each time a payment is made. (Page 126)

59. **A.** Karen Kodiak is a young investor with a relatively small amount to invest and a goal of maximum diversification. An asset allocation fund allows her small investment to benefit from the return potential of the stock, bond and short-term debt markets. (Page 95)

60. **B.** Voluntary accumulation plans are just that—voluntary. The client can terminate at any time if she so chooses, and she incurs no penalty for doing so. (Page 122)

61. **D.** Contract holders receive one vote per $100 of cash value funded by the separate account. Additionally, if the insurance company votes the shares, the company must vote according to proxies received from the contract holders. (Page 149)

62. **C.** The insurance commissioner has the authority to change an investment objective if the objective violates state law; otherwise, the objective may be changed only by majority vote of the separate account's outstanding shares. (Page 149)

63. **B.** According to the act of 1940, a separate account may begin operations as long as the insurance company offering the contract has a net worth of $1 million or the account has a net worth of $100,000. (Page 136)

64. **B.** The minor owns the securities in an UGMA account while they are held in the custodian's name. (Page 119)

65. **A.** Capital appreciation funds seek growth, not current income. (Page 94)

66. **A.** The investor paid a total of $500 for 49 shares of stock, or $10.20 per share. The average price of the shares during this time was the total of the share prices ($70) divided by the number of investment periods (5), or $14. The difference between the two is $3.80. (Page 122)

67. **A.** Closed-end investment company shares trade in the secondary market; therefore, supply and demand determine price. (Page 82)

68. **B.** The annuitant will receive a payment equal to the previous payment if the separate account return for the period equals the AIR. (Page 142)

69.   **D.**   Sales charges could be paid on all types of open-end funds, while commissions are paid on securities traded in the secondary market, such as a closed-end company.   (Page 82)

70.   **A.**   NASD rules allow a maximum sales charge on a variable annuity contract of 8½ percent.   (Page 140)

71.   **C.**   The number of variable annuity accumulation units varies because during the accumulation period, the value of the units fluctuates relative to the value of the separate account. When a variable annuity contract is annuitized, the number of annuity units is fixed.   (Page 141)

72.   **C.**   An annuity with life and 10-year certain pays for the greater of 10 years or the life of the annuitant. Randy lived for 23 more years, which is more than the 10 certain.   (Page 140)

73.   **A.**   August should reduce his investment in the mutual fund and send the extra money to June.   (Page 71)

74.   **D.**   The separate account is used for the monies invested in variable annuities. It is kept separate from the general account and operated very much like an investment company. It is considered both an insurance product and an investment product.   (Page 137)

75.   **A.**   Both a mutual fund and a variable annuity's separate account offer professional management and a board of managers or directors, and the client assumes the investment risk. Only variable annuities have payout plans that guarantee the client income for life.   (Page 138)

76.   **D.**   Angus has a very short investment period. The most suitable recommendation is the money-market fund.   (Page 96)

77.   **D.**   Your client needs immediate income. Of the options listed, only the immediate annuity offers this.   (Page 139)

78.   **C.**   The contract earned 3 percent in September. The assumed interest rate for the contract is 3 percent. Payment size will not change from the payment made the previous month.   (Page 141)

79.   **C.**   The Bruins' substantial portfolio is diversified between equity and debt investments. However, to counteract the effects of the U.S. economy on their portfolio returns, they should invest a portion of their assets in the international stock fund.   (Page 94)

80.   **B.**   Members may give other members concessions, but must deal with the public and nonmembers at the public offering price.   (Page 99)

81.   **B.**   Cashing in an annuity before age 59½ is a taxable event. The amount withdrawn exceeding cost base is taxed as ordinary income. Additionally, the amount subject to tax is also subject to a penalty of 10 percent unless the distribution is annuitized for a period of at least five years or the distribution is the result of death or disability.   (Page 143)

82.   **D.**   The customer's beneficiaries would receive the current market value, but if the contract were insured, they would receive the greater of the amount invested or the current market value.   (Page 140)

83.   **D.**   Money withdrawn from an IRA after age 59½ is subject to ordinary taxation on the amount withdrawn, but there is no 10 percent penalty.   (Page 156)

84.   **C.**   The employer, not the employee, contributes to a qualified, noncontributory plan. Contributions are not taxed until the participant receives them as distributions. Because the benefits this type of qualified plan provides may vary (depending on the participant's age, sex, income, etc.), the contributions made on his behalf will vary. All distributions from the plan are taxed when the participant receives them.   (Page 157)

85.   **B.**   The purpose of dollar cost averaging is to obtain a lower average cost per share than average price per share.   (Page 122)

86.   **A.**   Keogh plans allow contributions for the lesser of 25 percent of postcontribution income or $30,000.   (Page 158)

87.   **B.**   Contributions to a TSA, as to all qualified plans, are made before taxes. Payments from these plans require the payment of taxes at the ordinary income tax rate.   (Page 162)

88.   **B.**   This arrangement is possible if both firms are NASD members and a sales agreement is in effect.   (Page 99)

89.   **C.**   The Investment Company Act of 1940 requires disclosure when all or part of the dividend payment comes from a source other than current income or accumulated undistributed net income.   (Page 108)

90.   **D.**   The principal of the firm must approve the use of the annual report as sales literature, and the figures contained must be current and complete. A prospectus is always required.
                                              (Page 193)

91.   **B.**   The sale of mutual fund shares requires that the client receives the prospectus before or during the sales solicitation.   (Page 173)

92.   **B.**   A person conducting business in the over-the-counter market must be a member of the NASD. Transacting business on the Exchange requires membership with the NYSE.   (Page 183)

93.   **B.**   Mutual fund performance statistics must show results for 1, 5 and 10 years. (Page 97)

94.   **D.**   None of the people listed may purchase hot issues.   (Page 175)

95.   **B.**   This is called a *breakpoint sale* and is contrary to just and equitable principles of trade.
                                              (Page 202)

96.   **B.**   A registered rep may continue to be compensated for sales he made while working for the firm that were in accordance with the contract.   (Page 201)

97.   **D.**   No investment is suitable for all investors. Statements about future prices and earnings may be used if they are clearly labeled as forecasts.   (Page 192)

98.   **D.**   Supervision of business solicitation or training requires that a person be registered as a principal.   (Page 186)

99.   **D.**   Regulation T regulates the extension of credit by brokers and dealers for investment company shares.   (Page 178)

100. **A.**   The Code of Procedure contains the guidelines for handling violations of the NASD Rules of Fair Practice.   (Page 204)

52

Final Exam Three

1. T bills are issued with all of the following maturities EXCEPT

   A. 1 month
   B. 3 months
   C. 6 months
   D. 12 months

2. Which of the following statements about a bond selling above par value is(are) true?

   I. The nominal yield is lower than the current yield.
   II. The yield to maturity is lower than the nominal yield.
   III. The yield to maturity is lower than the current yield.
   IV. The nominal yield always stays the same.

   A. I and IV only
   B. II, III and IV only
   C. III only
   D. I, II, III and IV

3. All of the following statements are true of a Treasury receipt EXCEPT

   A. it may be issued by a securities broker-dealer
   B. it is backed by the full faith and credit of the federal government
   C. the interest coupons are sold separately
   D. it may be purchased at a discount

4. Which of the following does NOT issue commercial paper?

   A. Commercial bank
   B. Finance company
   C. Service company
   D. Broker-dealer

5. A newly issued bond has call protection for the first five years after it is issued. This feature would be most valuable if, during this five-year period, interest rates are generally

   A. fluctuating
   B. stable
   C. falling
   D. rising

6. The newspaper indicates that T bill yields have gone down. This means that T bill prices

    A. are up
    B. are down
    C. are mixed
    D. cannot be determined

7. A 5 percent bond is purchased with an 8 percent yield to maturity. After the capital gains tax is paid, the effective yield is

    A. less than 5 percent
    B. 5 percent
    C. between 5 percent and 8 percent
    D. 8 percent

8. If a registered representative violates NASD rules, which of the following statements is true?

    A. The NASD may impose a fine only.
    B. The rep may be expelled, but nothing further, by the NASD.
    C. The NASD may recommend that disciplinary action be taken, but only the SEC can take such action.
    D. NASD may fine, censure, suspend or expel the rep.

9. Which of the following statements about general obligation municipal bonds is(are) true?

    I. They are second only to U.S. government bonds in safety of principal.
    II. They are backed by the taxing power of the municipality.
    III. They are nonmarketable.
    IV. They pay higher interest rates than corporate debt securities.

    A. I and II
    B. I, II and IV
    C. II, III and IV
    D. III

10. ABC Company issues a 10 percent corporate bond due in 10 years. The bond is convertible into ABC common stock at a conversion price of $25 per share. The ABC bond is quoted at 90. Parity of the common stock is

    A. $22.50
    B. $25
    C. $36
    D. $100

11. All of the following statements are true of taxable zero-coupon bonds EXCEPT

    A. the discount is accreted
    B. tax is paid annually
    C. interest is paid semiannually
    D. the bonds are purchased at a discount

12. Which of the following statements is true about a bond quoted as QRS Zr 12?

    A. The bond pays $12 interest annually.
    B. The bond pays $120 interest annually.
    C. The bond pays no interest until maturity.
    D. None of the above statements is true.

13. Greta Guernsey, age 60, is retired and living alone in a home with a fully paid-off mortgage. Her portfolio contains growth stocks and high-quality bonds. She has invested in the stock market all of her adult life and is comfortable with risk, but her objective is a moderate level of current income to supplement her corporate pension plan distributions and the earnings from her IRA. Which of the following mutual funds is the MOST suitable for Greta?

    A. ACE Equity Income Fund
    B. ArGood Stock Index Fund
    C. ATF Capital Appreciation Fund
    D. ATF Biotechnology Fund

14. The Code of Arbitration is used when disputes arise between a broker-dealer and

    A. the Securities and Exchange Commission
    B. another broker-dealer
    C. the general public
    D. the National Association of Securities Dealers

15. A fund seeks maximum capital appreciation by investing in common stocks of companies located outside the United States. The management selects well-established companies that are listed on their native stock exchanges and that have demonstrated high earnings potential. Although the fund may be affected by fluctuations in currency exchange rates, over the long term it may provide protection against downturns in U.S. markets. This information describes which of the following mutual funds?

    A. ATF Biotechnology Fund
    B. ATF Overseas Opportunities Fund
    C. ArGood Stock Index Fund
    D. ATF Capital Appreciation Fund

16. Which of the following statements best describes the federal funds rate?

    A. It is the average rate for short-term bank loans last week.
    B. It is the rate major New York City banks charge.
    C. It is a rate that changes daily and that banks charge each other.
    D. It is the rate major New York City banks charge broker-dealers.

17. An owner of common stock has which of the following rights?

    I. To determine when dividends will be issued
    II. To vote at stockholders' meetings or by proxy
    III. To receive a predetermined fixed portion of the corporation's profit in cash when declared
    IV. To buy restricted securities before they are offered to the public

    A. I, III and IV
    B. II
    C. II, III and IV
    D. II and IV

18. A company in which you own stock is about to have a stock rights offering. You do not plan on subscribing to the offer. Therefore, your proportionate interest in the company will

    A. increase
    B. decrease
    C. remain the same
    D. More information is needed to answer this question.

19. Under a defined contribution plan, which of the following statements are true?

    I. The participant is guaranteed a contribution based on an agreed-upon percentage or rate.
    II. The participant's retirement benefits are based on the balance in his individual account.
    III. The employer may discriminate among employees as to participation.

    A. I and II only
    B. I and III only
    C. II and III only
    D. I, II and III

20. An investor's portfolio includes 10 bonds and 200 shares of common stock. If both positions increase by ½ of a point, what is the gain?

A. $50
B. $105
C. $110
D. $150

21. A mutual fund's investment policy can be changed by a majority vote of the

A. board of directors
B. fund's managers
C. SEC investment committee
D. outstanding shares

22. What of the following attributes of 401(k) thrift plans is NOT allowed in most other retirement plans?

A. Tax-deferred earnings
B. Deductible contributions to the plans
C. Matching employer contributions
D. No penalties for premature distributions

23. Which of the following statements is true regarding an open-end investment company's calculation of its expense ratio?

A. The expense ratio is computed exclusive of the management fee.
B. The expense ratio is computed inclusive of the management fee.
C. The expense ratio is computed taking into account the management fee only.
D. The expense ratio shows the extent of leverage in the fund.

24. Bud Charolais opened an account about 12 years ago with ACE Mutual Fund. Today, his NAV is $20,000. ACE offers rights of accumulation, and its breakpoints are as follows:

$1 to $24,999	8 percent
$25,000 to $49,999	6 percent
$50,000 to $99,999	4 percent

Bud wishes to deposit $6,000 in the account today. Which of the following would represent his sales charge?

A. $1,000 at 8 percent, and $5,000 at 6 percent
B. $4,999 at 8 percent, and $1,001 at 6 percent
C. Full $6,000 at 6 percent
D. Full $6,000 at 8 percent

25. June Polar has invested in a mutual fund and has signed a statement of intention to invest $25,000. Her original investment was $13,000, and her current account value is $17,000. For her to complete the letter, she must deposit

A. $8,000
B. $12,000
C. $13,000
D. $27,000

26. Adam Grizzly invests $3,000 in open-end investment company shares. After 60 days, he signs a letter of intent for a $10,000 breakpoint and backdates the letter two months. Six months later, he deposits $10,000 into the fund. He receives a reduced sales charge on

A. the $3,000 investment only
B. $7,000 of the investment only
C. the $10,000 investment only
D. the entire $13,000 investment

27. Some open-end investment companies offer their investors a conversion privilege, which permits investors to

    A. exchange general securities for shares in a mutual fund's portfolio
    B. delay payment of taxes on investment company shares that have appreciated in value
    C. purchase additional fund shares from dividends a fund pays
    D. exchange shares of one mutual fund for those of another fund under the same management, at net asset value

28. ArGood Mutual Fund permits rights of accumulation. Klaus Bruin has invested $9,000 and has signed a letter of intent for a $15,000 investment. His reinvested dividends during the 13 months total $720. How much money must he contribute to fulfill the letter of intent?

    A. $5,280
    B. $6,000
    C. $9,000
    D. $15,000

29. If an investment company offers rights of accumulation and an investor wishes to get a reduced sales charge, she must deposit sufficient funds within

    A. 45 days
    B. 13 months
    C. There is no time limit.
    D. Each fund has its own requirements.

30. The death benefit of a life insurance contract funded by a separate account and offered with fixed premiums is determined at least

    A. daily
    B. weekly
    C. monthly
    D. annually

31. A husband and wife are both employed, and each qualifies to open an IRA. To make their maximum allowable contributions, they should open

    A. a joint IRA and deposit $2,000
    B. a joint IRA and deposit $4,000
    C. two separate IRAs and deposit $2,000 each
    D. two separate IRAs and deposit $2,250

32. Which of the following persons would be eligible under a Keogh plan?

    I. Self-employed doctor
    II. Engineer receiving extra compensation as an outside consultant
    III. Advertising executive who made $5,000 during the year freelancing
    IV. Executive employed by a corporation who received $5,000 in stock options

    A. I, II and III only
    B. I, III and IV only
    C. II and IV only
    D. I, II, III and IV

33. Which of the following statements are true regarding the withdrawals from a qualified retirement plan?

    I. The employee will be taxed at the ordinary income tax rate on his cost base.
    II. Funds may be withdrawn after retirement (as defined) with no tax on the withdrawn amount.
    III. Funds may be withdrawn early by the beneficiary if the covered person dies.
    IV. All qualified plans must be in written form.

    A. I and II only
    B. II, III and IV only
    C. III and IV only
    D. I, II, III and IV

34. A registered representative may avoid arbitration proceedings by doing which of the following?

    A. Selling only mutual funds
    B. Changing firms every two years
    C. Refusing to submit to arbitration
    D. A registered representative cannot avoid arbitration.

35. All of the following statements concerning IRA contributions are true EXCEPT

    A. between January 1 and April 15, you may make contributions for the current year, the past year or both
    B. you may make contributions for the past year after April 15, provided you have filed an extension on a timely basis
    C. if you pay your tax on January 15, you may deduct your IRA contribution even if it is not made until April 15
    D. you may contribute to this year's IRA from January 1 of this year until April 15 of next year

36. If you invest in a mutual fund and choose automatic reinvestment, you would expect that

    I. dividend distributions will be reinvested at net asset value
    II. dividend distributions will be reinvested at the public offering price
    III. capital gains distributions will be reinvested at net asset value
    IV. capital gains distributions will be reinvested at the public offering price

    A. I and III
    B. I and IV
    C. II and III
    D. II and IV

37. Which of the following may own a Keogh plan?

    A. S corporation owner filing Schedule K1
    B. Small-business owner filing Form W-2
    C. Small-business owner filing Schedule C
    D. Unemployed lottery winner filing Form 1099G

38. In a nonqualified variable annuity, which of the following risks does the annuitant bear?

    A. Taxes on the earnings in the current period
    B. Mortality risks
    C. Separate account performance risks
    D. Operating expense risks

39. A 65-year-old woman seeks income and preservation of capital. Which of the following should you recommend?

    A. Small-cap fund, mid-cap fund, government bond fund
    B. Aggressive growth fund, mid-cap fund, growth and income fund
    C. Large-cap fund, small-cap fund, government bond fund
    D. Government bond fund, corporate bond fund, municipal bond fund

40. What is the capital gains tax rate that an individual pays on appreciation in the reserves held for his variable annuity in a separate account while the contract is in the accumulation period?

    A. 0 percent
    B. 10 percent
    C. 25 percent
    D. 50 percent

41. A customer, age 42, has been depositing money in a variable annuity for five years. He plans to stop investing, but has no intention of withdrawing any funds for at least 20 years. He most likely is holding

    A. accumulation units
    B. annuity units
    C. accumulation shares
    D. mutual fund units

42. During the accumulation period of a periodic payment deferred variable annuity, the number of accumulation units

    A. varies and the value per unit is fixed
    B. is fixed and the value per unit is fixed
    C. is fixed and the value per unit varies
    D. varies and the value per unit varies

43. A doctor has compensation of $160,000. What is the maximum he may contribute to his Keogh plan?

    A. $5,000
    B. $22,000
    C. $28,000
    D. $30,000

44. In the sale of open-end investment company shares, which of the following statements is true of the prospectus?

    A. It is not necessary.
    B. It must be delivered to the client either before or during the sales solicitation.
    C. It must be delivered before the sales solicitation.
    D. It must be delivered at or before the delivery of the fund share certificate.

45. A retired man has $100,000 to invest for growth. He also owes a $10,000 note due in six months, a $20,000 note due in one year and a $25,000 note due in two years. How much of the $100,000 should he allocate to growth investments?

    A. $45,000
    B. $65,000
    C. $70,000
    D. $100,000

46. Which of the following constitutes a discretionary account?

    A. Registered representative's trading account
    B. Broker-dealer's trading account
    C. Account in which the investor gives the broker-dealer the authority to buy or sell securities
    D. Mutual fund account allowing periodic withdrawals

47. When a client opens an account, which of the following information must be noted on the application?

    I. Client's name and Social Security number
    II. Whether the client is employed by an NASD member firm
    III. Registered rep's signature
    IV. Signature of the office manager, a partner or another designated principal
    V. Statement that the client understands the risks involved

    A. I only
    B. I, II, III and IV only
    C. II and IV only
    D. I, II, III, IV and V

48. In general, a registered representative could have power of attorney for accounts of each of the following EXCEPT a(n)

    A. corporation
    B. individual
    C. partnership
    D. custodian

49. Which of the following statements is true of a limited power of attorney that a customer gives his rep?

    A. The rep needs written permission from the customer for each trade.
    B. The customer must renew the power of attorney every year.
    C. The customer can still enter independent orders.
    D. The branch manager must initial each order before it is entered.

50. An investor has $20,000 to invest. She requires $500 per month to pay for her mother's nursing home care. Which of the following funds should you recommend?

    A. Money market
    B. Aggressive growth
    C. Biotechnology
    D. Foreign stock

51. A registered representative of a member firm who wishes to work outside the firm after hours must notify the

    A. member firm
    B. NASD
    C. NYSE
    D. SEC

52. General communications by a broker-dealer firm, such as advertising or research reports, must be approved by which of the following?

    A. Member
    B. Principal of a member
    C. Supervisory analyst
    D. Certified financial analyst

53. Which of the following statements is true of sales literature for a mutual fund?

    A. It must promise delivery of a prospectus when the shares are delivered to the purchaser.
    B. It must contain a warning that SEC supervision of the company does not guarantee against a decrease in the shares' market value.
    C. It must be preceded or accompanied by a prospectus.
    D. It must contain the following statement: "A prospectus relating to these securities is available upon request."

54. Which of the following must review sales literature and advertising material that have been prepared by a firm's principal underwriter and will be used by a member firm in connection with the offering of investment company shares?

    I. Firm's advertising manager
    II. NASD
    III. SEC

    A. I
    B. I and II
    C. II
    D. II and III

55. Which of the following funds may issue more than one class of common stock?

    A. ArGood Open-end Growth Fund
    B. ACE Closed-end Fund
    C. NavCo Unit Investment Trust
    D. ATF Open-end Bond Fund

56. Joe and Bea Kuhl, both 34 years old, are employed in their own computer software business. They have one daughter, Vera, age 4. The Kuhls want to begin accumulating the money required to send Vera to one of the nation's top universities in 14 years. In addition, they have not yet begun to accumulate money for their retirement. Which of the following mutual funds is the MOST suitable for the Kuhls?

    A. ATF Capital Appreciation Fund
    B. ZBEST Government Income Fund
    C. NavCo Cash Reserves Money-Market Fund
    D. NavCo Growth & Income Fund

57. A customer indicates that he wishes to invest $50,000 in mutual funds. The investments are to be split among three unrelated funds, each with its own management company. The registered representative should advise the client that

    A. this is an excellent idea because it significantly spreads the risk of investing
    B. the customer will pay greater commissions on the investment when she splits the money between three funds than she would if she invested the money in only one fund
    C. the customer will be able to exchange shares between funds as conditions change without incurring a new sales charge
    D. the investor should buy individual stocks because mutual funds are only for smaller investors

58. Sales literature and advertising used in connection with the solicitation or sale of variable life products include which of the following?

    I. Circulars and leaflets describing a variable life product
    II. Prepared presentations used at a seminar open to the public
    III. Newspaper advertisement detailing the benefits of variable life insurance
    IV. Letter sent to 50 of an agent's present clients describing variable life insurance

    A. I and II only
    B. I and III only
    C. III only
    D. I, II, III and IV

59. Which of the following situations might constitute a hot issue?

    A. New issue is offered at $30 and immediately appreciates to $35
    B. New issue is offered at $30 and immediately decreases to $25
    C. Market maker buys at $17 and immediately sells with a spread of $2
    D. Broker-dealer sells inventory at $60 three weeks after buying at $30

60. Except under limited circumstances, NASD rules on freeriding and withholding prohibit the purchase of a hot issue by which of the following people?

    I. Finder
    II. Bank officer who has a significant relationship with the issuer
    III. Officer of a broker-dealer firm that is a member of the NASD
    IV. Registered representative

    A. I and II only
    B. I, III and IV only
    C. III and IV only
    D. I, II, III and IV

61. Which of the following is(are) actively traded?

    I. Warrants
    II. Nondetachable rights
    III. Common stock
    IV. Options on stock

    A. I, III and IV only
    B. II only
    C. II and IV only
    D. I, II, III and IV

62. Belle Charolais, age 45, is single and in search of maximum capital appreciation. She inherited a substantial amount of money a few years ago and has taken an active interest in managing her investments. Currently, her portfolio is diversified among common stocks, tax-exempt bonds, international investments and limited partnerships. She has a long-term time frame and is not risk averse. Which of the following mutual funds is the MOST suitable for Belle?

    A. ArGood Balanced Fund
    B. ATF Biotechnology Fund
    C. NavCo Cash Reserves Money-Market Fund
    D. ZBEST Asset Allocation Fund

63. An oral recommendation by a registered representative must be

    A. followed by a statement of risks
    B. followed by an example of the strategy recommended
    C. followed by a prospectus
    D. approved by a registered principal

64. Chip Bullock owns 100 shares of TCB Company. A dividend declared on August 30 will be paid to stockholders of record on Thursday, September 15. When will the stock sell ex-dividend?

    A. September 11
    B. September 12
    C. September 13
    D. September 15

65. A fund seeks maximum capital appreciation through investment in stocks of companies providing innovative products in the biotechnology sector, including pharmaceutical developers and medical equipment suppliers. Fund management seeks to evaluate emerging economic and political trends and to select individual companies that may benefit from technological advances. This information describes which of the following mutual funds?

    A. ATF Overseas Opportunities Fund
    B. NavCo Growth & Income Fund
    C. ATF Capital Appreciation Fund
    D. ATF Biotechnology fund

66. Your firm is underwriting a new mutual fund organized under a 12b-1 plan. Which of the following statements may you make in any mailings or phone calls to your clients?

    A. "The fund has the added advantage of being a no-load investment."
    B. "You will not have to pay any sales charges with this fund because we're buying it as a long-term investment."
    C. "Investments in no-load funds of this type do have some risks, and you will want to review the prospectus carefully."
    D. None of the above

67. Some mutual funds that are in a family of funds managed by the same company offer an exchange privilege. This privilege gives a shareholder the right to

    A. convert mutual fund shares to securities listed on the New York Stock Exchange
    B. reinvest dividends and capital gains without a sales charge
    C. convert shares to a different investment company within the family of funds on a dollar-for-dollar basis
    D. switch shares to an investment company within the family of funds and defer the taxes on any capital gains due to the exchange

68. An annuity is purchased with a life contingency offering a fully paid contribution to the annuity in the event of the owner's death. This life contingency applies during

    A. the accumulation period
    B. the annuity period
    C. both A and B
    D. neither A nor B

69. A shareholder's failure to provide her Social Security number to the investment company results in which of the following taxes?

    A. Surtax
    B. Alternative minimum tax
    C. Noncertification tax
    D. Withholding tax

70. For a registered investment company to terminate its 12b-1 plan, the termination must be approved by a majority of the

    I. outstanding voting shares of the company
    II. board of directors
    III. uninterested members of the board of directors
    IV. investment advisory board

    A. I and II
    B. I, II and III
    C. I and III
    D. II, III and IV

71. How often are 12b-1 fees paid?

    A. Monthly
    B. Quarterly
    C. Semiannually
    D. Annually

72. All of the following are benefits to owning an IRA EXCEPT that

    A. earnings accumulate on a tax-deferred basis
    B. contributions may be tax deductible
    C. no penalty is charged for failing to withdraw funds after age 70½
    D. funds may be withdrawn without penalty because of permanent disability

73. A Series 6 registered representative can sell which of the following securities?

    I. Real estate limited partnership
    II. Secondary market closed-end investment company
    III. Open-end investment company
    IV. Unit investment trust

    A. I and II
    B. II, III and IV
    C. II and IV
    D. III and IV

74. 12b-1 fees may be used to pay

    A. distributor expenses not identified in the plan document
    B. sales and promotional expenses
    C. transfer fees
    D. investment advisory fees

75. The maximum fee that can be charged under a 12b-1 plan is

    A. an amount equal to the shares' net asset value
    B. the difference between the shares' POP and NAV
    C. an amount that is reasonable in light of the distribution services offered and described in the plan
    D. 9 percent over the life of the plan

76. A college graduate has $1,000 in savings and owes $15,000 on college tuition loans to be paid over the next 10 years. What would you recommend that he do?

   A. Open an account in an income fund with $1,000 and invest periodically using dollar cost averaging
   B. Invest $1,000 in a capital appreciation fund
   C. Invest $1,000 in any fund; because he is young, he can absorb any losses
   D. Defer investment of the $1,000 until he has enough money accumulated to allow investment without adversely affecting his ability to meet emergency expenses

77. Hugh Heifer is 29 years old and seeks a long-term growth investment. He is concerned about the loss of purchasing power as a result of inflation, and he often complains about high commissions and charges that reduce his investment returns. When he was in college, he took a few economics courses and firmly believes that securities analysts cannot consistently outperform the overall market. Which of the following mutual funds is the MOST suitable for Hugh?

   A. ZBEST Asset Allocation Fund
   B. NavCo Growth & Income Fund
   C. ATF Biotechnology Fund
   D. ArGood Stock Index Fund

78. An individual has periodically invested $24,000 in a unit investment trust over 10 years. What is the maximum sales charge?

   A. $2,040
   B. $2,160
   C. $4,800
   D. $12,000

79. A 45-year-old woman wants the greatest possible monthly income. Preservation and stability of capital are important, although secondary, objectives. Which of the following investments would you recommend?

   A. Money-market mutual fund
   B. High-grade bond fund
   C. Growth mutual fund
   D. Combination fund

80. Gwinneth and Porter Stout, both 42 years old, have two children, ages 14 and 12. The Stouts have spent the last 10 years accumulating money to provide for their children's education. Their oldest child will enter college in four years, and the Stouts are not willing to take risks with the money they worked hard to accumulate. They need a very safe investment that provides regular income to help them meet tuition payments. Which of the following mutual funds is the MOST suitable for the Stouts?

   A. ArGood Stock Index Fund
   B. ATF Overseas Opportunities Fund
   C. ArGood Investment-grade Bond Fund
   D. ArGood Balanced Fund

81. Gwinneth Stout invested $10,000 in the ACE Fund in February. Gwinneth sold the shares the following January for $9,000. The result is a capital

   A. loss in the year of sale
   B. gain in the year of sale
   C. loss in the year of purchase
   D. gain in the year of purchase

82. ATF Mutual Fund has incurred the following on a per-share basis: dividend income of $1.10, interest income of $.90, long-term gains of $1 and management fees of $.50. What is the maximum dividend the fund can distribute per share?

   A. $1.50
   B. $2.00
   C. $2.50
   D. $3.00

83. Under the Code of Arbitration, the statute of limitations for filing a complaint against a member or an associated person is

    A. six months
    B. one year
    C. two years
    D. six years

84. Tex Longhorn, age 60, and Sadie Longhorn, age 58, are married and have raised three children. Both Longhorns have decided to retire this year. They have accumulated a nest egg of about $1 million, which they will use to travel around the world, pursue their hobbies and care for each other's health. Both are concerned about rising inflation and are comfortable with a reasonable level of risk. Which of the following mutual funds is the MOST suitable for the Longhorns?

    A. NavCo Cash Reserves Money-Market Fund
    B. NavCo Growth & Income Fund
    C. ZBEST Government Income Fund
    D. ArGood Investment-grade Bond Fund

85. Which of the following statements is true of the District Business Conduct Committee?

    A. It may expel a registered representative from the securities business.
    B. It may fine a registered representative an amount not exceeding $15,000.
    C. It may not bar a registered representative from associating with other members or associated persons.
    D. It may not suspend a member.

86. When you inherit a mutual fund upon the death of the owner, what is your cost basis in the shares?

    A. Market value of the shares upon the decedent's death
    B. Same as the decedent's cost basis
    C. Decedent's cost basis plus the final distribution the fund makes
    D. Market value of the shares 12 months from the date of death

87. A fund's objectives are to maintain a stable net asset value and to provide current income. The fund invests in high-quality, short-term obligations, including U.S. Treasury bills, commercial paper, certificates of deposit and repurchase agreements. Check-writing privileges are available. This information describes which of the following mutual funds?

    A. ZBEST Government Income Fund
    B. NavCo Tax-free Municipal Bond Fund
    C. ArGood Balanced Fund
    D. NavCo Cash Reserves Money-Market Fund

88. A fund seeks to maximize safety of invested principal while providing current income. By investing in a broad range of debt securities issued by the U.S. Treasury as well as by government agencies such as the Government National Mortgage Association, the fund provides reduced risk. It aims for a current yield higher than the yield of short-term debt instruments and money-market funds. This information describes which of the following mutual funds?

    A. NavCo Cash Reserves Money-Market Fund
    B. ACE Equity Income Fund
    C. ZBEST Government Income Fund
    D. NavCo Tax-free Municipal Bond Fund

89. A fund seeks maximum tax-exempt current yield. It invests in a portfolio of high-quality municipal debt obligations. The portfolio is diversified among securities issued by many state and municipal taxing authorities. Income distributions the fund provides are exempt from federal income tax. This information describes which of the following mutual funds?

    A. ArGood Investment-grade Bond Fund
    B. NavCo Tax-free Municipal Bond Fund
    C. ACE Equity Income Fund
    D. NavCo Growth & Income Fund

90. ALFA Enterprises, which has 7 percent $100 par cumulative preferred stock outstanding, has the following dividend record: last year, 5 percent was paid to preferred stockholders; the full preferred dividend was paid until last year. Now ALFA wishes to declare a common dividend. Before ALFA can pay dividends to the common stockholders, how much must it pay on each preferred share outstanding?

    A. $3
    B. $7
    C. $9
    D. $15

91. What sales charge is refunded in a variable life contract after six months?

    A. No refund is allowed.
    B. All sales charges collected are refunded.
    C. Sales charges exceeding 30 percent are refunded.
    D. Sales charges less management fees are refunded.

92. A 12b-1 asset-based fee must be disclosed

    A. in the prospectus
    B. on the share certificate
    C. on the application for investment
    D. on all of the above

93. A fixed-premium variable life insurance contract offers a

    I. guaranteed maximum death benefit
    II. guaranteed minimum death benefit
    III. guaranteed cash value
    IV. cash value that fluctuates according to the contract's performance

    A. I and III
    B. I and IV
    C. II and III
    D. II and IV

94. Acme Sweatsocks has issued both common stock and convertible preferred stock. The convertible preferred has a par value of $100 per share. It is convertible into the common at $25 per share. Acme convertible is trading at 110. What is the parity price of the common?

    A. 25
    B. 27½
    C. 35
    D. 37½

95. Which of the following describes the prime rate?

    A. Interest rate offered to a bank's best corporate customers
    B. Interest rate at which banks borrow from the Federal Reserve Board
    C. Interest rate at which individuals borrow from banks for mortgages on residential purchases
    D. Points or premium paid to obtain a mortgage on a residential purchase

96. Tex Longhorn, age 65, will receive a lump-sum distribution from his pension plan. He had invested the money in a growth fund in the pension plan. Tex is reconsidering his investment options and doesn't want to commit the funds for at least eight or nine months. What would you recommend that he do?

    A. Reinvest the money in a growth fund to match his previous objectives until he decides what he wants to do
    B. Reinvest the money in a one-year CD to preserve capital
    C. Reinvest the money in a money-market mutual fund
    D. Hold onto the check from the pension plan until he decides what he wants to do

97. If a registered representative uses a prospectus as a sales aid, what must accom-
pany the prospectus in her presentation?

    A. All sales literature describing the invest-
       ment
    B. All advertising describing the invest-
       ment
    C. Company's balance sheet
    D. No other information is required unless
       requested.

98. Acme Sweatsocks has issued both common
stock and convertible preferred stock. The
convertible preferred has a par value of $100
per share. It is convertible into the common
at $25 per share. Due to a change in interest
rates, the market price of the Acme preferred declines to $90 per share. Assume
that the common is trading at 20 percent
below parity. What is the market price of the
Acme common?

    A. 15¾
    B. 18
    C. 22½
    D. 25

99. Which of the following is a statutory disqualification preventing an individual from
participating in the securities business as a
registered person of the SEC or another self-
regulatory organization?

    I. The individual has been convicted
       within the past 10 years of a securities-
       related crime.
    II. The individual has willfully violated the
       provisions of a federal securities act.
    III. The individual has been expelled or sus-
       pended from an SRO.
    IV. The individual is subject to an order of
       the Commission denying, suspending
       or revoking registration.

    A. I only
    B. I and II only
    C. II and III only
    D. I, II, III and IV

100. A $1,000 Consolidated Codfish bond can be
converted at $50 per share into COD com-
mon stock. The bond is currently selling at
110 percent of parity, while the stock's current market value is $55 per share. What is
the bond selling for in the market?

    A. $1,000
    B. $1,100
    C. $1,210
    D. $1,350

Answers & Rationale

1.   **A.**   T bills are issued with 3-, 6- and 12-month maturities.   (Page 36)

2.   **B.**   Nominal yield is fixed and stays the same on all bonds. A bond selling above par is selling at a premium, so the current yield and yield to maturity are less than the nominal yield.   (Page 28)

3.   **B.**   Although the Treasury securities underlying Treasury receipts are backed by the full faith and credit of the federal government, the stripped securities are not.   (Page 37)

4.   **A.**   Commercial banks do not issue commercial paper. The commercial paper market was developed to circumvent banks so that corporations could lend to and borrow from each other more economically. Commercial paper is unsecured corporate IOUs.   (Page 46)

5.   **C.**   In this case, "call protection" means that the issuer cannot call the bonds for at least five years. If interest rates are falling, the issuer would have reason to want to call the bonds in and, perhaps, issue new bonds at a lower interest rate. Therefore, the call feature protects the investor for a specific period of time.   (Page 26)

6.   **A.**   If the yields have gone down, the discount has been reduced; therefore, the dollar cost of bills has gone up.   (Page 36)

7.   **C.**   Because the yield is above the coupon, this bond is trading at a discount. Therefore, if it is held to maturity, the customer will realize an 8 percent return on the bond and will incur a capital gains tax. Because the tax paid will reduce the return on the customer's investment, the effective yield will be less than 8 percent.   (Page 28)

8.   **D.**   Under the Code of Procedure, a member or its employees may be censured, suspended, expelled or fined for a violation of NASD rules.   (Page 205)

9.   **A.**   General obligation bonds are backed by the general taxing authority of the municipal issuer. As such, they are often considered very safe investments. Municipal issues are marketable and are bought and sold in the secondary marketplace. Because interest received on municipal debt is exempt from federal taxation, yields offered on municipal debt are lower than yields offered on corporate debt.   (Page 44)

10.   **A.**   The bond is quoted at 90; therefore, it is selling for $900. Parity of the stock into which the bondholder can convert equals $22.50, calculated as follows: The bondholder could convert the bond into 40 shares of stock ($1,000 face amount × $25 per share = 40 shares) because the bond has a current price of $900; dividing $900 by 40 equals the underlying stock's parity price.   (Page 34)

11.   **C.**   A portion of the original issue discount on a taxable zero-coupon bond must be declared as income and taxed annually until the bond matures. This is known as *accreting the discount.*   (Page 32)

12.   **C.**   The QRS is a zero-coupon bond maturing in 2012. Zero-coupon bonds are bought at a discount and mature at face value. If a bond is held to maturity, the difference between the purchase price and the maturity price is considered interest.   (Page 31)

13.   **A.**   Greta Guernsey is retired and requires current income, which might at first indicate a fixed-income fund. However, she can probably expect to spend 15 years or more in retirement and, therefore, should maintain some of her portfolio in conservative equity investments. An equity fund that aims to achieve current income and growth of income best matches her objectives.   (Page 94)

14.   **B.**   The Code of Arbitration covers inter-dealer disputes.   (Page 207)

15. **B.**   Foreign funds invest in common stocks of companies located outside the United States. (Page 94)

16. **C.**   The federal funds rate is what banks charge each other for overnight loans. It can fluctuate hourly. (Page 47)

17. **B.**   The stockholder has the right to vote and the right to dividends if and when declared (although not to a fixed dividend). A restricted security has prescribed limits on resale generally requiring registration. (Page 6)

18. **B.**   A preemptive right enables you to maintain a proportionate share of ownership in the corporation. Because the shares have already been authorized, should you decline to participate in the rights offering, your interest will be reduced. (Page 6)

19. **A.**   Under a defined contribution plan, contributions may depend on years of service or, more frequently, salary. Benefits are based on what the accumulated contributions will provide at retirement. The plan is qualified and may not discriminate. (Page 163)

20. **D.**   The gain would be $50 for the bonds (½ point for one bond is $5 times 10 bonds) and $100 for the common stock (½ point is $.50 times 200 shares). (Page 22)

21. **D.**   Any changes in a mutual fund's investment policies must be made by a majority vote of the fund's outstanding shares. (Page 93)

22. **C.**   Thrift or 401(k) plans allow the employer to match employee contributions up to a stipulated percentage. (Page 164)

23. **B.**   The expense ratio includes the costs of operating the fund compared to fund assets. Expenses included in the ratio are management fees, administrative fees, brokerage fees and taxes. (Page 97)

24. **C.**   Under rights of accumulation, if an additional investment plus the client's current account value (or money invested) puts the client's account value over a breakpoint, the entire additional investment qualifies for the reduced sales charge. In this case, Bud's additional investment of $6,000 plus his account value of $20,000 puts his account value over the $25,000 breakpoint. Therefore, the entire $6,000 investment qualifies for the 6 percent sales charge. (Page 105)

25. **B.**   Under a letter of intent, the full contribution stated in the letter must be contributed for the letter to be completed. Appreciation is not considered. (Page 104)

26. **D.**   The entire investment qualifies for the reduced load. A letter of intent covers purchases within a 13-month period and may be backdated 90 days. Adam actually had 11 months in which to make the additional investment. (Page 104)

27. **D.**   The exchange or conversion privilege allows an investor to exchange shares of one fund for shares of another fund under the same management without paying an additional sales charge (although the exchange is still a taxable event). (Page 105)

28. **B.**   Klaus must contribute the full $15,000, which means he owes an additional $6,000. Reinvested dividends and changes in the NAV do not affect the amount required. (Page 105)

29. **C.**   Rights of accumulation are good forever, while the letter of intent has a 13-month limit. (Page 105)

30. **D.**   The variable death benefit of a scheduled premium variable life contract is determined annually. (Page 147)

31. **C.**   Each individual with earned income may open an IRA and deposit 100 percent of this earned income up to $2,000 per year. (Page 154)

32. **A.**   Only an individual with self-employment income may open a Keogh Plan (HR-10). (Page 158)

33. **C.** Cost base in a retirement plan is money contributed after taxes; upon receipt, there is no tax liability. Money withdrawn from a qualified plan is taxed as ordinary income upon receipt. (Page 164)

34. **D.** A registered representative may not avoid arbitration proceedings. (Page 207)

35. **B.** You may contribute to an IRA only until the first tax filing deadline (April 15) even if you filed an extension. Anyone with earned income can contribute to an IRA. (Page 154)

36. **A.** Most mutual funds offer automatic reinvestment of income and gains distributions at net asset value. If income distribution reinvestment is subject to a sales charge, the maximum allowable sales charge for any purchase is reduced. (Page 108)

37. **C.** A small-business owner filing Schedule C may own a Keogh plan. (Page 157)

38. **C.** In a variable annuity, account performance is not guaranteed; the investor accepts the risk that the account will not perform at the assumed interest rate. (Page 137)

39. **D.** The most suitable investments for this woman are bond funds. (Page 95)

40. **A.** Gains in a separate account are tax deferred. The annuitant pays ordinary income tax on the distribution upon receipt. (Page 143)

41. **A.** The customer, in the deferral stage of the annuity, is holding accumulation units. The value of the customer's account would be converted into annuity units when and if the customer decides to annuitize the contract. (Page 140)

42. **D.** An accumulation unit's value varies according to the value of the insurance company's separate account. During the accumulation stage of a variable annuity, the number of units also varies as the income distributions and additional contributions purchase more units. Only at the conversion of accumulation units into annuity units is the number of units fixed, but their value still fluctuates according to the separate account's value. (Page 140)

43. **D.** Keogh contributions are limited to 25 percent of after-contribution income (the equivalent of 20 percent of precontribution income) to a maximum of $30,000. In this case, the doctor's $160,000 income times 20 percent equals $32,000— $2,000 more than the maximum contribution. (Page 158)

44. **B.** The sale of mutual fund shares requires that the client get the prospectus before or during the sales solicitation. (Page 90)

45. **A.** The man will pay a total of $55,000 over two years. This period is too short to invest in stocks for growth. The man can invest the remaining $45,000 because he will not need it to pay the notes. (Page 71)

46. **C.** In a discretionary account, a representative has been given authority to select the amount and type of investment for a client. The authorization must be in writing. (Page 118)

47. **D.** When a customer opens an account, the minimum information needed is the customer's name, whether the customer is employed with another NASD firm and the customer's tax identification number. Additionally, the registered representative must have discussed the risks of the investment with the customer and must sign the appropriate forms. A supervisor (principal of the firm) reviews all accounts. (Page 114)

48. **D.** A custodian for an UGMA account cannot grant trading authority to a third party. (Page 120)

49. **C.** The registered rep must have prior written authority from the customer and must have received approval from a supervisory person before accepting discretionary authority. While a designated principal must review the account frequently, the branch manager need not initial each order before it is entered. (Page 118)

50. **A.** The money-market fund is the most suitable of the choices given. (Page 96)

51. **A.** A rep must notify the firm before working for another company. (Page 200)

52. **B.** A qualified principal of the firm must approve all advertising and other communications by a broker-dealer. (Page 190)

53. **C.** All sales literature or advertising used in connection with the solicitation of mutual fund shares must be accompanied or preceded by the prospectus. (Page 189)

54. **C.** All sales literature used in connection with a new offering must be filed for review with the NASD. A principal of the firm must approve its use and is responsible for corrections the NASD requires. (Page 196)

55. **B.** Closed-end investment companies may issue more than one class of common stock, preferred stock and bonds. (Page 81)

56. **A.** The Kuhls require maximum capital appreciation. Their long-term time frame allows them to ride out the stock market fluctuations. The best investment for them is the stock mutual fund that concentrates solely on achieving long-term growth rather than generating current income. (Page 94)

57. **B.** Because the funds are under separate management, the load charged on each separate investment will likely be at the maximum. If the client invests the entire sum within one fund or a family of funds, a reduced sales charge may be available. (Page 103)

58. **D.** All of the materials listed are considered either sales literature or advertising when used in connection with the solicitation of variable life insurance. (Page 188)

59. **A.** When a stock goes up in price dramatically upon issue, it is said to be *hot*. Although no mathematical formula exists, a rise in price of ⅛ of a point or more upon issue is generally considered an indication of a hot issue. (Page 175)

60. **D.** Registered reps, officers and directors of broker-dealers can never buy a hot issue and neither can a firm for its own inventory. Those persons listed in choices I and II, as well as their relatives, cannot buy a hot issue unless the amount they purchase is insignificant and they have an underwriter to assist in the solicitation of public interest during the 20-day cooling-off period. (Page 175)

61. **A.** Warrants, common stock and options all have an active secondary market. (Page 18)

62. **B.** Belle Charolais has a high net worth and substantial investment experience. She is capable of assuming the higher risk and return potential of a speculative investment such as the biotechnology sector fund. (Page 94)

63. **A.** Any recommendation implying that an investor can make a gain must be followed by a statement of the attendant risks of the transaction. (Page 68)

64. **C.** The ex-dividend date is always two business days before the record date. In this case, the record date is Thursday, September 15, so the ex-date is Tuesday, September 13. (Page 58)

65. **D.** Sector funds invest in stocks of companies providing innovative products in specific industries. (Page 94)

66. **D.** Any statement or reference to a mutual fund offered under a 12b-1 plan implying that the fund is a no-load fund is considered misleading and a violation of the Rules of Fair Practice. (Page 102)

67. **C.** The exchange privilege allows a shareholder to exchange shares from one fund for shares from another fund within a family of funds under the same management without paying an additional sales charge (dollar for dollar). The shareholder is liable for any tax on gains as a result of the exchange. (Page 105)

68. **A.** An annuity with a life contingency (death benefit) promising a full contribution amount applies to the annuity during the accumulation stage. A guaranteed payout to a beneficiary in the event of an annuitant's death applies to the annuity period.   (Page 140)

69. **D.** Failure to provide a Social Security or federal tax identification number results in an automatic withholding tax on the account.
(Page 111)

70. **C.** For a registered investment company to terminate a 12b-1 charge, the termination must be approved by a majority vote of the shareholders or a majority of the uninterested members of the board of directors. Approval by the full board of directors is not required.   (Page 101)

71. **B.** A 12b-1 fee is a percentage of a fund's annual average net assets. The fee is typically paid in quarterly installments.   (Page 101)

72. **C.** Sufficient IRA withdrawals must begin in the year after the year the account owner reaches age 70½.   (Page 155)

73. **D.** A Series 6 licensed representative may sell open-end investment companies and unit investment trusts. A Series 6 representative also may sell closed-end investment companies, but only in the primary market.   (Page 185)

74. **B.** Amounts paid under a 12b-1 plan may be used only to cover specific sales or promotional services or activities described in the plan. Such services or activities must be provided in connection with the distribution of the shares.
(Page 101)

75. **C.** The maximum charged under a 12b-1 plan must be reasonable and bear a relationship to the distribution services offered. The fee charged may cover only those distribution, selling and promotional expenses specifically described in the plan. Shares offered under a 12b-1 fund are sold at net asset value; there is no POP. The 9 percent maximum refers to shares sold under contractual plan agreements.   (Page 101)

76. **D.** Without knowing more about the graduate's financial situation, you should tell him that he is better off deferring the $1,000 investment at this time. Should he invest the full $1,000 in any of the mutual funds described in the question, and should an emergency occur, he would most likely have to liquidate his investment. However, if one of the choices were a money-market fund and Hugh invested the $1,000 as an emergency fund, this type of investment would be appropriate.
(Page 68)

77. **D.** Hugh Heifer requires a mutual fund that offers the potential for long-term capital growth. Also, he believes money managers cannot consistently outperform the overall market. This indicates that an index fund that attempts to match the stock market's performance is the most appropriate investment for him.   (Page 94)

78. **B.** First, the method of investment describes a contractual plan (i.e., a periodic investment into a unit investment trust over a period of time). The maximum sales charge over the life of a contractual plan is 9 percent. In this case, 9 percent of $24,000 equals $2,160.   (Page 123)

79. **B.** A high-grade bond fund would provide income that is greater than that provided by a money-market fund while still offering stability and preservation of capital. Many bond funds provide for monthly payment of interest income, whereas stock funds typically offer distributions on a quarterly or less frequent basis. A growth fund's objective usually is not to offer income distributions; rather, the objective is appreciation. A combination fund invests in growth and income stocks and attempts to provide both growth and current income; however, the NAV can fluctuate widely.   (Page 95)

80. **C.** The Stouts' investment goal of providing for their children's education is about four years away. They cannot afford to take the risk that a downturn in the stock market will occur within that time. A safe alternative that also provides additional returns is the high-quality corporate bond fund.   (Page 95)

81. **A.** A gain or loss is claimed in the year of sale, not in the year of purchase. (Page 109)

82. **A.** A mutual fund may distribute net investment income as a dividend. "Net investment income" is defined as interest and dividends less fees. Long-term gains must be distributed separately and no more often than annually. Therefore, dividend income of $1.10 plus interest income of $.90 minus expenses of $.50 equals a maximum $1.50 per-share dividend distribution. (Page 107)

83. **D.** The time limit for filing a grievance under the Code of Arbitration is six years. However, the six-year limitation cannot extend the limitation under state law, which is typically two years. (Page 207)

84. **B.** The Longhorns are preparing for retirement. They want to maintain a comfortable standard of living, which means staying ahead of inflation. A combined fund that offers both current income and growth potential is the best choice for this couple. (Page 94)

85. **A.** Following hearings by the District Business Conduct Committee or the Board of Governors, penalties for violation of the NASD Rules of Fair Practice may be assessed as follows: fines (unlimited) on a member or person associated with a member; censure of any member or person associated with a member; suspension of membership of any member or suspension of the registration of any person associated with a member; expulsion of any member or revocation of the registration of any person associated with a member; suspension or barring of a member or person associated with a member from association with all firms; or any other penalty deemed appropriate. (Page 205)

86. **A.** The basis of property inherited is either stepped up or stepped down to its fair market value (FMV) at the date of the decedent's death. No adjustment of basis is necessary for a period before the decedent's death. (Page 111)

87. **D.** Money-market funds invest in high-quality, short-term debt obligations. (Page 96)

88. **C.** Government income funds invest in U.S. Treasury and agency securities. (Page 95)

89. **B.** Municipal bond funds invest in municipal debt obligations. (Page 95)

90. **C.** To pay this year's common dividend, the corporation must pay the preferred stockholders the 2 percent not paid last year and this year's 7 percent dividend—in total, 9 percent, or $9. (Page 9)

91. **C.** The refund provisions for variable life contracts extend for two years from issuance of a policy. If, within the two-year period, the contract holder terminates participation in the contract, the insurer must refund from the premium the cash value on the contract (the value calculated after receiving the redemption notice) *plus* all sales charges deducted exceeding 30 percent in the first year of the contract and 10 percent in the second year. After the two years have lapsed, only the cash value need be refunded; the insurer retains all sales charges collected to date. (Page 149)

92. **A.** The 12b-1 fee must be fully disclosed in the prospectus used as the offering document for the mutual fund. (Page 101)

93. **D.** A fixed-premium variable life contract offers a minimum death benefit (typically $25,000) and a cash value that fluctuates with the performance of the separate account funding the variable life contract. The separate account performance determines the amount of life benefit exceeding the minimum guaranteed by the contract. (Page 147)

94. **B.** Acme preferred may be converted into four shares of common (100 ÷ $25 = 4). With the convertible preferred trading at 110, the common stock must be trading at 27½ for four shares of common stock to be equal in value to one share of preferred. To calculate the common stock's parity price, divide the preferred stock's current market

price by the number of shares of common stock that an investor would receive for converting to the preferred ($110 ÷ 4 = 27½).   (Page 34)

95. **A.** The prime rate is the interest a bank charges its best corporate customers. Choice B describes the discount rate (set by the Fed).
(Page 47)

96. **C.** Tex wants to park the money from his pension plan distribution for a short period of time, so he requires a short-term investment vehicle. The money-market fund is best suited to his needs. The CD has a maturity that exceeds Tex's time horizon. The growth fund likely entails a load. To do nothing prevents Tex from earning any money during his decision period. (Page 96)

97. **D.** Although the prospectus is required before or during any solicitation for sale, no other literature or documentation is needed. (Page 90)

98. **B.** The parity price of the common would be 22½ (90 ÷ 4 = 22½). Because the common is trading at 20 percent below parity, you know that its market price is 80 percent of 22½ (.80 × 22½ = 18).   (Page 34)

99. **D.** Conviction of a securities crime, suspension or expulsion from a self-regulatory organization, infraction of a securities law or suspension by SEC ruling represent a statutory disqualification. The term "statutory" means *written in law*. If an individual is found to fall under any of the above categories, he can be summarily barred from participation in the securities industry.
(Page 186)

100. **C.** This is a two-step problem. First, you must find the bond's parity price. A bond's parity price equals the market value of common stock times the conversion rate. $55 multiplied by a 20 conversion rate (which is $1,000 divided by $50) equals a parity price of $1,100 for the bond. If the bond's price is 110 percent of parity, parity times 1.1 equals the market price ($1,100 × 1.1 = $1,210).
(Page 34)

How Many Business Days?

Same **Business** Day	The settlement date on cash transactions for securities
One **Business** Day	Regular way settlement on U.S. government securities
Two **Business** Days	The relationship of the normal ex-dividend date to the record date
Three **Business** Days	Regular way settlement for securities other than U.S. government securities (corporate and municipal)
Five **Business** Days	Regulation T settlement for cash account purchases

How Many Calendar Days?

Seven **Calendar** Days	The maximum time for mutual funds to redeem shares
Twenty **Calendar** Days	The minimum time between the filing date and the effective date of a security registration (cooling-off period)
Thirty **Calendar** Days	The IRS time restriction on purchases to avoid wash sale designation (thirty days before or thirty days after)
Forty-five **Calendar** Days	The maximum period within which one can receive a 100 percent refund of sales charges in an investment company contractual plan (free-look period)
Sixty **Calendar** Days	The maximum time within which the free-look letter can be sent by the custodian bank to the contractual planholder
	The maximum time permitted to roll over qualified money from one qualified retirement plan to another qualified retirement plan
Ninety **Calendar** Days	The maximum length of time for a letter of intent to be backdated

How Many Months?

Six **Months**	The frequency with which investment companies must send reports to shareholders
Thirteen **Months**	The maximum duration of a letter of intent
Sixteen **Months**	The maximum time that an investment company prospectus may be used
Eighteen **Months**	The time after which refunds of sales charges in excess of 15 percent on front-end load contractual plans expire (act of 1940)